THE PHILOSOPHER'S PLANT

THE PHILOSO PLANT

AN INTELLECTUAL

PHER'S

HERBARIUM

MICHAEL MARDER

DRAWINGS BY MATHILDE ROUSSEL

COLUMBIA UNIVERSITY PRESS   NEW YORK

COLUMBIA UNIVERSITY PRESS
Publishers Since 1893
New York   Chichester, West Sussex

cup.columbia.edu

Library of Congress Cataloging-in-Publication Data

Marder, Michael, 1980–
The philosopher's plant : an intellectual herbarium / Michael Marder ;
with drawings by Mathilde Roussel.
pages cm
Includes bibliographical references and index.
ISBN 978-0-231-16902-8 (cloth) —
ISBN 978-0-231-16903-5 (pbk.) —
ISBN 978-0-231-53813-8 (e-book)
1. Botany—Philosophy. 2. Botany—History.
3. Plants—Adaptation. 4. Human-plant relationships. I. Title.

QK46.M36 2014
580—dc23

2014010349

COVER DESIGN: MATHILDE ROUSSEL
BOOK DESIGN & TYPESETTING: VIN DANG

For Patrícia—
To grow together . . .

ALL MY BOTANICAL WALKS, THE VARIED IMPRESSIONS MADE ON ME BY THE PLACES WHERE I HAVE SEEN STRIKING THINGS, THE IDEAS THEY HAVE STIRRED IN ME, AND THE INCIDENTS CONNECTED TO THEM HAVE ALL LEFT ME WITH THE IMPRESSIONS, WHICH ARE RENEWED BY THE SIGHT OF THE PLANTS I COLLECTED IN THOSE VERY PLACES.... [A]LL I HAVE TO DO IS OPEN MY HERBARIUM AND IT QUICKLY TRANS-PORTS ME THERE.

JEAN-JACQUES ROUSSEAU, *REVERIES OF THE SOLITARY WALKER*

[THE] FLOWERS ARE OF COURSE DRY AND LIFE HAS VANISHED FROM THEM. BUT WHAT ON EARTH IS A LIVING THING IF THE SPIRIT OF MAN DOES NOT BREATHE LIFE INTO IT? WHAT IS SPEECHLESS BUT THAT TO WHICH MAN DOES NOT LEND HIS SPEECH?

G. W. F. HEGEL, LETTER TO NANETTE ENDEL, JULY 2, 1797

THERE IS, ABSENT FROM EVERY GARDEN, A DRIED FLOWER IN A BOOK . . .

JACQUES DERRIDA, *MARGINS OF PHILOSOPHY*

NOT ENOUGH TIME TO COME AND GO AROUND A THOUGHT, NOT ENOUGH TIME TO MAKE THE HERBARIUM OF THOUGHTS . . .

HÉLÈNE CIXOUS, *MANNA: FOR THE MANDELSTAMS, FOR THE MANDELAS*

CONT

Part I. Ancient Plant-Souls

ENTS

Part IV. Postmodern Plant-Subjects

ACKNOWLEDGMENTS

This book reconsiders Western philosophy from the perspective of plant life, which has been systematically marginalized throughout its history. Given the vast scope of the subject, it will be impossible for me to thank everyone who has indirectly contributed to this project. I cannot, however, fail to mention the inestimable support that Wendy Lochner of Columbia University Press has provided to *The Philosopher's Plant* since its very inception. Luis Garagalza has been my interlocutor in the last few years and has indicated a number of sources crucial for chapter 5. Alan Read and the participants in a daylong event, Plant Science, at King's College, London, which took place in May 2013, have helped me sharpen my thoughts on "the place of plants" and on the relation between Plato's and Heidegger's approaches to the vegetal. In June 2013, students in my Critical Plant Studies seminar at the Forum for Contemporary Theory at the University of Goa, India, have provided valuable feedback on the second half of the manuscript. Luce Irigaray has been generous in her comments on the chapter dedicated to her work. Mathilde Roussel's creativity, expressed in beautiful and thought-provoking drawings, has turned *The Philosopher's Plant* into a veritable "intellectual herbarium." Patrícia Vieira has been a constant companion in the practical and theoretical contemplations of vegetal nature. This book is a small token of my gratitude to her.

Between November 2012 and September 2013, samples from chapters 1 through 10 appeared in a blog hosted by Project Syndicate (project-syndicate.org). Parts of chapters 11 and 12 were published on my blog, *The Philosopher's Plant*, hosted by *The Los Angeles Review of Books*. All these texts are reproduced with the permission of the copyright holders.

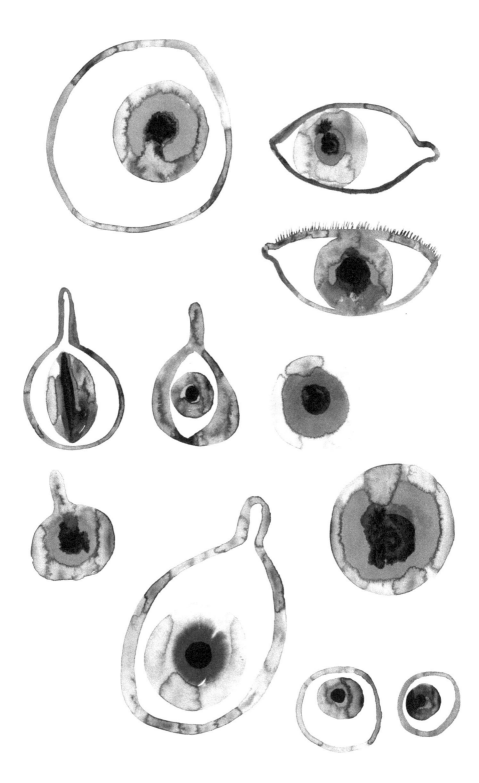

Few among the intellectual giants of the West professed a greater love for plants than Jean-Jacques Rousseau. Through his immersion in a meticulous study of botany, which surpassed the limited scope of an empirical science and became for him an instance of *l'art divin*, the philosopher hoped to get back to our natural origins, which were obstructed by the perversions of civilization. Alexandra Cook fittingly grouped Rousseau's botanical reflections and practices under the heading of "the salutary science," a therapy for curing the modern soul by purging it of destructive passions and putting it back in touch with the simplicity, calm, and truth of nature.[1]

In light of this sublime botany, philosophy itself changes beyond recognition: *philo-sophia*, the love of wisdom, is brought to life with the help of *phyto-philia*, the love of plants.[2] The stunted growth of the human psyche receives a vital impetus from the flourishing of plants, which instigate thought, itself as prone to metamorphosis as the dandelions Rousseau described in one of the botanical letters to his cousin, Madame Delessert, in 1793.[3]

Already for Socrates, care for the soul was a preeminent philosophical concern. The goal of philosophy was to save the soul from its corruption and degradation by putting it in touch with its immortal provenance in the realm of Ideas. Much of the Western intellectual history that ensued accepted, without questioning, the Socratic recipe for salvation: thought had to discover a way back to its own immutable logical, metaphysical, and ontological foundations so as to dwell there in a lasting respite from the vicissitudes of everyday reality. The utopian, placeless place of salvation, exempt from the effects of time, is at the furthest remove from the plant, for which constant change and the environment wherein it flourishes are paramount. That is probably why most philosophers were not phytophiles but instead viewed growth along with its unavoidable double, decay, as anathema to true philosophizing.

Despite its widespread conceptual allergy to vegetable life—indeed, its phytophobia—the philosophical tradition in the West could not skirt the issue of plants altogether. Philosophers allotted to them a generally inferior place in their systems; used their germination, growth, blossoming, fruition, reproduction, and decay as illustrations of abstract concepts; mentioned them in passing as the natural backdrops for their dialogues, letters, and other compositions; spun elaborate allegories out of them; and recommended appropriate medicinal, dietary, and aesthetic approaches to particular specimens.

Most of these engagements with the flora were fleeting and marginal, as though plants did not deserve the same careful reflection and theoretical attention due to other beings. But our rehashing of the philosophical record, sketchy at best in the case of plants, is not doomed to repeat the failures of the past. *The Philosopher's Plant* turns the tables on the metaphysical tradition and illuminates the elaborate centerpieces and the hidden kernels of theoretical discourse from the perspective of what has been relegated to its vegetable margins. Briefly put, this book lifts the curtain on the significance of plants to the making (and growth) of thought.

On the journey that lies ahead we will visit fields and gardens, forests and groves, vineyards and backyards. Both seasoned philosophical fellow travelers and novice voyagers will discover something for themselves along the path, be it an unexpected angle on the intellectual history they are already steeped in or an introduction to some of its most important figures and concepts.

Traveling through the entangled roots and dense undergrowth of philosophy can take various forms. Readers may choose to move *along*, roughly following the chronology of Western philosophy from Plato to Luce Irigaray, or they may wish to wander *across* the parallel sections of each chapter. For those who prefer the second option, four additional byways and shortcuts open up. Readers interested in stories that mingle the episodes from the lives (and, in some cases, the deaths) of philosophers with the life of plants may browse the first section of each chapter. If you would like to glean theories of vegetable existence and how they bear upon the main ideas of each philosopher in question, you are advised to consult the second sections (and, at times, the third). The third section of each chapter explores the implications of human interaction with plants. The concluding sections offer critical vistas for reassessing the place of plants as well as the legacies of the thinkers discussed in the book.

Whatever itinerary readers decide to pursue, they will encounter in *The Philosopher's Plant* an interactive web of associations, one where ideas and their authors are linked to certain plant specimens. You will reminisce about Plato while resting in the shade of a plane tree; have a flashback to Avicenna as you cook celery soup; recall Hegel, eating grapes or drinking wine; and think of Irigaray in the blissful moments of contemplating a water lily. Philosophical dialogues, treatises, lectures, and meditations will grow, flourish, blossom in greater proximity to vegetable life. The philosophers and their thought will appear, quasi-magically, in the guise of the specimens that represent them—from magnificently tall trees to humble but all-pervasive grasses, from enchanting flowers to nourishing sweet fruits.

Resuscitated upon contact with plants, systems of metaphysics both ancient and modern will receive a second chance to do justice to the life they have devalued, instrumentalized, and rendered banal. In effect, the three final chapters in our intellectual herbarium will display an attitude to plant growth that is markedly dissimilar to the rest, the attitude consistent with their modification of (if not their rebellion against) the metaphysical tradition. Ultimately, in the shape of Irigaray's water lily, thought and growth will, once again, melt into each other, opening this tradition to Eastern philosophies and inflecting it with feminist modes of intellection.

The Philosopher's Plant is not, however, the philosopher's stone—that mysterious alchemical substance that was supposed to turn base metals into gold. The stories you are about to read do not put plants to the task of a simple mediation between the so-called natural world and the gold standards of conceptuality. Each of the twelve specimens featured below promotes our appreciation of the ideas associated with the respective author as much as it thwarts understanding, for instance, by dissolving this faculty of the human mind in pure aesthetic pleasure, as Immanuel Kant would put it. The trees, flowers, vines, and cereals collected in this book are cultivated at the edge of the traditions they illustrate, since *the history of what ideally does not grow, namely metaphysics, is told here from the perspective of what grows, including the very plants that have surreptitiously germinated within this history.*

Hence the second reason *The Philosopher's Plant* is not the philosopher's stone: it is not, nor does it claim to be, a monumental contribution to the history of thought à la Bertrand Russell's widely read tome, precisely because it refuses to force thought, whether past or present, into rigid, inorganic, stonelike molds.[4] Rather than cast a panoramic gaze over this history, I have *selected*, *arranged*, and *displayed* some of its most prominent representatives. And rather than emphasize the deep conceptual connections among them, I have pointed out certain family resemblances running across their genealogical tree. In short, I have compiled an "intellectual herbarium."

The German philosopher and literary critic Walter Benjamin dreamt of writing a book consisting of little else than quotations, collecting morsels of works that had influenced his thinking and interspersing them with his own reflections. His mammoth, albeit unfinished, *Arcades Project* is a partial realization of this dream. Indeed, citations are somewhat like the botanical specimens collated in a herbarium. To get a foretaste of this comparison, consider the etymology of "anthology," a book containing assorted texts, poems, or epigrams by different authors, which originally meant "a collection of flowers" (from the Greek *anthos*, "flower" + *logos*, derived from *legein*, "to gather"). A book of citations, an anthology, an intellectual herbarium is distinct from the canonical endeavor that assembles the core of a discipline. Flowers are the least essential (and, on the evolutionary scale, the latest to have emerged) parts of plants, which have asexual means of reproduction at their disposal, and so are their textual analogues in an anthology.

Both the fragments of texts and those of the plant world are selected with great care and attention, cut off from the "natural" context of their growth, and displayed in a book, where they are juxtaposed with their casual neighbors. For J. Hillis Miller, such is the effect of translation: "Use of a translation uproots the work, denatures it, transforms it into a *hortus siccus*, or dried, specimen flower ready to be stored in the bottomless archives."[5] The denaturing and transformation evoked here are not exclusive to the work of translation. To return to Benjamin, a book of citations (and no book is ever free of citation) is a veritable *hortus siccus*, a desiccated garden, which makes thought grow. It allows the reader to make unexpected connections among different passages and to open a passage between these passages, to let them dialogue with one another, much like a botanist working with an herbarium studies and compares plant morphology, notably the shapes of leaves. Just listen to the conversation that is beginning to unfold among the epigraphs to this volume! Unwittingly, those practitioners who dried leaves and entire small plants between the pages of thick books have always been complicit in an act of repetition, which redoubled the preservation of tidbits drawn from other texts in these same books.

Though not as inflexible as a row of monuments to philosophers and their works, *hortus siccus* is still a far cry from a living garden. Metaphysics robs the living of their immediate life, promising, in return, their resurrection in the ideal world of its chimeras—the Ideas, substance, Spirit... At the tail end of the metaphysical tradition, Hegel expresses what he sees as the upside of this tendency in his melancholic reflection on the dry flowers he kept as a memento of a dead friend: "[The] flowers are of course dry and life has vanished from them. But what on earth is a living thing if the spirit of man does not breathe life into it?"[6] It is after they are desiccated that the flowers can truly live, live *in* truth, animated by "the spirit of man," who, godlike, breathes a new and higher vitality into them. Thought finds itself in the same predicament, attaining its true life within the history it enters when its living impulse has all but waned. Refracted through the prism of this thought, *in extremis*, the entire earth comes to resemble a "living herbarium," as the Russian poet Anna Akhmatova notes in one of her poems. On the other hand, postmetaphysical philosophy, which overflows the confines of the final section in our intellectual herbarium, restores to plants and to thinking itself the life and being that are rightfully theirs. It could well be that both may carry on living after metaphysics only in an alliance they would forge between them. The name I have provisionally given to this alliance is "plant-thinking."

Just as a botanical herbarium cannot be compiled without the preserved plants themselves, so an intellectual herbarium is incomplete without the images of plants. The drawings by Mathilde Roussel included in *The Philosopher's Plant* are incalculably more than mere adornments to a scholarly text. They are the offshoots of thinking that draws its nourishment and produces its sap from the aesthetic medium where it thrives; the fruits of an ongoing and often tacit dialogue between the artist and the philosopher; and, in some sense, the main protagonists of this book. For while the images encapsulate the central ideas of the corresponding chapters, the text that follows may be read as an extended commentary on the images.

The complete title of Rousseau's *Reveries*, which frequently makes mention of his botanical observations, specifies the subject of these musings and daydreams as a "solitary walker." Feeling ostracized by humankind, Rousseau sought refuge in the world of plants, which he visited on his local botanical expeditions. Besides these peculiarities of his biography, the thinker's solitary stance is hardly surprising. By now it is something of a cliché to imagine a philosopher (in particular, a modern one) meditating in unperturbed solitude. The illustrious precedent of René Descartes, seated in his evening gown alone next to a fireplace, has served as the model for subsequent generations of thinkers. In turn, the readers of *The Philosopher's Plant* will not walk alone. On this decidedly nonsolitary stroll, which nonetheless promises to be full of reveries, you will be accompanied by a plethora of characters, past and present, who have shaped Western thought. You will witness a multifaceted conversation between philosophy and art. But, above all, you will come face to face with plants.

Rousseau might have been mistaken after all: he was not alone during his walks full of "happy reverie" amid "greenery, flowers, and birds."[7] Is it the case that we are—still or already—immersed in solitude when we are with animals or plants? What does being with these nonhuman beings mean? Doesn't "being *in* nature," as we say in everyday language, ineluctably create a broad transhuman community: being *with* nature? If so, then what is our place, and that of our thought, within such a community, and where are we situated with respect to the place of plants? The intellectual herbarium you are about to view is, at once, a cartographic record of these places and a set of indications for their scrupulous remapping.

THE PHILOSOPHER'S PLANT

PART I

ANCIENT PLANT-SOULS

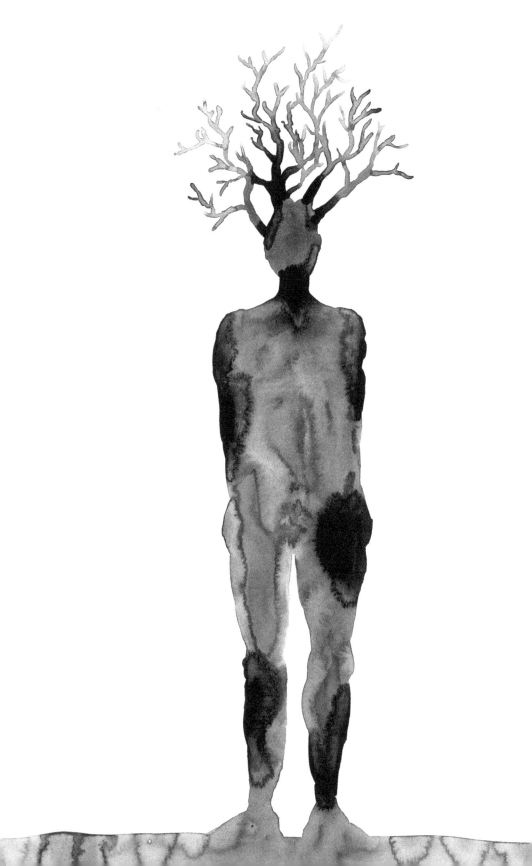

1 | PLATO'S PLANE TREE

In the Shade of a Plane Tree

Plato was notoriously averse to the arts of rhetoric. In florid discourses and techniques of persuasion he saw the trademarks of his sworn enemies, the sophistic sleights of hand that dispensed with the real work of thinking at the heart of true philosophizing. No other negative attitude of his rivaled this aversion, except a glaring distaste for myths. Churning out dogmatic answers to humanity's quest for origins, the received wisdom of mythological narratives interfered with the philosopher's relentless questioning of reality and of himself. Myth beckoned with the exact opposite of the Socratic profession of not-knowing, which, if we are to believe the hallucinogen-induced prophesies of the Delphic oracle, made Socrates the wisest of all mortals. Myth's promise of easy knowledge (and, to the sophists, easy money) inevitably shortchanged those naïve enough to put their trust in it.

Tempted though he was, Plato could not bring himself to forgo intricate rhetorical devices, metaphors, subtle similitudes, and clever allegories, with which he adorned his dialogues. Nor did he, counting on the credulity of the readers, really give up mythic storytelling, which was tightly woven into the fabric of his writings. An obsessive writer who worked with multiple drafts of his texts, he paid careful attention to the dramatic settings of the conversations he recorded. And, invariably, the initial setup of the dialogues contained clues to what was going to be discussed in them.

The Republic begins with Socrates relating to his listeners, "I went down to the Piraeus," a port city in the vicinity of Athens (Plato *Republic* 327a). Although at first glance this line is hardly significant, Plato's writings are calibrated all the way down to the last word, if not to the last sound, as J. B. Kennedy claims in his intriguing *The Musical Structure of Platonic Dialogues*.[1] For those who keep the esoteric subtext in mind, the expression "I went down" bristles with deeper meaning, in that it alludes to the philosopher's literal descent to the world of everyday appearances. In the celebrated Myth of the Cave, Socrates will echo these opening words with the story of the philosopher's allegorical descent to the chaos of unexamined ways of thinking. Read in retrospect, the statement deposited at the threshold of *The Republic* will reveal that the whole masterpiece proceeds along the jagged narrative lines of Socrates' meeting his interlocutors at the exact place where they are in their own cognition and in his making a herculean effort to elevate them above the darkness of this conceptual cave. "I went down" is a laconic summary of what is to follow, at least from the viewpoint of Socrates himself.

In *Phaedrus*, a dialogue overtly hostile to *ars rhetorica* and even more so to writing, the dramatic setting is equally telling. Socrates and his companion, who lends his name to the title of the exchange, find themselves in the countryside. Phaedrus singles out a particularly auspicious place for the rest of the conversation—a soft patch of grass shaded by a tall plane tree, *platanos* (229a–b). Does the idyllic natural setting stand for a counterweight to writing and rhetoric, those despised excesses of civilization? Not quite. A few pages into the dialogue, Socrates will confess: "You see, I am fond of learning. Now the country places and the trees won't teach me anything, and the people in the city do" (230d). We cannot learn anything from trees, comfortable as it may be to converse in their shade on a scorching summer's day. The city with its marketplace (the *agora*) is still the preferred place for philosophizing. What, then, is the point of dwelling on the plane tree, under which Socrates and Phaedrus will rest?

As is often the case in Plato, the explanation is as unexpected as it is laced with irony. A rhetorical trick has permitted Plato to insinuate himself into the dialogue without really taking part in it. To the Hellenic readers of the text it will have been obvious that the plane tree, *platanos*, is a semantic play on the author's proper name, with both words derived from the Greek *platys*, meaning "broad." (Plane trees have remarkably broad leaves, as do all other sycamores. No wonder, then, that a variety known as the London plane predominates in New York City, with over ninety thousand specimens scattered throughout the five boroughs.)[2] So, the irony is that Plato has literally overshadowed Socrates and Phaedrus, who linger in the shade of a plane tree. The exaggerated modesty of a mere "reporter" of his teacher's thoughts and great deeds is a rather thin veneer that hides the towering presence of the student over the Socratic legacy. More than that, Plato's shadow has turned out to be broad enough to shelter the rest of Western philosophy, which, as Alfred North Whitehead once put it, is but a series of "footnotes to Plato."

To complete the ironic overview I have presented, consider Phaedrus's suggestion that the grass is there "to sit on, or, if we like, to lie down on" (229b). Where is the punch line? Well, Phaedrus was one of the main characters in Plato's *Symposium*, the great dialogue on the subject of love. His playful offer to recline together under the tree makes part of a string of the all-but-evident seductions. As for Plato, he silently and, perhaps, voyeuristically observes the entire scene from the heights of his position as a scribe and of the plane tree he has dramatically metamorphosed into.

The overtones of sexual seductiveness that permeate this strange love triangle of Phaedrus-Socrates-Plato are inseparable from the allure of vegetal nature. Having arrived at the foot of the plane tree, Socrates lavishly praises the place as "charming," not the least thanks to the "very spreading and lofty" tree and the grass "thick enough to be just right when you lay your head on it" (230b–c). Phaedrus has conducted the Athenian gadfly well outside the confines of the city, with its strict laws and opportunities for learning, to the place of sheer enchantment. The charming environment, rife with mythic insinuations, is populated with the nymphs Pharmaceia and Oreithyia, as well as the river god Achelous and the god of the northern wind, Boreas. In a word, trailing after Phaedrus, Socrates has arrived at the *ur*-place of myth framed on all sides by lush vegetation. All that remains is to lower one's head on the grass, to recline, and to forget oneself in blissful slumber, which is the sleep of reason itself.

Not on Plato's watch, though! (Remember the plane tree vigilantly towering over the scene.) The only thing that will enchant a true philosopher will be the seductive promise of knowledge, comparable to the charms of vegetation—leafy branches or fruit—that attract herbivorous animals. Listen to Socrates once again:

> But you seem to have found the charm to bring me out. For as people lead hungry animals by shaking in front of them a branch of leaves or some fruit, just so, I think, you, by holding before me discourses in books, will lead me all over Attica and wherever else you please. So now that I have come here, I intend to lie down, and let you choose the position in which you think you can read most easily, and read.
>
> (230d–e)

From here onward, Phaedrus's moonlighting as a guide is over. Despite the Socratic pretense of acquiescence to the reading of a speech his companion has prepared, it will be Socrates alone who will lead the way out of the labyrinths of myth. He will spare nothing and no one as he ranks and judges, discerns and criticizes (for instance, good writing and bad) with the view to establishing a comprehensive tribunal of reason itself. The frantic activity of philosophizing will retrace the initial contrast between the plane tree and the grass, the high and the low, for the floral embodiments of mythic reality have already outlined a hierarchy of judgment in the most palpable terms conceivable. The human figures of Socrates and Phaedrus—but also of the dialogue's readers: you and I— will thus be suspended between the two extremes, caught up in a vertical valuation and hierarchical organization of the world. Neither as low as the grass nor as tall as the majestic plane tree.

When the torch passes to Socrates, who has never really relinquished it, vegetal imagery does not disappear; on the contrary, it is cultivated, refined, and transplanted into what Kenneth M. Sayre felicitously named "Plato's literary garden."[3] An elevated, serious discourse is one that "plants and sows in a fitting soul intelligent words" and that is fruitful, yielding as it does "the seeds, from which there spring up in other minds other words capable of continuing the process forever" (276e–277a). If harvest is scarce, it is safe to say that the soul, where intelligent words were sown, was not a good fit for the semantic seeds *or* that the words themselves were not intelligent. At any rate, the Platonic soul is a kind of ethereal soil for the growth of *logoi*, that is to say, of speeches, discourses, and words, not to mention logic and reason. We will keep circling around this cross-fertilization of philosophy and agro-botanical discourse in Plato's work.

The time has not yet come for us to leave the cool shade of the plane tree, into which the author of *Phaedrus* has fashioned himself. Would we be justified in viewing this ironic metamorphosis as anything other than a symptom for Plato's unbridled poetic license, if not his down-right bad taste? It is not unheard of that humans, even those as excellent as the legendary heroes, tired of their human countenance and elected noble animal incarnations in Platonic dialogues. The striking and orig-inal Myth of Er at the close of *The Republic*, where Plato contemplates the idea of an afterlife, puts forth precisely this scenario, which sees Or-pheus choosing the life of a swan, Agamemnon embracing that of an eagle, and so forth (620a–b). Why, then, wouldn't a soul adopt the life of a plant (say, of a plane or an oak)? After all, in the same dialogue where Plato disguises himself as a tree, Socrates invokes a prophesying oak "in the holy place of Zeus at Dodona" (*Phaedrus* 275b). The Socratic point here is that it does not matter where the voice comes from—a tree or even a rock—insomuch as it speaks the truth. In other words, *logos* (or the voice of truth) is powerful enough to level down qualitative distinc-tions among different classes of beings. How so?

Suffice it to say that the modern systems of biological classification, formalized at the time of Carl Linnaeus, were foreign to the ancients. True: every being had a niche of its own and existed for a particular end, or *telos*. But the contours of these teleologies were not as we tend to pic-ture them. A noble human (e.g., Odysseus), a noble animal (e.g., a lion), and a noble plant (e.g., bay laurel) had more in common with one an-other than two members of the same "kingdom," such as a laurel tree and a stalk of corn. Nor were the boundaries between biological kingdoms set in stone. As we will learn in the next chapter, for Aristotle, a dumb human, incapable of abiding by the strict principles of logic, literally became no better than a vegetable. Contemporary transgenic research, too, violates these boundaries all the time. Plants with bacterial genes that presumably improve their growth, salmon with the genes of the eel-like ocean pout, or mice expressing human growth hormone genes are no longer oddities in our world. So, what if the mélange of otherwise dis-similar classes of beings, passing into and out of one another in ancient modes of thinking, is not a fanciful invention but an astute description of our transgenic present and future?

Heavenly and Earthly Plants

The grand cosmological narrative preserved in *Timaeus* holds the kernel of Plato's theory of plant life. It is futile, he implies, to treat plants as a unified and homogeneous category of beings. Along with other ancient thinkers, Plato recognizes that what botanists now define as the "higher" plants, including trees, are qualitatively different from the less individuated "lower" varieties, such as the grasses. Staggering as it may sound, the higher plants were assumed to share the physical substance of which humans were made. In the middle of an account focused on the divine creation of humanity, this nobler kind of plant emerges as a living creature consubstantial with us. The gods, Timaeus speculates, "engendered a substance akin to that of man, so as to form another living creature: such are the cultivated trees and plants and seeds which have been trained by husbandry and are now domesticated amongst us" (77a). Among Plato scholars, consensus is lacking as to whether we should take the speculation seriously. *Timaeus* is the least Socratic and the least dialogic of the Socratic dialogues. Essentially a monologue—or, as Socrates sarcastically puts it, as a euphemism for verbal diarrhea, "a feast of words" (20c)—delivered by the text's eponymous character, it is a compilation of a dizzying array of ancient cosmological and cosmogonic beliefs. Having said that, certain hallmarks of Platonic thought are stamped onto Timaeus's discourse, most notably when it comes to the subject of plant life.

In what is surely the most remarkable statement of the plant-human relation in the history of Western thought, the dialogue portrays humans in the shape of "heavenly plants":

> We declare that God has given to each of us, as his *daemon*, that kind of soul which is housed in the top of our body and which raises us—seeing that we are not an earthly but a heavenly plant—up from earth towards our kindred in the heaven. And herein we speak most truly; for it is by suspending our head and root from that region whence the substance of our soul first came that the divine power keeps upright our whole body.
>
> (90a–b)

In and of itself, the classification of the human as a kind of plant underscores the affinities between the vegetal kingdom and us. The contrast between the earthly and the heavenly plants retraces the difference between the higher and the lower varieties of actual vegetation. Still, humans are so much spiritually higher than the highest of plants that the entire system of spatial coordinates ("above" and "below") flips, revealing an entirely distinct reality. While our bodies may have a stake in the stuff of which other creatures are made, the substance of the rational soul derives from another region altogether: the eidetic sphere, or the realm of Ideas. It is this superior realm that nourishes our psyches, attached to the eidetic soil as though by invisible roots. In the earthly plant, the root is the lowest part immersed in the moist darkness of the earth. But in the heavenly plants that we are, the root is the highest point and the most lucid part of our bodily constitution—the head, which is also closest to Ideas. Just as vegetation clings to the earth for support, so the heavenly plant stands upright and grows in strength the more it is bound to its own ethereal ground. We are, so to speak, topsy-turvy plants rooted at the head in the eidetic soil above us. Compared to this firm anchorage, our locomotion is as haphazard as the movement of tree limbs and branches flapping in the wind.

The conceptual image of a heavenly plant teaches us an important lesson about the nature of Platonic Ideas. Now, these are not found in our heads, even though the rational soul housed there has sprouted from the substance of which Ideas are made. Beauty, Goodness, and Truth are not to be conflated with beautiful, good, and true things, themselves the hazy reflections of their corresponding Ideas. Even if, in a terrifying thought experiment, all sensible reality were to disappear, Beauty, Goodness, and Truth, not to mention the Idea of a tree, would remain untouched in their own autonomous sphere. This is because, eternal and immutable, Ideas exist independently of us, who pass like shadowy silhouettes over the face of the planet. They are the sole things that truly and fully *are*, neither coming into being nor passing away. More stable than the earth itself, which is prone to landslides and earthquakes, Ideas form the cornerstone of Plato's philosophy. Only by rooting ourselves in them, only by embracing the view of the human as a heavenly plant, can we hope to partake of the stability they promise.

To recap: in Plato, the meaning of human life and the key to our salvation are totally unrelated to the physical substance and activities we share with the rest of the living, be they plants or animals. Our *daemon*, or guardian spirit, is our capacity for reasoning: everything depends on how skillful we are in reconnecting with our celestial roots and, ultimately, with the substratum of what makes us human. To survey the marvelous region of Ideas is not to press on with the open-ended, future-oriented progress of knowledge. It is, instead, to return to our half-forgotten eidetic origins, keeping to the trajectory of Platonic *anamnesis*, remembrance, or, more precisely, un-forgetting.

As heavenly plants suspended from the eidetic sphere by invisible roots that converge on our heads, we are like marionettes that move with a sense of purpose when guided by the rational *daemon*. Cut those ties loose, and the human body will be reduced to a set of chaotic movements or a pile of incoherent actions, seeing that a solid connection to Ideas is responsible for keeping "upright our whole body." With the same degree of success we could sever a tree from its roots and hope that it would survive detached from the source of its vitality! As for the human, we occasionally glimpse this collapse in the temporary numbing of the rational *daemon* in us. In a state of inebriation—to take a familiar example—not even our limbs obey us; the body loses its bearings without the support it habitually draws from the eidetic soil.

But the fable of the earthly and heavenly plants is still more encompassing than that. Vegetal roots are the figures of depth as much as of hiddenness, which cannot be violated without inflicting major damage upon the entire plant. Does the same stipulation hold for the roots of the heavenly plant? Can *they* be revealed? One pointer is that Plato deems a direct contemplation of Ideas impossible. The impenetrable darkness of the soil conceals the subterranean portions of plants from view; the dazzling light of Ideas makes gazing at them straight on with our mind's eye unbearable. Platonism would have bordered on mysticism (an all-too-common misinterpretation, alas!) were it to bet on a direct intuition of Beauty, Goodness, and Truth. Yet Plato forbids going right to the root of the heavenly plant and, without further ado, exposing the soil from which it obtains nourishment. That is why he interposes dialogues and, more generally, speech or discourse as a mediation between the readers (and the speakers) and eidetic luminosity.

Where does the plane tree, *platanos*-Plato, fit in the division between the earthly and the heavenly plants? No matter how tall, actual plane trees, such as those that adorned the legendary Academy in Athens, do not reach the heights of the heavenly plant. More than that, when Plato identified with one of those trees, as he did in *Phaedrus*, he became a strange specimen, to say the least—his roots hovering above him and reaching through the air toward the realm of Ideas. The near monstrosity of this composite image was outweighed by a projection of the human shape onto a tree, with its outstretched limbs and upright posture, which distinguishes it (and us) from most animals. Unwittingly trailing Plato, the French poet Paul Claudel quipped, "*L'arbre seul, dans la nature est vertical, avec l'homme*": In nature, the tree alone is vertical, along with man.[4] At this precise point the analogy nevertheless breaks down. Whereas plants flourish from the earth up, humans grow from the heavenly ground down, their uprightness inverted. In the more noble stirrings of our souls, we yearn for this distant support of our existence. Much in Platonism gives voice to the nostalgia of the heavenly plant on a quest for its celestial roots.

Desiring Plants, Rooted Animals, and Other Ideas

A little earlier, I noted that ancient systems of thought operated with classifications utterly distinct from those of the moderns. One reason for the fluidity of the ancient categories has to do with language. In the vocabulary of Plato and his contemporaries specialized words for "plants" and "animals" simply did not exist. (In English, both of these derive from Latin.) This does not mean, of course, that ancient Greeks could not speak of these living beings. Rather, for reasons of linguistic necessity, in referring to plants and animals, they had considerably broader categories of beings in mind. So, the word for animal, *zōon*, signified any "living being" whatsoever, and we still see vestiges of that etymology when we visit a zoo or decide to study zoology. The word for plant, in turn, was *phuton*. Related both to nature as a whole (*phusis*) and to light (*phōs*), this word referred to any "growing being." The difference between plants and animals, then, was a matter of emphasis: whether one wished to highlight the living aspect of growing beings or, conversely, the growing aspect of living beings. To assert that the plant is a rooted and impassive animal in this context was merely to aver that it was a rooted and impassive living creature.

That's exactly what's at stake in Plato's treatment of the plant as a kind of animal. Undeniably, both are living beings (*zōa*), though their respective vitalities may be somewhat different. "Plants seem to live," writes Aristotle, "without sharing in locomotion or in perception" (*De Anima* 410b). This observation sounds as little more than a reiteration of Plato, who sees no problem in calling plants *zōa*: "For everything, in fact, which partakes of life may justly and with perfect truth be termed a living creature (*zōon*)" (*Timaeus* 77a). But what are the telltale signs of plant life? If plants are incapable of either locomotion or perception, then what *do* they share with animals? How to pinpoint the vitality of a living being whose energy goes almost entirely into growth (and reproduction)?

Plato's answer was unambiguous. Using Timaeus as his mouthpiece, he determined that plants possessed an appetitive soul—the same as the one housed in humans "between the midriff and the navel." This soul, he added, "shares not at all in opinions and reasoning and mind but in sensation, pleasant and painful, together with desires" (77b). Upon hearing about the appetitive soul of plants, today's readers of Plato might run out of patience with his theory. They will raise a litany of ironical questions: What is it that my cactus desires? What are the pleasures of a rosebush—not the ones it gives to those contemplating its blossoms, *but of the bush itself*? And that is not even to speak of the pains of a liana, the sensations of a bamboo, or the desires of a palm tree.

Before brushing aside the Platonic insight with a dismissive smirk, why not give the philosopher the benefit of the doubt and let him explain himself. His train of reasoning is actually very simple. Plants cannot live without receiving nourishment by imbibing water through their roots. (Although the term is of a Greek pedigree, photosynthesis was as yet unknown at the time of Plato.) When water is in short supply, plants detect the lack of moisture and respond by wilting. If they can be "thirsty," and if desire is associated with the experienced lack of the desired thing in the desiring being, then the fern you have not watered for weeks is, in fact, desirous of water.

The remaining piece of the puzzle is the idea of plant experience. Does a water-deprived fern really feel the absence of the object of its desire? For Plato, such a feeling is the uncompromising baseline for any life deserving of the name. Further, contemporary botany confirms this intuition. The subdiscipline of "plant signaling and communication," in particular, demonstrates that plants are more complex than previously thought. In addition to registering adverse changes in their environments (a drought, an attack by herbivorous insects, you name it), plants communicate, through their roots, the onset of environmental stressors, a piece of information they encode in biochemical messages intended for their neighbors.

It is not silly to talk about plant experience so long as we specify that it is devoid of self-experience. In Plato's precise formulation, the plant "is not endowed by its original constitution with a natural capacity for discerning or reflecting upon any of its own experiences. Wherefore it lives indeed and is not other than a living creature, but it remains stationary and rooted down owing to its being deprived of the power of self-movement" (*Timaeus* 77c). This explanation leads us to a new question, and a potential can of worms at that: *On what grounds does Plato disentangle desire from knowledge?* Does desire not occasion a rudimentary discernment of its own? At the very least, a desiring creature must be able to differentiate between a desirable object and the undesirable ones.[5]

The plant, of course, does not ask what water is, and it has no "idea" of water as a distinct object. Its knowledge is not at all conceptual but a practical outcome of successfully identifying, through appropriate receptors, X and not-X (in this case, water and not-water). Plants "know," in this very elementary sense of knowing, more than we give them credit for. Recently, the plant scientist Danny Chamovitz summarized the findings of contemporary botany in a book appropriately titled *What a Plant Knows*. In chapters that explore "what a plant sees," "what a plant feels," and the rest of the vegetable "senses," we come across data that support the Platonic hypothesis. Take, for instance, some of the most intelligent observable plant behavior, the closing of mimosa leaves as soon as they are touched. The mechanism behind rapid leaf closure is the plant's regulation of water levels in its cells. Upon physical contact, mimosa leaves generate an electric charge, amazingly similar to the action potentials of animal neurons, that causes leaf cells to divest themselves of water. Once the miniature hydraulic pump finishes its work, water pressure on cell walls drops, and the leaf closes.[6] Not only does the plant know that it is being touched, but it also manipulates a particular substance, namely water, to achieve the desirable outcome of leaf closure—and, under certain conditions, it can learn *not* to close its leaves.[7]

To be sure, in Plato's estimation, vegetal desire does not reach these heights of sophistication. It is concentrated exclusively in the appetitive soul with its pleasures and pains, hungers and temporary satiety, physical desires and their frustrations. Plato's plants are purely hedonistic creatures, as there is simply no other faculty of the soul (that's to say: no capacity for reasoning) to impose a limit on their strivings. We humans also have an appetitive soul, housed roughly around the stomach. In us, this is but the lowest psychic region, and it is hemmed in by the spirited soul, which dwells close to the heart, and the rational psyche that corresponds to the head. Provided that the rational soul is firmly in control of my actions, I would not act as a stomach without reason; however hungry I am, I would not snatch a piece of bread from the hands of another person. A harmoniously functioning human soul is just that—the appetites submitting to the law of reason with the help of an intermediary spirit. And the same goes for the ideal political regime Plato described in *The Republic*, where the element cognate to the appetitive soul, the class of the producers (the workers), submits to the philosopher-king, who embodies the principle of reason, with the mediation of the spirited class of guardians. It follows that Plato's workers are not only the creatures of pure desire but also the most vegetal of humans.

Hierarchical valuations of heavenly and earthly plants come back with a vengeance, and in an unabashedly political form at that. Harmony does not magically spring from equality; it is made contingent on the axiom that the highest must "by nature" preside and rule over the lowest—reason over the appetites, the philosopher-king over the workers, the heavenly over the earthly plant. Crucially, Plato's unarticulated premise in this argument is that a harmonious arrangement always posits a minimal degree of complexity, requiring the differentiation and specialization of parts in a coherent whole. But what of my ensouled cactus? The lowest type of soul in a human is both the highest and the lowest in the plant, for which the appetitive psyche is a member in a set of one. The plant turns out to be the great equalizer, a leveler of hierarchies, and an embodied challenge to the very idea of a limit. How will Plato respond to this silent vegetable threat?

Predictably enough, he will valorize domesticated plants over the wild varieties. The cultivated plants "have been trained by husbandry and are now domesticated amongst us" (*Timaeus* 77a) and thus are substantially akin to the humans. Where an inner measure and moderation are missing in vegetable growth, something or someone other than the plant will enforce the limit from the outside. Agriculture is the birthright of culture and a trophy in the victory of human spirit over the terrifying exuberance of wild nature. Before long, Plato reintroduces a hierarchical system into the plant kingdom by elevating the domesticated varieties, symbolic of humanity as a whole, over the wild specimens. (I leave it up to the reader to guess where weeds, the undesirable companions of cultivated plants, would fit in this hierarchy. Theirs is a slightly different story, which I will tell in a little while.)

Plato's second recipe for neutralizing the vegetable threat has been the trademark of all (or almost all) subsequent Western philosophy. The ancient Greek thinker reinserted the entire flora into a system of negative comparisons to humans. Make no mistake: the presumed consubstantiality with domesticated plants and the fact of sharing the appetitive soul with them were not the tokens of our proximity to our green brothers and sisters. Heavenly plants were coded as spatially and conceptually opposed to the earthly vegetation, with which we intersect only in the lowest, messiest, and most physically dependent regions of our being. Left to their own devices, unbridled desire, the soul of plants, and the psychosocial character of the workers—things that, in Plato's mind, must have been structurally equivalent—sweep us off our feet or, more accurately put, uproot our heads from their true ground and thrust us into an extreme danger zone. To succumb to their dictates is to become no better than a tree, be it as majestic as a plane.

But behind the flurry of negative comparisons, Plato has never quite managed to rid himself of the obsession that has prompted him to translate plant growth, however altered and ethereal, into everything that makes us human. Having eagerly devalued the actual soil and the plants rooted in it, he has sanctioned and immortalized the image, the *eidos*, or the idea of the plant that holds the key to our self-understanding. His teaching that we are *plants in reverse*—turned upside-down, rooted in the celestial ground—contains the most abiding conclusions of his philosophizing.

Two Grounds, Two Plants, Two Worlds?

To put it succinctly, the contrast between heavenly and earthly plants anticipates Plato's so-called two-world theory. The worlds in question are those of Ideas open to intellection, on the one hand, and of appearances accessible to the senses, on the other. The first is the foundation of life everlasting and true, static being; the second is the ground of finite growth and fleeting becoming. As everything else in Platonic thought, this bifurcation is mapped on the vertical axis high-low: the celestial sphere of Ideas is higher, in spatial as well as evaluative terms, than that of appearances. But—*voilà* the master-paradox of Platonism!—"high" and "low" are relational terms that imply each other and therefore make the absolute separation between the two worlds impossible. The markers of transcendence cancel out the very transcendent push they announce. A vertical continuum cuts across differences and reconciles opposites. Ideas and appearances, the intellect and the senses, heavenly and earthly plants all find their proper places on this "divided line," as Plato christens it. Heavenly it may be, but the human remains a plant.

The paradox we have just spotted is also the crux of Plato's greatest pedagogic endeavor. The point is not to describe, in a dispassionate manner, the segregation of the two worlds but to assist the readers in making a transition from the immature reliance on the senses to a life illuminated by Ideas. Were this quasi-religious conversion to have worked on a mass scale, Plato calculated, Socrates would not have received a death sentence from the irrational jury of five hundred Athenians, most of them swayed by sophistic argumentation. Who would have guessed that a measly plant could illustrate the transition from one world (or from one life) to another?

The extravagant centerpiece of *The Republic* is the Myth of the Cave. According to this Socratic allegory, humans, enthralled by the world of appearances, are like prisoners in a dimly lit cavern, deprived of the light of the sun (the Ideas). The heroic philosopher descends to the gloomy underworld to initiate a prison break by delivering those living in the shackles of the senses to the heights of intellection. If we are to believe Luce Irigaray, whose philosophy will contribute the final leaf to our intellectual herbarium, the Platonic cave is a metaphor for the womb,[8] given that the Greek word for cave, *hystera*, also signifies the uterus and stands at the semantic origins of hysteria, originally thought to be a neurotic condition caused by the disorders of the womb. Irigaray's daring reading certainly makes sense, considering the self-definition of Socrates as a "midwife of Ideas," the catalyst in the event of his interlocutors' second birth into the world of the mind. An alternative interpretation I would like to submit in what follows does not invalidate but supplements her feminist take on Plato.

The vegetable vein of Plato's thought hints at the possibility of interpreting the Myth of the Cave not exactly as a story of animal birth but of seed germination. It describes how heavenly plants sprouted from the dark soil of appearances to the light of Ideas. The sun, so prominent in the Platonic narrative, quickens the process by lavishing its luminosity and warmth upon the young human sprouts. Evidently, the sun can also overwhelm—dazzle and burn—the burgeoning plants if the transition from the underworld to the eidetic realm is too abrupt (*Republic* 515c). That's why the role of Socrates is so vital: he is like a gardener tending to the growing souls and ensuring that supports are available for the spiritual vines to climb up on their own initiative, using the tendrils of their understanding. (The persona of a caring gardener will make its comeback in the chapter on Plotinus.)

Astute readers will readily identify an apparent flaw in this allegory. When the seeds of earthly plants germinate, they grow up and down simultaneously, drawing vitality from sunlight and from subterranean moisture and minerals. In their impressive grandeur, plane trees reach the heights of one hundred feet above ground, but their roots extend further dozens of feet below the surface. Assuming that the earthly growth processes were applicable to the Myth of the Cave, the sprouting heavenly plants would have had to receive nourishment from the world of appearances *and* the light of Ideas alike. Yet nothing could be further from the take-home message of *The Republic*, or so the conventional reading of the dialogue goes. In the event of their second birth, humans ought to release themselves from their earthly connections and, overcoming the confusion caused by this deracination, find their true roots elsewhere, in the sphere of Ideas. Could it be the case that the act of uprooting the heavenly plant from everyday reality smuggles the so-called two-world theory into our understanding of Plato? Is the theory's affirmation of a complete separation between the senses and intellection equivalent to a culling of the plant?

Assume the separation were perfect. In that case, those who have beheld the Ideas with their mind's eye would need to isolate themselves, as much as possible, from the life of the flesh with its sensory evidences and pleasures, symbolically (or perhaps literally) dying to this world. That is, most likely, what we would expect of philosophers: to carry on a monkish, self-denying existence away from the hustle and bustle of the everyday. They should be detached from mundane realities to the point of appearing otherworldly and eschew above all the messiness of public affairs.

Someone who does not in the least fit this stereotype is the model philosopher, Socrates. A notorious gadfly, he eagerly participated in the drinking parties (the *symposia*) of the Athenian aristocracy and lurked around the marketplace seeking, to no avail, a person wiser than him. Faithful to his own injunction, Socrates came back to the cave of appearances to give those imprisoned there a chance to emerge into the broad and luminous expanses of Ideas. He spanned two seemingly disparate worlds and, not unlike Plato-as-plane-tree, fashioned himself into a plant that/who was in touch both with the dimness of appearances and the luminosity of Ideas.

The philosopher, not by accident, repeats the courageous feat of Orpheus, who went down to the underworld in search of his beloved Eurydice. Leading an examined life means delving on a daily basis into the depths of one's psyche, rooted in the obscurity of the unconscious, just as the subterranean portion of the plant is mired in the darkness of the soil. On a reduced scale, each of us is at once an Orpheus and a Eurydice, a Socrates and a cave dweller, in relation to him- or herself. The arduous mission of conscious and finite creatures such as ourselves is not so much to uncover our celestial roots but to square them with the fleshly portions of the heavenly plants that we are. But we are not the first to perform this small miracle, in which two become one. Want to see for yourself? Just glance at a tree growing on your street to realize how successfully, if inconspicuously, it straddles the earth and the sky.

2 | ARISTOTLE'S WHEAT

Philosopher's Bread (and Butter)

Nicknamed "the Reader" by Plato himself and known as Ille Philosophus, or The Philosopher, in the Middle Ages, Aristotle was responsible for singlehandedly systematizing philosophy and gifting it with a unique technical vocabulary. Words with humble everyday meanings received a new lease on life when, at the hands of the Master, they were transfigured into abstract concepts. Nearly two and a half millennia after Aristotle, most of these have withstood the test of time and remain the indispensable tools of our trade. Philosophers of every historical epoch will keep on dreaming of a dispassionate and purely logical discourse of truth. But while Aristotelianism is the organizing matrix of the discipline, their reveries will inevitably fall short of reality. Just as, in large measure against his stated wishes, Plato forever allied philosophy with storytelling and myth, so Aristotle, perhaps involuntarily, anchored its fate in the vicissitudes of ordinary language. Daring as it may be, any attempt at a conceptual clarification will find itself under the obligation to return to the "impure" source of thinking and to grapple with its consequences. Hegel and Wittgenstein have little in common save for a sober realization of this necessity, which they convert from an irremediable flaw into the strength of their philosophizing.

We need not go far for an example. Matter, a term we tend to take for granted, is among Aristotle's enduring achievements. It, too, issued from an ordinary word, *hylē*, which in colloquial Greek meant "wood," whether the growing forests or timber.[1] Unlike its modern variation, Aristotelian matter does not refer to just about anything with volume and mass; nor does it describe a physical extended substance. Instead, it has to do with the stuff of which a thing is made, the thing's "material cause." Matter is simply materials (bronze, stone, and so forth) before they are shaped into a recognizable form. What is curious, though, is that one type of material, wood, lends its name to materiality as such. In line with its preconceptual origin, matter is essentially wooden!

Thus the world of plants was the inspiration behind the birth of a vital Aristotelian concept. Besides this vague allusion to vegetation, there is also a particular plant that crops up with notable consistency in texts as diverse as *Physics* and *Metaphysics*, *Politics* and *Nicomachean Ethics*. That plant is wheat. In *Metaphysics*, Aristotle's preferred cereal goes to illustrate the strongest sense of being entailed in the copula "is." We mean different things, Aristotle observes, when "we say Hermes is in the stone, and a half line is in the line, and that a growing stalk *is* wheat [*sitos*]" (*Metaphysics* 1017b). In the first case, the statue of a god is in the stone only potentially, awaiting the sculptor's chisel to bring it out in all its splendor to the light of day; in the second, half a line is contained in the entire line, of which it is a part; and, in the third, there is a felicitous coincidence, a necessary identity between "a growing stalk" and "wheat."

This stalk we are leaning over with Aristotle is a specimen of wheat, a tiny sample of the genus it represents. It may be neither a ripe nor a perfect specimen nor one that embodies the genus as a whole. Yet the growing stalk *is* wheat in a stronger sense than the yet uncreated statue of Hermes is in the rough stone or than a part is in the whole, half a line is in the line. Why? Because it is a momentary actualization of the cereal not as mere potentiality, inherent in the seed, but as the presence of the plant before us, even if its qualification as "growing" or "not yet ripe" disallows the attribution of full presence to this, or any other, living being. (A quick aside on the meaning of actualization and potentiality may be helpful. While the first term implies putting something into *action* or into play in the drama of existence, the second revolves around the sheer capacity or the power—in Latin: *potestas*—to do so.)

Let's pause for a moment here and flip back a page in our herbarium. We have just left Plato's plane tree behind. The contrast between Aristotle's lowly, albeit deliberately sown, cereal and Plato's magnificent, though wild, plant is not accidental. As you shift your mental gaze back and forth between the two pages in the intellectual herbarium, recall yet another image: the legendary depiction of Plato and Aristotle in Raphael's "The School of Athens." In the center of the Renaissance masterpiece, Plato points his finger up, gesturing toward the transcendent world of Ideas (or is it the crown of a plane tree outside the painting's frame he is bringing to our attention?), even as Aristotle brings the palm of his own hand down, grounding knowledge and humanity itself in the world of the here and now. Aristotle will implicitly reject his teacher's notion of humans as "celestial plants." Presented with a choice between the plane tree and the grass that framed the scene of Plato's *Phaedrus*, he will opt for the humble grass that stays close to the earth. Wheat would, in point of fact, be even better than grass, since the cereal is a useful, cultivated crop, indicative of hard labor, rather than a green carpet inviting us to a leisurely conversation. In other words, the cereal fulfills a definite mundane purpose—and Aristotle was partial to the network of purposes or ends that, according to him, made the entire universe what it is—and gives us a foretaste of what symbolizes all human sustenance: our proverbial daily bread.

Indeed, the Greek *sitos* applied more broadly to any staple food. Symbolically, it was an umbrella term for human fare. In Hesiod's *Works and Days*, for instance, humanity is defined as "men who live on *sitos*" (513). Homer in *The Iliad* relates that the mortals consume *sitos*, in contrast to the "blessed gods" who "eat no bread [*sitos*], drink no shining wine, and so are bloodless, which is why we call them deathless" (V.382–384). Not only was the same noun used as a label for the cultivated plant itself, the edible product into which it was transformed, and all kinds of human food, but it also betokened a variety of grains, including wheat and barley. This semantic confusion surely provided Aristotle with ample food for thought and became a liability in his persistent efforts at disambiguation and classification. Everyday language, in all its messiness, intruded upon the philosophical work of ordering and explication. And the unexpected harbinger of the intrusion was a measly stalk of wheat, which both exemplified and subverted Aristotle's reasoning.

Now, Aristotle spent a fair share of his intellectual energy on determining how the whole relates to its parts and the parts to the whole. To everyone who knew "the Reader," it was no surprise that this seemingly

obscure problem preoccupied him so. After all, he was extremely dissatisfied with Plato's gloss on the connection between the Ideas and their
shadowy reproductions, the things of the senses that somehow participated in eidetic immortal essence. History has shown that this problem was no passing fad: even the twentieth-century phenomenological
philosopher Edmund Husserl allocated to it many a dense page of his
monumental *Logical Investigations*.

One of Aristotle's targets in trying to solve the riddle of the whole
and its parts was rhetoric. In common discourse, we say that "a child
comes from father and mother, or a plant out of the earth." But, Aristotle
clarifies, "they come from a part of these" (*Metaphysics* 1023b). A stalk of
wheat does not germinate from the entire earth but from the tiny cubit
of land where it is rooted. Grasping this does not require much musing.
What to do, however, with the small linguistic conundrums in which one
word-label attaches itself to the part and the whole alike? How to ana-
lyze the relation of wheat to grains and of grains to staple foods, if each
of the three terms goes under the same name, *sitos*?[2]

When a part stands in for the whole, we are facing what rhetoricians
call *synecdoche*. We have already stumbled upon this rhetorical trap when
we discovered that the original concept of matter derived from one type
of material, namely wood. There are also less abstruse usages of synecdoche: for instance, a news reporter, who evokes a capital city (say, Paris)
in place of the entire country (here, France). Aristotle is acutely aware of
this phenomenon, which in *Rhetoric* he groups under the heading of metaphor. With equal acuteness, he feels the blows these rhetorical tropes
deal to the philosopher's "bread and butter," that is, to reason and formal
logic, built on the axiom that X and not-X cannot be true at the same
time. The assertion that something is simultaneously the whole and not
the whole, a part and not a part, grossly violates the principle of noncontradiction, which was so dear to Aristotle's philosophical heart. Although
he concedes that metaphors can promote learning, he would vehemently
object to the mystifying rhetorical force of the synecdoche that erases
the lines of demarcation between parts and wholes.

We would overlook the other half of the story if we were to concentrate solely on the synecdochic nature of *sitos*. In the jargon of rhetoric,
it is also a homonymy, where dissimilar things receive the same name,

as in *race*, in the sense of a racial group, and *race*, in the sense of a running contest. While it is still possible to dismiss synecdoche as "mere metaphor," decidedly less serious than a pure concept, the paradoxes of homonymy call for more drastic measures. Julie K. Ward, who dedicated a book to this subject, recommends a radical move of turning to extra-linguistic referents in order to reintroduce some order into the chaos wreaked by homonymy.[3] In all fairness, her solution is a bit like throwing the baby out with the bathwater. What impels us toward these referents outside of language if not further explanations, weaving and casting the webs of words a little farther than before, and so on *ad infinitum*? At best, we would be urged to continue weaving this web, supplementing *sitos* with the appropriate discernment "in the sense of" wheat, grain, staple food items, food of the mortals—fill in the blank.

What a moment ago looked like an explanation of being stands in need of yet another explanation. The conclusion "the growing stalk is *sitos*" is—far from determining its actual being—an open invitation to a vast assortment of interpretations. The word immediately following the copula "is" signifies anything from the actual plant *wheat* to the general category *grain* and from the even more general notion of staple food to the yet unbaked (i.e., potential) bread, the nourishment of mortals. Can we learn anything about the relation of parts to wholes in the rhetorical Babel where the elements are hopelessly mismatched?

Aristotle must have found some solace in his investigations of the animal world that shed light on the part-whole connection, which fascinated him. When it comes to the body of an animal, the whole is an organism, and the parts are distinct organs dependent on the entity they comprise. Outlining organismic logic in *The Movement of Animals*, Aristotle does not withhold from his readers a helpful simile:

> And the animal organism must be conceived after the similitude of a well-governed commonwealth. When order is once established in it there is no more need of a separate monarch to preside over each several task. The individuals each play their assigned part as it is ordered, and one thing follows another in its accustomed order. So in animals there is the same orderliness—nature taking the place of custom—and each part naturally doing his own work as nature has composed them.
>
> (703a)

The orderly arrangement of the organs (parts, or individuals) in the organism (the whole, or the commonwealth) rests on a clear division of labor instituted by nature itself. Further, the organs are both dependent on the organism and interdependent among themselves, thanks to a connection properly termed "organic." Does this hold true for the plant? Does the plant exhibit the same natural orderliness as that evident in animal constitution?

The answer Aristotle secures makes matters worse. For one, plants have "no great variety in their heterogeneous parts" as a result of the presumed simplicity of their vital functions: "For, where the functions are but few, few also are the organs required to effect them" (*Parts of Animals* 656a). The relative lack of differentiation in plant organs makes it doubtful that plants are organisms, coherent wholes with distinct and interdependent parts. Animal order gives way to vegetable anarchy of parts that step into the role of wholes and wholes that are interchangeable with parts, of plants growing upon other plants (681a), and of severed branches that "live on and attain the perfect form of the whole" (682b). A stalk of wheat turns out to be a stick in the wheel of the well-oiled organismic (and philosophical) machinery that functions so smoothly in the case of animals.

Potential and Actual Plants

By the time *sitos* resurfaces in *Metaphysics*, Aristotle's philosophy has already entered the thicket of issues surrounding potentiality and actuality. Simply put, the old chicken-and-egg question hangs in the balance: did an actual, fully grown plant first produce a seed (i.e., a potential plant), or did the seed give rise to a plant? What was the cause and what the effect in the process of natural generation?

Compared to the idea of material causality, these questions do not sound remote to us, and for a good reason. When we speak of causes in the modern context, we hone in on a subclass of Aristotelian causality known as "efficient." Their efficiency has nothing whatsoever to do with competence; rather, it pertains to the unity of causes and their effects. British empiricists, among others, pictured efficient causality in terms of one billiard ball hitting another, prompting the latter to move with a speed and in a trajectory determined by the first ball. As for Aristotle, he distinguished among four kinds of causes. In addition to the material, which we have already touched upon, and the efficient, he postulated formal and final causality. Intimately linked to his ontology, or theory of being, the four causes explain in the most detailed way what a thing *is*, how it *came to be*, and what it is *for*.

Back to efficient causality, the chicken, the egg, the grain, and the plant! In the contest between the chicken and the egg (the actual bird and the potential one), the chicken wins. Actuality must be "prior to potentiality" both logically and temporally. "I mean," Aristotle writes, "that this man who is already active and this grain crop [*sitos*] and this seeing animal are temporally ahead of the material for a man, the grain of wheat, and the animal whose eyes are not yet open; for they are not yet in operation, but can become an actual man, plant, or seeing animal" (*Metaphysics* 1049b). Potentiality is comparable to a bridge leading from one actual being to another of its own kind. But there is a caveat: the bridge vanishes as soon as the second actual being appears before us. In her immensely perceptive *Aristotle's Ethics as First Philosophy*, Claudia Baracchi elegantly recaptured this Aristotelian insight that "actuality comes to be out of actuality."[4] In the beautiful quasi-tautology of this movement, we can make sense of the miracle of the vanishing bridge—the disappearing potentiality—with reference to the new appearance that has absorbed or actualized the potential, leaving no remainder behind. Between one stalk of wheat and another, which will have germinated from it, there is a grain anticipating the new plant it will grow to be.

It's worth noting that a mature plant is inserted into a continuous line of examples alongside an actual human and a "seeing animal." Why does Aristotle bestow an honor so high upon it? Because, at bottom, all three are actual beings with a potentiality to generate other beings akin to themselves? If so, then the plant, the animal, and the human must have a special generative capacity enabling them to reproduce themselves (i.e., to produce other actual creatures). In *De Anima*, this capacity is a part of *tō threptikon*—the vegetal soul, shared by all three types of creatures. Actual living beings are also *actualizing*, that is to say, productive of other real beings in their own image and of potential replicas of themselves. Those searching for something like "plant agency" will find the Aristotelian acumen enlightening. Irreducible to the modern mechanical causality of colliding billiard balls, the efficient cause "in the sense illustrated

by a seed, a physician, and advisor, and any agent generally is the factor whereby a change or state of being is initiated" (*Metaphysics* 1013b).
And so, obliquely harkening to Aristotle, Immanuel Kant will chide his
nineteenth-century contemporaries for their mechanistic thinking. "It is
utterly impossible," the German thinker will remark, "for human reason
to hope to understand the generation even of a blade of grass from mere
mechanical causes."[5]

On the side of potentiality, a grain of wheat joins the list that includes "the material for a man" and an "animal whose eyes are not yet
open." Some philosophers have taken the substantial identity of a potential human—an embryo—and an actual human to be fodder for an
Aristotelian argument against abortion. One of them, the late Professor
Alfonso Gomez-Lobo, of Georgetown University, was appointed to the
Presidential Bioethics Council by George W. Bush and to the Pontifical
Academy for Life at the Vatican. His argument for the personhood of
the fetus developed directly out of Aristotle's thinking of potentiality.
"It is because we are humans right from the beginning," Gomez-Lobo
wrote in his *Morality and the Human Goods*, "that we slowly develop into
human adults (and not into monkeys or whales)."[6] But the same is true,
in a banal way, for any being with a unique genetic makeup, which is why,
for once, Aristotle positions plants and animals on the same level as humans. Would the textual evidence we have uncovered stir philosophers
such as Gomez-Lobo to respect the ownmost potentialities of wheat,
monkeys, and whales? And, if actuality in Aristotle's philosophical narrative is both temporally and logically prior to potentiality, does it not become the true locus of reproductive ethics? That is, doesn't the primacy
of the actual human being (a woman) entail her "right to choose"?

The deep reason behind Aristotle's untiring insistence on the priority
of the actual is that, for the Greeks, something could only come from
something else; *creatio ex nihilo*, creation out of nothing, was a much later
Christian invention that made no sense in ancient Greece. In *Physics*,
Aristotle puts this bluntly: "There is always something already there,
out of which the resultant thing comes; for instance, the seed of a plant
or animal" (190b). But a new dilemma immediately rears its head as
a consequence of this commonsense observation—the dilemma of infinite regress. Assuming that before every living creature there was another nearly identical creature, where does the chain of actualities, or of

self-actualizing potentialities, start? Is the origin infinitely pushed back, in time and in the space of thinking? Is it ultimately unknowable? Or, is there, after all, no such thing as the true beginning?

Aristotle could not tolerate the impression that the chain of actualities was winding down to infinity. Giving up on the concept of the beginning, *arkhē*, would be underwriting a purely chaotic world because the Greeks understood *arkhē* at the same time as the origin and as the commanding principle, the order-creating first cause. So, to avoid philosophical chaos, Aristotle came up with a bold hypothesis, an assumption that—he knew full well—was not borne out by any factual evidence. At the beginning of the chain of becomings, of actualities traversing the vanishing bridge of potentiality, he posited a fully actual being, the primary *unmoved mover*. A useful theoretical fiction, this metaphysical construct, reminiscent of the monotheistic God, was the non-natural origin of nature, exempt from the laws governing generation and decay. This pure agency, unaffected by anything outside itself, was diametrically opposed to a growing plant—the quintessential thing of nature dependent on the external elements (sunlight, moisture) and embodying the reproductive principle.[7]

But what exactly does Aristotle have in mind when he mentions *nature*? In a nutshell, the overall movement of generation or production that harmoniously unites three out of four Aristotelian causes: the material out of which natural beings are produced, their form or blueprint (i.e., the genetic code), and the efficient cause of their generation (other creatures like them) (*Metaphysics* 1032a). Conspicuously absent from this list is the final cause, which answers the question, "For the sake of what is the power of generation applied?" We will tackle this shortly.

For now, observe that a being that has a nature "such as a plant or an animal" is "what has been generated" (*Metaphysics* 1032a). This is yet another tautological statement, for nature is nothing but the total generation of beings governed by their material, formal, and efficient causes. The ongoing generative process does not permit actuality to rest but awakens its ownmost potentiality, out of which a new actual being will flourish. The unmoved mover, though, has no nature because it has not been generated: the origin has no origin. Like the Mosaic God, it is absolutely what it is. In comparison to it, we humans are no different from plants that take time to grow and flourish, sometimes wilting before

actualizing any of our potentialities. How, in the Aristotelian philosophical universe, can we become all we can be? How do plants attain their
actualized "planthood"? And at what crossroads do human and vegetal
destinies intersect?

On Being All You Can Be (Without Becoming a Plant)

The U.S. military has learned a thing or two from Aristotle. The recruit-
ment slogan it favored at the end of the last century, "Be all you can be!"
is an eerie echo of the ancient desideratum for a maximum actualization
of one's hidden potentialities. Of course, the capacities prized by the
recruiters are definitely not those Aristotle had in store for humans. For
the Greek philosopher, the highest and the most proper potentiality we
have is that of rational thinking aided by the principle of noncontradiction. So elevated is this theoretical activity that it manages to peek behind the curtain of the divine realm (*theoria* is, literally, a contemplation
of divinity). Failure to actualize this capacity threatens our very status as
humans. Those who disregard the principle of noncontradiction sink all
the way down to the state of a vegetable: "If, however, all men alike are
both right and wrong, no one can say anything meaningful; for one must
then at the same time say these and also other things. And he who means
nothing, but equally thinks and does not think, in what respect does his
condition differ from that of a plant?" (*Metaphysics* 1008b).

It was, perhaps, Aristotle's outrage that blinded him to the fact that
he was engaging in the activity he criticized at the exact moment of criticizing it. A human who snubs the principle of noncontradiction "equally
thinks and does not think," which is itself a contradiction in terms! The
point Aristotle tries to bring across could well be that it is impossible
to describe the violations of formal logic in formal-logical terms. However, much more than this impossibility is riding on his enigmatic verdict. Those who, at the same time, think and do not think find themselves in the condition of plants: unable to say anything meaningful,
to make sense, or to activate their properly human psyche. Aristotle of
course alludes to the flexible gradation of beings we have come across
in Plato—an ontological framework where one could happen upon all
kinds of creaturely mixes. An orderly universe is guaranteed only while
each being actualizes the potentialities that belong to it: a stalk of wheat,

those of wheat; a dog, those of dogs; and a human, those of humans. When a lapse, whether accidental or not, creeps into the process of actualization, nothing prevents the barely thinking (thinking and not thinking) human specimen from sliding down to the level of a plant, which specializes exclusively in the acquisition of nutrients and reproduction. Couch potatoes, be forewarned!

To his credit, Aristotle does not state that those who violate formal logic (let alone the plants themselves) are unthinking. They both think and don't think, which may mean that they think differently, in a less abstract way. Life is already intellection, dispersed into as many modes of thinking as there are forms of life. *Tō threptikon*, or vegetal soul, traversing the biological kingdoms and species, is neither a symbolic nor a conscious form of thought, but it is thought nonetheless (or, twisting formal logic a little more: thought that is not thought). In contemporary terms we might say that evolutionary adaptation, in which plants have excelled as evidenced by their successful spread across the surface of the earth, is a sign of lived intelligence. All the same, the nutritive and reproductive excellence of a plant, which is the bare minimum for the maintenance and perpetuation of vital functions in any organism, is insufficient for safeguarding our humanity. It is up to the readers to infer what Aristotle could contribute to the euthanasia debate and how he would assess the medical condition known as "persistent vegetative state" in humans.

In striving to be all it can be, how does a natural being endowed with a set of potentialities actualize them? Precisely by putting them into action, practicing them, phenomenalizing them, bringing them to the light of day. A plant that draws nourishment from the soil and from sunlight, that bursts forth with seed-bearing fruit, and that, in this abundant fertility, gives rise to other plants of its kind practically actualizes itself. A human guided in her discernments by logical thinking and engaged in theoretical contemplation actualizes her humanness. Of course, humans may botch or altogether ignore the precepts of theoretical and applied reason. We have already recorded the ontological side-effects of this fiasco. But plants, too, can fail in what *they* are supposed to do. Aristotle's verdict? A " 'seedless' fruit is in a sense imperfect" (*Metaphysics* 1023a), in that it does not live up to its purpose (*telos*), elucidating the entire nature of a plant. Though it holds reproductive potentiality, a barren plant does not put this power into action, does not actualize it. To avoid endangering his carefully constructed teleology—the system of purposes or ends—Aristotle dismisses barrenness as a mere accident, a chance privation, an exception to the normal course of affairs. As a rule, coming-to-fruition will provide him, as well as many subsequent philosophers, with a tangible model of teleological actualization.

Considering that fruit and seed exhibit the excellence of the vegetal soul, whose potentialities pass into living actuality, it is all the more amusing that Aristotle viewed these parts of a plant as the excretory byproducts of its nutritive process. (Plants indeed use their own waste to their advantage, as they convert it into the outer hard layers of their bodies—a sort of vegetal exoskeleton. Thus, they attain stability in the absence of something like the animal skeletal structure.) In *Parts of Animals* the philosopher marvels at the fact that plants have no equivalent to the intestine in animals: they are "without any part for the discharge of waste residue." "For the food which they absorb from the ground," he continues, "is already concocted, and they give off as its equivalent their seeds and fruit" (*Parts of Animals* 655b). In other words, plants can only eat (with their roots functioning as subterranean mouths) and shit (with fruit as the equivalent of waste). It is this ingenuous solution that paves the way to the conception of *tō threptikon* as the seat of a single capacity for nourishment, where reproduction is reduced to a byproduct of nutrition. The actualized potentiality of plants mingles the highest and the basest; were we to psychoanalyze Aristotle, we would have concluded, in the spirit of Freud, that his theory of plant life is the sublimation of shit.

Since Aristotle adhered to the axiom of a fixed natural order and shrugged off any and all explanations contingent on chance, he took it upon himself to detail the strict regularities of actualization. Two of these are exceptionally pertinent to our discussion.

First, the development of potentialities always and necessarily tends toward a predetermined limit inherent to each developing being. More so than the form of past actuality, this limit regulates the movement of actualization from the future, as it were. Along these lines, "it is impossible that an animal or plant should exceed all limit in greatness or smallness," and "the same must be true of any part of it" (*Physics* 187b). Aristotle goes on to cite flesh and bones as animal parts and fruit as their vegetal analogues, subject to the limitations of size. The earnest efforts of bodybuilders and agronomists notwithstanding, they will not manage to produce a set of muscles or pieces of fruit so sublime as to exceed all measure. The phenomenon of the exploding Chinese watermelons reported in 2011 and likely instigated by growth-promoting chemicals is a good illustration of this impossibility.

All this is true for physical measures. But the actualization of our uniquely human potentialities introduces an unexpected twist into Aristotle's philosophical narrative. Indisputably, there are objectively set limits to growth and to the activities that promote it; to say this somewhat crudely, there is a non-negotiable constraint to how much a human (or a plant) can eat and shit. The human capacity for rational thought and for theoretical activity, too, is limited. We cannot be purely rational like the gods: our finite bodily existence stands in the way of that. Nonetheless, at the summit of *theoria*, glimpsing something of divine nature, we achieve the sort of self-reflexivity that results in "thought thinking itself." That is how we can finally be all we can be. Akin to the unmoved mover, unaffected by things outside itself, thought thinking itself puts in place a peculiar self-limitation, for it is not limited by anything save for itself! It does not do away with the limit but appropriates it, and in this subjection to itself, it glimmers with the promise of freedom. This circularity, symbolized by a snake biting its own tail, is foreclosed to plants, which, in Aristotle's view, lack self-reflexivity and subjective interiority, an inner world of thoughts, dreams, memories, and hopes. The plant does not get a hold of—does not appropriate—itself. We can only speculate on how Aristotle would have reacted to the recent findings of plant scientists, who have pointed out the existence of vegetable memory, self- and kin-recognition, learning, etc.[8] In any event, the exciting implication of this research is that even "advanced" psychic structures like memory need not be actualized in subjective consciousness or self-consciousness but can be inscribed in the bodies of organisms.

The *second* regularity of actualization worth highlighting is that neither the process nor its outcome is haphazard: "It is not a matter of chance what springs from a given seed, since an olive comes from such an one, and a man from such another" (*Physics* 196a). And, in the treatise *On Generation and Corruption*, Aristotle will add wheat to the equation: "What then is the cause [for the fact] that man is generated from man, and wheat from wheat, and not an olive?" (333b). Rather than chance, the essential nature of a propagating being is responsible for what is generated. In the same passage, Aristotle admits that exceptions to this general rule (i.e., what we know as genetic mutations) are attributable to "chance or luck." As we know, genetics did not exist as a scientific discipline when Aristotle penned these lines. Drawing a vast majority of his theoretical inferences from animal life and utilizing the "generation of animals" as a paradigm case for everything that lives, Aristotle could not have suspected that plants exhibit a much greater genetic flexibility than animals. Apple seeds, for instance, never reproduce the mother tree but give rise to a novel species each time they are planted.[9] On average, plants show more plasticity than animals in their development, producing changes that often go as deep as their genetic makeup and that are passed on to the subsequent generation.[10] A veritable Aristotle's nightmare, genetic plasticity in plants does not spell out outright chaos, where a stalk of wheat can somehow morph into an olive tree. But it does challenge his bid to neutralize chance in the process of actualization. Plants would be all they could be on the condition that they could realize their infinite potentialities for being—a complete and utter impossibility, to say the least.

Wishing to exorcise chaos from thinking and from being, Aristotle stresses in his *Physics* the idea that it is not "a matter of chance what comes up when you sow this seed or that," but he is forced to grant that the "indications of purpose" in plants are not "elaborately articulated" (199b). His long-lost tractate on botany would have likely helped explain the nonarticulateness of the vegetal purpose. (The book *De Plantis*, or *On Plants*, attributed to Aristotle, was likely composed roughly three hundred years after his death by Nicolaus of Damascus.) Absent the original text, we can reconstruct the Aristotelian hypothesis, which likely sounded something like this: The purpose, or the final cause, is evident in the parts of plants but not in the whole. Plants, Aristotle maintains, "produce organs subservient to their perfect development—leaves, for instance, to shelter the fruit" (*Physics* 199a). But while leaves exist "for the sake of" fruit, the plant does not exist for itself. Its goal is to exercise its generative capacity, to give rise to another like it, which means that its actualization does not culminate in itself but in that other being, and so forth, to the *nth* degree. Reproduction, the final cause of plants, is not exactly final, because a potentially infinite series of offspring cannot reach natural closure. The open-endedness of plant life encroaches on Aristotle's orderly universe.

Chaotic Proliferations: Collapsing Distinctions

The philosopher's heroic fight against chaos ends in disappointment and is blamed on the rudimentary and relatively undifferentiated state of plant existence. Not even the most fundamental division between nature and culture withstands the destabilizing power of vegetation. Blurring this line of demarcation, cultivated crops are the products of both domains: culture, in a sense, is born of cultivation. Hence, their appearance in Aristotle's texts leads to a sudden implosion of conceptual boundaries and to the explosion of internal contradictions menacing the entire philosophical enterprise with an imminent breakdown.

Only apparently unrelated, the Aristotelian critique of moneymaking follows directly from his notion of the final cause. To lend or invest money so as to gain more of it upon its maturation date is to plunge into a never-ending routine. Since money is a pure potentiality of purchasing power, this activity does not serve any final end; instead, it treats the financial means as an actual aim. But neither does the life of plants have a clearly defined final end! This coincidence is, itself, not coincidental. Similar to vegetal growth, the expansion of capital has no internally necessary limit, that "for the sake of which" it grows. This is why the terminology of financial operations—yields, maturation, and so forth—borrows so heavily from botanical life processes.

The ambiguous entwinement of plants with finance is apparent in Aristotle's texts. Again, wheat is the main protagonist in this knotty story. Early on in *Politics* Aristotle gives a nod of approval to the barter customs of those "barbarian tribes," *barbarikōn*, that satisfy their mutual needs "by exchange: they exchange one class of useful goods for another—for example, they take and give wine and grains [*sitos*] and so on." But the barbarians do not carry the process farther than this. "Such a technique of exchange," Aristotle deems, "is not contrary to nature and is not a form of moneymaking; for it keeps to its original purpose to re-establish nature's own equilibrium of self-sufficiency" (*Politics* 1257a). The emblematic products of cultivation, wine and grains, revindicate nature, to the extent that their barter promotes self-sufficiency based on the mutual satisfaction of need. Quite tellingly, Aristotle sides with the barbarians, his version of the "noble savages," who are in touch with nature, as opposed to the hypercivilized, money-addicted Hellenes. His repudiation of purely financial transactions and nostalgic praise of barter economies are part of his not-so-veiled critique of the Athenian social, political, and economic corruption and decline.

But is it really the case that wheat and wine belong squarely on the side of nature? Isn't the proportion in which the two commodities are exchanged a matter of agreement, that is to say, of convention? This is the very point Aristotle himself makes in *Nicomachean Ethics*: "The rules of justice based on convention and expediency are like standard measures. Grain and wine measures are not equal in all places, but are larger in wholesale and smaller in retail markets. Similarly, the rules of justice ordained not by nature but by man are not the same in all places" (V.vii.5). Barter may not be *contra natura* but it does not hinge upon some invariable value set by nature itself, either. Thanks to a negotiated consensus among the parties, two measures of wheat are worth, for example, one measure of wine. Even if, as Marx claims openly, referring to Aristotle, the same amount of labor goes into producing a measure of wine and two measures of wheat, labor is nothing natural; it is, on the contrary, the linchpin of civilization, if there ever was one. And, besides, measures (*metra*: hence, the word "meter") are relative to the context where they are used: larger in wholesale markets and smaller in retail. The equivalences of wheat and wine are thus doubly unnatural—first, because the measure of each is place and time dependent, and, second, because there is no magical equation that would "naturally" settle the right proportion between them for all eternity.

We have not yet gleaned all the grain there is to harvest from the margins of Aristotle's texts. Another important distinction collapses when, with the help of an allegory, the difference between humans and plants evaporates into philosophy's thin air. The meltdown happens twice on those pages of *The Politics* that decry the tyrannical core of democracy, which is obsessed with formal equality. The story Aristotle narrates fea-

tures, in addition to grain stalks, the tyrant of Corinth, Periander, and
the tyrant of Miletus, Thrasybulus:

> It is said that to Thrasybulus' messenger, who had come for advice, Perian-
> der returned no answer; but while walking in a field, reduced all the ears of
> grain [*stakhus*] to one level by lopping off the tallest. The messenger did not
> understand the motive for this action but reported it to Thrasybulus, who
> perceived that he ought to remove the outstanding men.... Oligarchies and
> democracies are in just the same position, for ostracism has very much the
> same effect as lopping off and exiling the leading men.[11]
>
> (*Politics* 1284)

In this extended metaphor, the exceptional citizens *are* the tallest stalks
of grain, and the magnitude of human virtue is correlated with the physical size of the plants. You will have noticed that more than one conceptual frontier is trespassed in this brief excerpt. Among other things,
Aristotle levels the political difference between tyranny, oligarchy, and
democracy by showing a deep commonality among them, namely suspicion toward the best of citizens, who must be banished to ensure ho-
mogeneity and sheepishness in the rest of the body politic. Aristocracy,
on the other hand, is the ideal regime, where the best are nurtured, or,
figuratively speaking, the tallest stalks are encouraged to preside over
the rest.

We could have tracked many more instances of plants confounding
differences and oppositions in Aristotle. They cross the boundaries between male and female (*Generation of Animals*, 724b, 762b), between the
living and the dead (as in the case of *hylē*, the word for matter, which also
refers to "timber" and "growing woods"), and even between themselves
and what they are not (the kind of animals whose "principal organ," or
"cephalic part," is underneath, "motionless and destitute of sensation"
[*Parts of Animals* 686b].) The growing plant extends its reach well beyond
the confines of the philosophical vocabulary and the nascent body of
thought that aims to capture and freeze it. Everything that grows and
flourishes, from a single stalk of wheat to an oak tree, will thwart the
drive toward classification and categorization. From its very systematic
beginnings onward, philosophy sees in plants the dreaded reflection of
chaos it believes to have exorcised together with myth.

PLOTINUS' ANONYMOUS "GREAT PLANT"

A Portrait of the World as Plant

Plotinus did not just philosophize; he led a philosophical life. If we are to trust his most illustrious student, Porphyry, his existence was scrupulously self-effacing. Plotinus did not celebrate his own birthday but offered sacrifices on the birthdays of the long-dead Socrates and Plato. He did not wish his portrait to be painted, as he reckoned the body to be a worthless image of the soul, and its artistically produced likeness an image of an image. He also "seemed to be ashamed of being in the body" (Porphyry, *On the Life of Plotinus*, 1, 2), praising instead the virtues of the soul. A thinker of the absolute unity of the One, Plotinus succeeded like no other philosopher to combine the teaching of the pre-Socratic Parmenides with Platonism and Aristotelianism in the six books of his magnum opus, the *Enneads*, edited and compiled by the same faithful disciple, Porphyry.

There is no better point of entry into Plotinian philosophy than the allegory of the world, permeated by "the Soul of All," conceived in terms of a single plant, one gigantic tree, of which we alongside all other creatures (and even inorganic entities such as stones) are offshoots, branches, twigs, and leaves. The notion of a total soul was certainly not new at that point in the history of thought: Plato's *Timaeus*, for one, presented the whole universe in the form of an enormous animal. The groundbreaking aspect of the Plotinian image was the vegetal figuration he gave to the universal soul. What's behind the shift in perspective? Is it necessary, because in the plant the One and its fragmentation into the many coexist without a blatant contradiction? Because this fantasy frees Plotinus to think of the One without resorting to the organismic model and the zoocentric ways of moving and living? Or is something else going on here?

Although the portrait of the world as plant is painted most vividly in Book IV of the *Enneads*, its details are scattered through the rest of the treatise and shore up the most basic points of Plotinus' philosophical argument. Contrary to the classifications found on all the other pages in our intellectual herbarium, the world-plant does not belong to any recognizable genus or species. It is one of a kind, precisely, because it is a depiction of the One. Its anonymity coincides with its uniqueness, the uniqueness of a nonclassifiable origin and of a system of classification prior to its branching out. If there were a genus "world-plant," it would contain but a single example, which would overlap with the general category that lends it a name. (In saying this, I certainly do not take into account the conclusions of string theory in contemporary physics, with its hypothesis of multiple parallel universes. Assuming an infinite number of possible worlds, the genus "world-plant" would come to accommodate innumerable examples of vegetable totalities.)

In and of itself, world-plant is a useful theoretical fiction. In it, "the Soul of the All," as Plotinus imagines it,

> (that is, its lowest part) would be like the soul of a great growing plant, which directs the plant without effort or noise; our lower part would be as if there were maggots in a rotten part of the plant—for that is what the ensouled body is like in the All. The rest of our soul, which is of the same nature as the higher parts of the universal soul, would be like a gardener concerned about the maggots in the plant and anxiously caring for it.
>
> (*Ennead* IV.3.4, 25–35)

The Soul of All may envelop everything that is, but it is not undifferentiated in itself. Plotinus translates the Platonic division between the "highest" and the "lowest" into a separation between "the great growing plant," which is the ensouled body of the entire world, and a gardener who cares for it and who represents the soul in its pure state, unmixed with the corrupting bodily dimension of existence. Now, if a living body corresponds to the rotten part of the plant, we can begin to understand the reasons behind Plotinus' shame in the face of his own embodiment:

seeing death as a moment of liberation, he craved a return to the blessed condition of the gardener, his soul cleansed of its material incarnation. While many Christian authors, including St. Augustine, whose pear tree graces our herbarium, took this as a reference to the congenital sinfulness of corporeality and the inevitable fallenness of the soul trapped in a body, Friedrich Nietzsche will have brushed away the Plotinian metaphysical daydream as nihilistic.

The tremendous implication of Plotinus' vegetal portrait of the world is that there is nothing outside the soul, which, for all intents and purposes, cares for itself. The Socratic dictum that "all soul cares for the soulless" no longer applies there where a pure, because "unmixed," soul nurtures its tainted counterpart trapped in the dark cavern of the body. Even such inanimate things as rocks are not formless, as they exhibit crude material shapes that are the pale reflections of the soul's own formative capacity. And so it is with the gardener, who does not mold raw matter but cares for the preformed plant, the spontaneous, effortless, and noiseless growth of which should be, as much as possible, protected and redirected away from the deadly activity of the maggots that symbolize the self-forgetting of the soul in the body. As far as Plotinus is concerned, then, all pure soul cares for the embodied soul, so as to reduce its dependence on corporeality and hence to defend it from evil (provided that the "nature of bodies, insofar as it participates in matter, will be an evil," though "not the primal evil" [*Ennead* I.8.4, 1–2]).

Curiously enough, the singular image of the world as plant is sketched more than once in Plotinus' text. The ethical core of the soul's caring relation to the body is apparent in yet another variation on this memorable allegory. In Book II of the *Enneads*, the gardener turns into a farmer who worries about the external damage that hostile natural elements are causing to the crops. The soul that sets itself to work in the body, putting it in motion, "is like a farmer who, when he has sown or planted, is always putting right what rainstorms or continuous frosts or gales of wind have spoiled" (*Ennead* II.3.16, 30–5). The Plotinian soul is not akin to the deistic God, who rarely (if ever) intervenes in the course of His creation. The initial moment of animation gives rise to the ongoing concern of the cultivator for what is cultivated. The farmer has no respite in the task of "setting right" the otherwise self-directing growth of the crops that are endangered by the storms. The need for constant adjustments offers us an insight into the ancient idea of justice, in the thick, or substantive, sense of the term—as a being's return to the best condition possible. When the soul cares for the ensouled body, it fosters the well-being of the world, which it rescues from immersion in materiality. But do trees and well-being really mix? As we shall see, Plotinus adamantly claims that plants, too, have their share in happiness and welfare, which are desired by everything that lives.

We can spot the third picture of the world as plant while learning about the nature of the One. To flesh this out, Plotinus likens the One to "the life of a huge plant, which goes through the whole of it while its origin remains and is not dispersed over the whole, since it is, as it were, firmly settled in the root. So this origin gives to the plant its whole life in its multiplicity, but remains itself not multiple but the origin of multiple life" (*Ennead* III.8.10, 5–15). Life, to be sure, is multiplicity and dispersion; it is lived, always and everywhere, in the plural as lives. Yet, Plotinus implies, when we concentrate on living creatures, we are only seeing the upper segments of the world-plant with its intricate branching out at the tips. We literally miss the forest for the trees. A more radical vision aims at the radicle, the source, the root of life that is always one and the same, unaffected by the dispersion of the living. As a vegetal elaboration on the Aristotelian "unmoved mover," the ever-living root of the One, which is not split into the many, animates all finite lives without being in the least affected by their changeability or, indeed, finitude. It is an exceptional root that does not grow and that, remaining self-identical, upholds the origin's inviolability. Or, differently put, "the growth principle does not grow when it causes growth, nor increase when it causes increase, nor in general when it causes motion is it moved" (*Ennead* III.6.4, 30–40).

The root of the world-plant becomes, in Plotinus' philosophy, the yardstick for measuring the worth of multiplicities comprising this world. The closer a branch is to the root, the firmer its grasp on being, which it vicariously imbibes from the principle of growth. As for the tips of the branches, the leaves, and even the fruit, many of these are so distant from the root that they neglect "the image of that higher reality" they bear within themselves and, "flower[ing] into a divided multiplicity," desire "to be little trees" in their own right (*Ennead* III.3.7, 10–25). That is how contention and conflict flare up where unity and peace should, in principle, prevail. The One wages a war against itself the moment its most distal parts grow oblivious to their common emanation from the same root and, in an illusion of independence, assert themselves at the expense of other tree limbs, branches, and twigs. The more these parts identify with matter, which is thoroughly divisible, the more they violate the absolute wholeness of the One. Breaking out into finite lives ruled by the merciless cycles of growth and decay, the One is no longer (simply) one, even if its static root is appointed to serve as the guardian of unity.

All this is but a fragment of the fourth Plotinian image of the world-plant, which resists the gardener's efforts at pruning and orderly cultivation. In its excessive proliferation, the universal tree did not admit any empty spaces between its branches, filling them all "with shoots which also grow from the root, these, too, in a different way" (*Ennead* III.3.7, 22). What is the different way, *allon tropon*, Plotinus is referring to? It is *the way of evil*, where matter masters and dominates the formative principle, which is none other than the gardener's natural landscaping design for the plant. Those parts of the world-tree that, like weeds, grow unwelcomed, bespeak the growth of evil, of "unboundedness in relation to limit, and formlessness in relation to the formative principle," and are "always undefined, nowhere stable, subject to every sort of influence, insatiate, complete poverty" (*Ennead* I.8.2, 10–20). Despite the wild propagation of the world-tree, so extensive that there are no empty spaces between its branches, its untamed, uncultivated offshoots are the symptoms of poverty, indefiniteness, and lack of form. Beyond good and evil is the One, the common root whence they spring before their respective submission to, or rebellion against, the formative drive of the universal soul.

The growth of the world-plant is not identical to a preprogrammed development of the One toward the incontrovertible fulfillment of something like its destiny. The fifth depiction of the gigantic, universe-wide tree stands as silent testimony to this. Admittedly, the principle of the plant resides in the root, but it would be absurd "to call the direction which extends from there all over its parts and their mutual interrelation, acting and being acted upon, a single direction and, so to speak, destiny of the plant" (*Ennead* III.1.4, 1–10). There is nothing predestined about the clash between the distant twigs and blossoms that cease to obey the authority of the radical principle of unity they are no longer

PART I. ANCIENT PLANT-SOULS   44

in touch with. The growing multiplicity of the world does not advance in a single direction determined by its unitary origin; it spreads along multiple tracks at once, growing out of (and away from) the undying source of life. The more or less chaotic nature of growth should have irked Plotinus, but it didn't! Despite his adherence to the ideal of unity, he was a vehement antideterminist who indefatigably insisted on the need to keep open the space of freedom for human reason that alone makes us who we are (*Ennead* III.1.4, 15–25). But human liberty is not a standalone phenomenon: its prehistory includes the free development of the world-plant, divergent from its static root. If this is so, then actual vegetation must be privy to the same liberty as that enjoyed by the plant figuration of the Soul of All. What accounts for this prominence of plant life? In what sense is the plant, as Plotinus theorizes it, a desiring, intelligent (even contemplative!), and free creature aspiring to the good? These are the questions we must address next.

Traversing the Levels of the Vegetal Mind

The philosophy of Plotinus, who came up with a unique mix of Platonism and Aristotelianism, advances an overarching theory of the psyche indebted to both patriarchs of ancient Greek thought. Plotinus does not catch sight of any incompatibilities between the lower levels of the soul in Plato and Aristotle. The desiring and the nutritive parts belong together in living matter and comprise the most embodied aspect of the psyche. "Certainly," states Plotinus, "the desiring part is in matter, and so, too, is the part which governs nutrition, growth and generation, which is the root and principle of the desiring and affective form" (*Ennead* III.6.4, 30–40). In other words, nutrition is the "root and principle" of desire, because desire increases when the nutritive and other physiological needs of the organism are not satisfied and diminishes when the living are temporarily sated. But does it follow from this that plants, which have perfected the nutritive faculty and converted it into growth, are to be counted among the desiring creatures?

Plotinus indeed subscribes to this view, with the proviso that vegetal desire is peculiar because, dissimilar to that of animals and humans, it is drained of passion. Shorn of the spirited part of the soul (*thumos*), plants crave nourishment in a wholly dispassionate way that appears implausible to warm-blooded, at times hopeful and at other times desperate, animals such as ourselves. Consistent with Plato's view, the empirical evidence for the plants' desire is that they wilt without water and flourish when enough nutrients are provided; the sign for the absence of passion from their psychic life is that "they have no share of blood or bile" (*Ennead* IV.4.28, 60–65). The "otherness" of vegetable desire lies in its purity, that is, in its isolation from other emotive faculties of the soul, with which it is normally enmeshed in other living beings.

We should not, however, be under the impression that Plotinus merely repeats Plato's message on the appetitive soul of plants. Unlike his esteemed forerunner, Plotinus furnishes what we may term the "positive proof" of vegetal desire. Pervading the entire body of a plant, an animal, or a human, the principle of growth and generation (i.e., the plant principle) must also have its own motivation for action: "For that which generates and nourishes and produces growth must necessarily also have an appetite for generation, nourishment and growth" (*Ennead* IV.3.23, 40–45). Besides empirical hunger and thirst, Plotinus points out a certain metaphysical yearning for generation and nourishment that are themselves the more noble objects of desire! Keeping the Aristotelian final cause in mind, his implicit ultimate question is "Why?" Why do trees, for instance, bother to go through the cyclical process of growth, flowering, and bearing fruit? What is it for? What good is it?

With these questions, we are surveying the uncanny territory of the vegetal good, first demarcated by Plotinus. Section 4 of the first *Ennead*, "On Happiness" (*Peri Eudaimonia*), opens with an impassioned defense of the happiness of plants. *Eudaimonia*, of course, is a patently Aristotelian notion, which literally means "good spirits" and which, in Aristotle's thought, applies exclusively to humans who act in accordance with reason and hone their capacity for contemplation, *theoria*. Although plants lack sensations, Plotinus holds, they can act in accord with *their* reason, pursuing "a life which unfolds to its end." Their bearing fruit is a symptom of the plants' well-being, of their growth in harmony with reason underlying vegetal life: "one life can be good, another the opposite, as plants too can be well or badly off, and bear fruit or not bear fruit" (*Ennead* I.4.1, 15–30). Despite contradicting the letter of Aristotle's text, the non-emotive happiness of plants makes sense within the Aristotelian logic as the fulfillment of their purpose or final end. More interestingly yet, to the extent that it is purged of emotion, vegetable well-being anticipates the happiness of contemplative life, through which humans inch closer to the unmoved, self-contained, and unperturbed living of the gods.

In the current discussions of plant ethics, the intrinsic good of vegetation often turns into a stumbling block. My 2012 debate with the animal rights activist Professor Gary Francione, of Rutgers University, nicely exemplified this point. Francione's refrain throughout the debate was that, since plants are not sentient, they cannot have any interests to speak of. "That is," he explained, "they cannot desire, or want, or prefer anything. There is simply no reason to believe that plants have any level of perceptual awareness or any sort of mind that prefers, wants, or desires anything." Nor can you "act with speciesism with respect to a being that has no interests, such as a plant."[1]

We do not require a Plotinian philosophical prism to realize that the opponents of plant ethics are, so to speak, mixing apples and oranges when they judge the value and the possibilities of every kind of life against the arbitrary standard of perceptual awareness. The objective harm caused to a living being is not neutralized depending on whether or not this being registers the danger. In fact, plant science has churned up study after study describing how mechanical damage to but one leaf of a plant triggers a chain of biochemical reactions, communications, and frantic electrical signaling from the site of injury to the faraway (distal) leaves and plant parts.[2] Those who are convinced that plants have no interests have not bothered to learn that, for example, a damaged tomato plant produces proteinase inhibitors that fulfill the role of defense mechanisms in its injured and undamaged parts alike. Across millennia, Plotinus seems to respond, *avant la lettre*, to Francione with a warning: "Those who deny it [a good life] to plants because they have no sensation run the risk of denying it to all living things" (*Ennead* I.4.2, 1–5).

Especially germane to the philosophical climate of the twenty-first century is Plotinus' relativization of the mind and its linkage to the phenomena of life. How so? To be concise, there are as many varieties of intellect as there are lives, so that each form of life—the vegetable, the animal, and the human, among others—is a practical and material instantiation of a corresponding form of intellection. Against this background, another of Francione's grave mistakes lies in his premise that the basis for the mind is perceptual awareness, which would automatically exclude plants, as well as some other living organisms, such as bacteria, from the category of conscious beings. Surely, sentience as a "baseline" for ethical treatment furnishes a broader foundation than human exceptionalism, predicated on rational thought, would permit. But this baseline is still insufficiently inclusive, in that it admits into the moral community solely those organisms that are similar to us. The comparative advantage of the Plotinian notion of mind is that it surpasses the ambit of sentience while both dehumanizing and deanimalizing the intellect.

The mind immanent in life and dispersed into different forms of vitality in growth, sensation, and abstract thought is nothing else but the One practically thinking itself. As Plotinus argues, "the other lives are thoughts in a way, but one is a growth-thought [*phutikē noesis*], one a sense-thought, and one a soul-thought. How, then, are they thoughts? Because they are rational principles [*logoi*]. And every life is a thought, but one is dimmer than another" (*Ennead* III.8.8, 10–20). Growth-thought names the thinking of plants, where *phuton* signifies, at the same time, "plant" and "growth." My book on vegetal philosophy, *Plant-Thinking*, is deeply influenced by this Plotinian concept.

So, in plant, animal, and human lives, the One thinks itself, though with different degrees of clarity. thought is all the dimmer the more it is bogged down in bodily existence. On this gradation, the life-thought of plants is the dimmest because it permeates the entire living body that grows and requires nourishment in every one of its parts. All this makes Plotinus a crucial precursor to another thinker of the one (substance)— Baruch Spinoza, who similarly maintained that there was no qualitative difference between rational thoughts and their muddled manifestations, the emotions.

Take another look at the passage where Plotinus delineates his theory of mind embedded in life. Regardless of the shape it takes, life-thought is still a rational principle, a *logos*. With this bold assertion, the author of the *Enneads* breaks decisively with the teachings of Plato and Aristotle. Reason suffuses the entire universe and is no longer circumscribed to the rational part of the human psyche or to the eternal abode of the gods. Growth-thought, too, has its reason, discernable already in the "quiet seed" that, in growing, practically "thinks itself to largeness" as it unfolds itself under the guidance of its "formative principle [*logos*]" (*Ennead* III.7.11, 20–25). Life, soul, the formative principle, reason, and intellect are interchangeable in the Plotinian body of writings. Growth is a thought that acquires extension and that physically augments this extension as it actualizes (practically thinks) itself.

The characterization of the seed as "quiet" should stand as a reminder of how Plotinus represented the world-plant, directed by the Soul of All "without effort or noise." The actual germinating seed is, at once, a model for and a fragment of the all-encompassing *logos*, which animates the physical universe. But why qualify the mode of the rational principle setting itself to work as noiseless? The finer point of the argument has to do with the multiple senses of the Greek *logos*. In addition to reason, logic, and a slew of other meanings, this word is used to connote "voice" or "speech." Still today we often use the expression "the voice of reason" and agree that human reasoning is virtually unimaginable without discursivity,[3] or at least the possibility of vocalization.

Plotinus nonetheless amplifies the scope of reason and demonstrates that our "noisy" kind of *logos* is but a morsel of what the rational principle, spread through the universe, entails. Things much smaller than us, like mustard seeds, and those that are infinitely larger, like the entire world, obey a *logos* without voice no less (if not more) effectively than humans with our discursive rationality. Spoken *logos* is, perhaps, a weird mutation as far as the default rational principle is concerned, for "Intellect, by giving something of itself to matter, made all things in unperturbed quietness; this something of itself is the rational formative principle flowing from Intellect" (*Ennead* III.2.2, 15–20). Our speaking breaks this silence, heavy with meaning and full of life. In purporting to express it more authentically, we disrupt the quietness inherent to *logos* and forget about the existence of that reason which is not straightforwardly human.

Plotinus' example of the voiceless formative principle in plants has to do with the timing of their blossoming. Construing the soul as "a herald summoning" the body, he cites "the ordered development" of the living, including the trees, where every stage happens "at its appointed time" (*Ennead* IV.3.13, 5–20). Such noiseless summons is actually substantiated by botanical research. What Plotinus understood as the soul or the mind is the combination of calculation and memory factored into every leaf of a tree: detecting far-red rays of light at sunset and storing this information at the cellular level, plants are able to determine whether and by how much the days are increasing or decreasing and when it is most appropriate for them to blossom.[4] This calculus of life, with its flexibility and attunement to environmental conditions, supplements the relative rigidity of the instructions for organismic development stored in the DNA. It fleshes out the Plotinian growth principle as a mode of thinking woven into the very bodies of plants and of other living organisms.

Through our interpretation of the *Enneads*, we have come to a better appreciation of the multilayered nature of the vegetable soul. Subjects of desire, seekers of happiness, silent expressions of the rational principle of growth—Plotinian plants do not at all match the caricaturized view of them as simple, barely living, and totally predetermined impassive things. Plotinus further admits that the growth principle (or plant-thinking) is a thought of multiplicity and dispersion, everywhere interlaced with the corporeality it animates. There are two exceptions to this rule: the seed and the root. In its unity, the seed contains all the abstract possibilities for growth, without as yet coming out of itself and thinking itself to largeness. In this, it is consonant with the Soul of All before it has produced the world of sense. But, after germination, the seed becomes literally ec-static; it stands outside of itself, like the Soul of All that acquires a material extension. Plotinus laments this inexorable dispersion of the soul and of the seed in growth. "Instead of keeping its unity in itself, [the seed] squanders itself outside itself and so goes forward to a weaker extension; in the same way Soul, making the world of sense . . . first of all put itself into time" (*Ennead* III.7.11, 20–30).

Plotinian philosophy will be awash with the acute nostalgia for the lost unity of the seed, as much as of reason. Plotinus will strive to recapture this original oneness in the soul and in the root that survive the death of the body and the withering away of the plant. So much so that he will convert the retreat of vitality into the roots of perennial plants, subsequent to the "death" of other plant parts, into a proof for the immortality of the soul. In the section of *Ennead* IV dedicated to this very topic, we discover that "when the rest of the body of the plant withers up, in many plants the soul remains in the region of the root and the lower parts [and] it is obvious that it has left the other parts and gathered itself into one" (*Ennead* IV.7.8, 25–35). Before the birth and after the death of the body, in the seed and in the root, the soul is most genuinely what it is in its essence, that is, a simple unity that does not squander itself outside itself, does not waste itself on precarious and finite bodies.

The last and the highest stratum of plant soul in Plotinus is its theoretical activity. As if it were not enough that the confines of Aristotelian happiness expanded so as to welcome the well-being of plants, the contours of *theoria* too had to be redrawn to accommodate the plants' contemplative reason. Intriguingly, we are invited "to talk about the earth itself, and trees, and plants in general, and ask what their contemplation is," independent of the "power of forming mental images" (*Ennead* III.8.1, 15–25). Plotinus' response to this question is instructive. Since in plant life there is no separation between the subject and the object or, indeed, between practical living and theoretical activity, the plants' contemplation is identical to what they are and what they do according to their type of animating reason. In growing, they practically contemplate life!

Needless to say, a plant does not entertain abstract thoughts, which we usually associate with theory (*Ennead* III.8.3, 10–20). It is nonetheless an embodiment of *logos* masquerading as the principle of growth; in growing, in bringing itself to maturity, it thinks itself into existence, combining reason and corporeal being. "Making, for it, means being what it is," and "its making has been revealed to us as contemplation" (*Ennead* III.8.3, 15–25). Does this imply that plants share something with divine nature? Like God, they possess an essence, which is the same as their existence (growth), and, like Him, they have a power of thinking that is immediately creative and that produces the object they think. It is enough for God to think of the world to bring it into being; it is sufficient for a seed to think itself into extension to grow into a mature tree. The plant not only *expresses* a truth but also *makes* a truth by growing, by being, or by becoming what it thinks.

So majestic are the qualities Plotinus finds in plants, it may be hard to believe that he urges humans to uproot and to flee from the plant in us, which is to say, from everything we have in common with the vegetable mind. What is behind this sudden change of face in the attitude of a thinker who, arguably, displays the greatest kindness to plants in the history of Western philosophy?

To Stem Out the Plant in You!

Despite an overwhelmingly positive evaluation of plant life in the *Enneads*, there are mounting indications concerning its relative deficiency vis-à-vis other kinds of living and intelligence. We have already stumbled on Plotinus' assessment of the dimness of growth-thought compared to sensory perception and abstract intellection. We have also become cognizant of his critique of dispersion (both of the world-plant and of actual vegetation), tempered by hopeful pronouncements on the subject of the unity and the simplicity of the seed and the root. Things get ever more complicated when it comes not to the plant per se but to the lingering reminder of its soul in the human, or, simply—the plant in us. This vegetal heritage is nothing to scoff at, as it is etched into our corporeality and unconscious life of the mind.

Above all, Plotinus cautions the reader not to conflate the essence of humans, who contain a trace of plant soul, with the vegetal activity of growth that turns out to be an alien force operative in us. "When our growth-activity is active," he writes,

> no perception of it reaches the rest of the man through our sense faculties; and if that in us which grows were ourselves, it would be ourselves that would be active [irrespective of the fact that we were unconscious of it]. Actually, however, we are not it, but we *are* the activity of the intellect; so that when that is active, we are active.
>
> (*Ennead* I.4.9, 25–30)

There is something in the human that does not define the human, namely our growing, feeding, needing, procreating bodies. We cannot sense the activity of this growth, much less comprehend it, and, therefore, it would be a mistake to determine what or who we are by resorting to something we do not even register. The ideal would be to disentangle ourselves, as much as possible, from this strangeness within, to " 'fly from here' and 'separate' ourselves from what has been added to us, and not be the composite thing, the ensouled body in which the nature of the body (which has some trace of soul) has the greater power" (*Ennead* II.3.9, 20–25). Differently put, we ought to uproot the plant within us and, bearing witness to its withering away, rejoice in the simple unity of the cogitative soul that remains.

Plotinus is pragmatic enough to realize that many beings that appear human will not have heeded his warnings and, consequently, will have descended to the status of a plant. Before detailing ways in which such descent may occur, we can venture a Plotinian reading of the same event in Aristotle. You will remember that, in *Metaphysics*, a human who does not obey the principle of noncontradiction is no better than a plant, at the same time thinking and not thinking. This way of putting it was plagued by a noticeable contradiction, and now it turns out that only Plotinus can rescue the Aristotelian intuition from the grave charge of violating formal logic. To say that the illogical humans both think and do not think requires a qualification: they no longer think following the precepts of the cogitative soul but, instead, think like plants, whose growth activities are the expression of their embodied intellect. In this sense, people who contradict themselves subscribe to a different sort of *logos* that does not pertain to humans as humans.

According to Plotinus, we may contribute to our own dehumanization if we give free rein to the appetitive or the nutritive soul in us. The descent that terminates in our becoming-plant is gradual. First, we become animal-like, when we "sink to the level of sense-perception by pursuing the images of sense" (*Ennead* III.4.2, 5–10). Chasing after sensuous pleasures with their allure of entertainment, we betray the distinctly human formative principle, which is closest to the universal One. Our mental dispersion and distraction in particular violate the unity of the cogitative mind. Second, we would turn plant-like (becoming trees, really) if we "did not even live by sense along with desires but coupled them with dullness of perception" (*Ennead* III.4.2, 20–25). At least sensory acuteness, thanks to intense stimulation, imparted to us a semblance of energetic action, not one proper to the human intellect but one of physical animation. This is precisely what is missing from desire wedded to dull perceptions and redolent of the stupor of vegetable existence. All that remains in individuals who abide exclusively by the growth principle is the "urge for generation and the 'gluttonous love of good eating'" (*Ennead* III.4.2, 15–20). What used to be the noblest, theoretical activity of plant soul is now the basest, most deplorable impassiveness of the human vegetable.

While we live in the material world, the imbroglio of the plant, the animal, and the human in us is unavoidable. But it is up to us to prioritize one mode of intellection over the others and to realize, in theory as well as in practice, what is essential to who we are and what may be discarded without a sense of irreparable loss. Taking a page from the Socratic dictum that a good man cannot be harmed, Plotinus contends

that an exemplary human does not depend on the whims of bodily reality, because "man, and especially the good man, is not the composite of
soul and body" (*Ennead* I.4.14, 1–5). The words "is not" in this statement
are normative rather than descriptive, meaning that someone who has
dominated the animal and vegetable components of her or his existence
should not be seen as a cultural-biological, soul-body unit. The road to
such self-actualization passes through asceticism; having embarked on
it, we must renounce the phony goods of the body, or, as Plotinus puts
it, "reduce the body . . . so that it may be made clear that the real man is
other than his outward parts" (*Ennead* I.4.14, 10–15).

For our purposes, the reduction of the body is a counterweight to the
plant's principle of growth, or quantitative augmentation. Be it in the everyday form of dieting or in Christian practices of the "mortification of
the flesh," the soul's independence from the body betokens the levity of
what is no longer enchained to the earth. The reduction of the body uproots the vegetal heritage in us, all the while delivering us to ourselves,
that is to say, to the human reality in revolt against its "outward parts"
that subsist like organs of an animal or of a plant. To discover the real or
authentic "you," Plotinus seems to suggest, you should stop looking at
yourself in the mirror and, instead, look within.

The flight of the soul from its imprisonment in the flesh is the leit-
motif of Plotinian thought. Technically, this escape is the opposite of
biological death, where the body loosens its hold on the psyche, which
"it is unable to bind anymore" (Plotinus, *Ennead* I.9, 5–10). The body
"departs" out of weakness; the soul flees out of sheer determination and
spiritual strength. Furthermore, both the body and the soul draw their
force from the One. In the body's divisibility, the One is furthest from
itself, and the phenomena of death and decomposition merely bring the
inherent fragmentation (hence, the weakness) of the body to its logical
conclusion. Plant soul merges with the bodily extension, in that it is
"also divisible among bodies" (*Ennead* III.4.6, 35–45) and "is not absent
from any part of the body" (*Ennead* IV.3.23, 35–40). It suffuses the body
through and through. That is why to retreat from the body is actively
to contend with the corrupting influence of the vegetal principle and
to mend the fragmented One. It is to recover the "unboundedness" of
the soul, an unboundedness no longer limited by a material form, "un-
measured, because greater than all measure and superior to all quantity"

(*Ennead* I.6.9, 15–25). Bidding the body not to grow, not to conform to the vegetal injunction for a quantitative increase, the reduction of our material dimension thus triggers the soul's expansion toward the sublimity of disembodiment.

In Augustine's *Confessions*, the gathering of the soul from its worldly dispersion and distraction expresses the Plotinian aspiration to the One, appropriately renamed "God." For Augustine, psychic consolidation is made possible by a withdrawal not only from material space but also, above all, from the temporal order, responsible for the humans' noncoincidence with themselves. The eternal Now of God puts an end to the fleetingness of earthly time and offers the soul a lasting respite, liberating it from the succession of past, present, and future moments. The metaphysical thrust of the Plotinian and Augustinian philosophies quells the disquietude of the vegetal principle at the price of the living-breathing body itself, which overlaps with the part of the soul responsible for our nourishment and growth. But does the escape from a mere vegetal "shadow" or "echo" of the soul (*Ennead* IV.4.18, 5–10; see also IV.4.22, 1–5) to the reality of the One (or to God, for that matter) successfully dispense with plant imagery?

The Revenge of the Plant

The thought of Plotinus belongs in a venerable tradition of the philosophies of immanence, that is, of philosophies that deny the existence of anything outside the totality of the world, the One, God, life, and the like. Far from leading up to transcendence, the road we have just traveled—from measurable and divisible formed matter to the immeasurable and simple form of a "pure" soul—zigzags between different folds of the One. Even the coveted freedom from the plant in us is already anticipated and neutralized in the logic of vegetal life with its periodic flourishing and wilting, expansion into a full-grown sequoia and contraction to a miniscule seed. The extreme scenario where the entire world-plant withers away (that's how Plotinus would conceive the end of the world) still contains provisions for the survival of the plant's ideal root as a refuge place for the Soul of All. The reduction, diminution, and contraction of the body do not break with the vegetal principle; at worst, they are this principle's negative modalities and, at best, they allow for the reinvigoration of the soul in the unity of the seed and root before the resumption of growth. After a harsh winter comes the spring with its promise of regeneration.

Unity and multiplicity, too, are reconciled on the terms of plant soul that both underwrites the divisibility of the body in the processes of growth and facilitates the recovery of simple unity in a seed. The entire intelligible realm is akin to a single moment in plant reproduction: "There, in the intelligible world, everything is substance because all are one . . . ; just as in the seed all things are together and each is all" (*Ennead* II.6.1, 5–15). Plotinus wishes to flee from the One divided against itself to the One gathered back into itself. But, in any case, this flight takes place within the One. The alternating periods of plant growth and reproduction are the poles between which the dialectic of the One and the many wavers.

The revenge of vegetation is that, just when it seems that the plant has been fully uprooted, it regrows with more tenacity than before, there where thought rejects the very principle of growth. How could it not, given its kinship with nature as a whole? Plotinus carries on the Platonic and Aristotelian exploration of the links between nature (*phusis*) and the plant (*phuton*) in his speculations concerning the unity of nature, on which particular natures of diverse creatures grow as branches on a tree. "For," he argues, "one nature rules over all the natures, and they come after it, depending on and from it, growing out of it so to speak, as the natures in branches grow out of that of the whole plant" (*Ennead* IV.4.11, 5–15). The image of the world as a gigantic plant matches the concept of the inner constitution (i.e., the nature) of the universe as a tree, with branches that diverge from, though they are ultimately traceable back to, a shared trunk. Anthony Preus, in his analysis of the *Enneads*, gives this scheme a scientific spin, detecting in it a nascent biological system "closer to modern viewpoints than the apparent immutability characteristic of Aristotelian biology."[5] But in less obvious, political terms the one nature is a de facto monarch that rules over all the others, dominating the branches that draw their sap from a common source. In the same vein, centuries after Plotinus, Hegel will explicate the essence of the Trinity by resorting to the metaphor of a tree with three major branches, each of them a part of a single tree and a tree in its own right.[6] And another German thinker, the philosopher-poet Novalis, will recycle it in a legendary aphorism: "*Über die Nature als einen* geschlossenen Körper —*als einen* Baum—*woran wir die* Blütenknospen *sind* [On nature, as a *closed body*—as a *tree*—on which we are the *blossom buds*]."[7]

What eludes the attention of Plotinus, Hegel, and Novalis alike is the nonorganismic life of plants that does not add up to the unity of the One. It is not monarchy but vegetable anarchy that reigns there where parts are interchangeable with the whole. Neither political nor ontological hierarchies are sustainable on the grounds of the world-plant. Despite the togetherness of parts (of "all things," as Plotinus puts it) in the simple unity of the seed, we should take with a grain of salt any and all strict contrasts between the activity exclusive to the human, on the one hand, and the "alien" vegetable and animal forces within us, on the other. A philosophy of immanence precludes anything like absolute foreignness. If all are One and the One is all, then we must be able to identify and accept the plant in us and ourselves in the plant, the gardener in the garden and the garden in the gardener. Interiority and exteriority are two dimensions of a unified whole, viewed under the lenses of intelligibility and visibility, respectively. To discard as superfluous any part of the One—specifically, its vegetal aspect—is to throw away the unity made possible by this part. The reduction of the body and the uprooting of the plant literally impoverish the One, which grows anemic and deficient without "squandering itself," without stepping outside of itself, growing, and expanding into corporeality.

The plant regrows with a vengeance. If there is a lesson to be learned from this obstinate regeneration, it is that the philosophies of immanence have no choice but to be affirmative, the primary object of their affirmation being life itself. They cannot cogently say "no" to a plant while maintaining the consistency of their philosophical outlook. It falls to us to think with and against Plotinus, striving to be more Plotinian than the ancient thinker himself, who not only lived but also died philosophizing. To begin with, we would have to paraphrase his final words, recorded by Porphyry. We ought to repeat them, substituting the word "plant" for "god." The outcome would be suggestive: "Try to bring back the plant in you to the Plant in the All!"[8]

PART II

MEDIEVAL PLANT-INSTRUMENTS

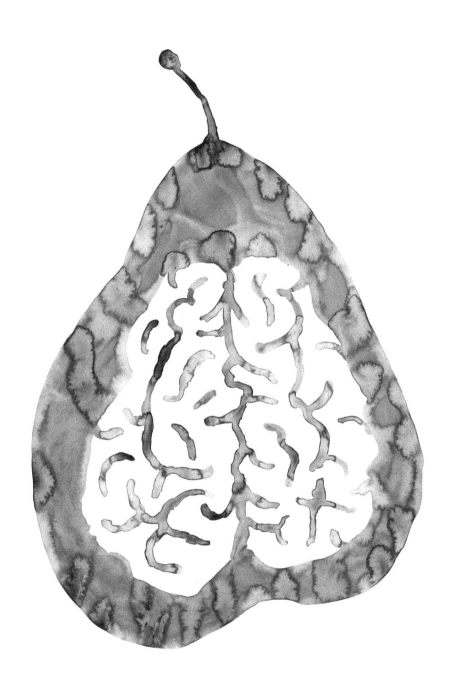

4 AUGUSTINE'S PEARS

When a Saint Stole Pears

After the publication of his *Confessions*, Augustine was unable to rid himself of a nagging suspicion. What if the success of the book was attributable to something other than the moral-pedagogic purpose he had in mind? It quickly became obvious that readers were attracted to the text out of perverse curiosity provoked in them by Augustine's narrations of his sexual tribulations. They were excited to learn about the carnal temptations that had continually thwarted his conversion. In short, the book of repentance was received in some circles as an erotic bestseller of the fourth century AD.

Nonetheless, the first comprehensive confession of *Confessions* is not related, at least not explicitly, to the author's fight against his sexual urges. Instead, it revolves around an act of theft. The stolen objects could not have been more trivial: what the adolescent, not-yet-saintly Augustine and his fellow gang members took without permission were pears. But the fruits were not desirable in and of themselves. "My desire," Augustine recounts,

> was to enjoy not what I sought by stealing but merely the excitement of thieving and the doing of what was wrong. There was a pear tree near our vineyard laden with fruit, though attractive in neither color nor taste. To shake the fruit off the tree and carry off the pears, I and a gang of naughty adolescents set off late at night.... We carried off a huge load of pears. But they were not for our feasts but merely to throw to the pigs.
>
> (*Confessions* II.iv.9)

Most will dismiss stealing pears as a relatively innocent teenage prank, as pettifogging as the stolen things themselves. To Augustine, however, the act is symbolic. His judgment of the pears' quality—"attractive in neither color nor taste"—is of the essence. Why did he steal mediocre fruits? Because what he craved were not the pears but the forbidden fruit of committing a crime and the thrill of breaking a law. Or, as he succinctly states, "I loved my fall, not the object for which I had fallen but my fall itself" (II.iv.9). In much the same manner, he will later love not the blessings of God but divine love itself. The material object, for instance a fruit, is a pure means, a vehicle for the satisfaction of desires that may be physical (e.g., hunger) or may not be straightforwardly oriented to anything in the order of nature (e.g., craving the acceptance of one's peers). This thoroughgoing instrumentalization of the fruit and of the world it represents is a necessary moment in the Augustinian ontology, or, more precisely, in his ontotheology.

Seeing that the pears themselves and the thievery are but foils for Augustine's confessional self-flagellation, we cannot be certain whether the recounted event really happened or is an allegory of the narrator's fallenness in general. Much is in favor of the latter interpretative option, with the attendant conclusion that the theft was figurative. Think back to the eating of the forbidden fruit from the tree of knowledge that triggered the fall of Adam and Eve or to Augustine's habitual interpretation of good works qua spiritual fruits. There is no reason to doubt the allegorical connection of the stolen pears to both of these tropes. And the same goes for other—presumably real-life—occurrences described in *Confessions*, not the least of which is the author's emblematic weeping under a fig tree, reminiscent of the first humans' postparadisiac sorrow (VII.xii.28). The plant is a symbol (*symbolum*: a token for or a mark of something other than itself), if not the symbol of a symbol. But so is everything else in the world accessible to the senses, along with this very world, which, as a whole, is a token for God's benevolence. The work of Christian hermeneutics proves indispensable for matching these marks with the hidden meaning they both reveal and encrypt.

The speculation on whether the events in question actually happened is beside the point. To demand a careful sifting of the real from the imaginary is to turn one's back on Augustine's fundamental message and his method. Literalness in the eyes of the Christian philosopher is typical of a Judaic approach, enamored with that law which is etched on stone and that covenant which is inscribed on the flesh. The New Covenant, conversely, demands a "circumcision of the heart" and, with this emphasis on spiritual interiority and on faith comes the depreciation of literalness. For Augustine, the world is a matter of interpretation, not for knowledge's sake but as an intermediary step toward the divine. Whatever pertains to the empirically real pales in comparison to the "fictions" of love, faith, and hope with which the road to heaven is paved.

It is all the more dumbfounding, then, to hear Jacques Derrida, an enthusiastic proponent of indeterminacy and of the porous lines of demarcation between faith and knowledge, agonizing over the truthfulness of the confessed theft. As a matter of fact, Derrida does not doubt the veracity of the Augustinian account but that of his own compatriot's, Jean-Jacques Rousseau, who confesses to having stolen apples from the master of engraving under whom he served as an apprentice. Does Rousseau cite without citing his predecessor? Did he "really steal those things, or is he simply, as an exercise, trying to inscribe himself in this great tradition of confession?"[1] How would such "plagiarism" sit with Rousseau's opening statement to the effect that his literary performance is without precedent? The questions may be multiplied further, but what makes them meaningful and worth our while in the first place? After all, confessions, as opposed to autobiographies, belong to an ethicoreligious genre predicated on faith and exempt from the order of verifiable knowledge. While it may be possible to ascertain whether a particular event in the life of a confessor indeed took place, it would be absurd to hold the inner, psychic world of the subject—the world born in the pangs of a confession—to the same restrictive empirical standard. And what if the confessor confesses to a history of lying, as Augustine does, saying that he used to make up stories of sexual exploits so as to impress his peers, "to pretend I had done things I had not done at all, so that my innocence should not lead my companions to scorn my lack of courage" (*Confessions* II.iii.7)? What guarantees that his confessions, starting with the episode of the pears, are not another collection of "so many empty boasts"?[2] Augustine's short and invariable response to this last question is "God"—the ever-present inner witness of the narrated events. But the answer does not produce any more certainty in the epistemological sense of the word; if anything, it confirms the fact that confessional discourse is built on the shaky foundations of faith.

In his *Circumfessions*, Derrida also admits to stealing grapes as an adolescent in Algeria. He is anxious for the reader to believe him, though he realizes that the "fact is that it *did* happen, but it looks like an exercise, a quotation in a genealogy of literary genres."[3] None of this would have impressed Augustine, according to whom faith, which is to be placed in God and only secondarily in the confessor, trumps knowledge. It is, in effect, God who is both the addressee of confessional discourse and the guarantor of its truthfulness, having already observed what is recounted in it from the depths of the confessor's soul. Within the abysses of the psyche, the mere thought of stealing or of sinning, even if not acted upon, already amounts to a recriminating piece of evidence. The hard and fast difference between reality and fiction is of no consequence, where fallen intentions are as serious as sinful acts.

Still, we must confess that there is something ominous in the decision to feature the theft of fruit so prominently in philosophical confessions. Why stealing? And why stealing fruit, of all things?

Let us try to advance in the symbolic, allegorical spirit required by the genre Augustine has pioneered. First, the readers of *any* confessions are unable to shake off the impression that they are breaking into a forbidden space—a private, secretive, and usually carefully protected domain of the psyche. Our opening the book (hence, the confessor's soul) is already, in some sense, a burglary. Of course, the authors willingly let us in and guide us through selective and highly structured narratives of their inner and outer lives. But they also indicate, in so many words, that their subjective interiority is, from the start, broken into, invigilated from within by God or by the Other. Far from a late disruption, it is this divine breaking-and-entering that makes the psyche what it is.

Second, if the act of stealing harkens back to the confession, then the object of theft, the fruit, must be associated with the broken-into psychic interiority. Confessing is like peeling a fruit—an orange, an apple, or maybe a pear—whose juicy core is analogous to the confessor's denuded soul. An open-heart surgery in the sphere of spirit, it is an attempt to get "inside and under the skin," *intus et in cute*, as the epigraph to Rousseau's *Confessions* mandates, or a quasi-surgical "de-skinning of oneself," as Derrida terms it. The confessor steals himself, wrenches his self through his own confessional performance, though in the end he must throw the stolen fruit away or feed it to the pigs starved for sensational yellow journalism and eager to learn every spicy detail about the sex lives of intellectual celebrities. The spiritual "open-heart surgery" invents, lifts up for everyone to see, and eventually trashes the very heart it operates on.

Confessions thus commence with and proceed through a series of burglaries. At sixteen, Augustine may have stolen pears. At forty-something, the period of his life when the book was composed, he graduated to grand theft, spiriting away the inherent value of the fruit. In reflecting on the shameful event of his youth, Augustine is reluctant to attribute physical seductiveness to the pears themselves. The beauty is not properly theirs; it is the stamp of God who created them: "The fruit which we stole was beautiful because it was your creation, most beautiful of all Beings, maker of all things, the good God, God the highest good and my true good" (II.vi.12). There is no discrepancy between the initial qualifications of the pears as, at best, mediocre and this reference to the fruit as "beautiful." Unremarkable when considered in and of themselves and in the light of sensory appreciation, they become magnificent as the bearers of the divine signature, the *signatura rerum*. Those who steal them are impotent to undo the bountiful goodness of creation; a rebellion against God does not evacuate the rebel from the world made possible by and bound to the divine Word.

Augustine himself would have refuted the charge of having disregarded the inner value of the fruit by arguing that this value has never been *of* the pears, even though it has rested *in* them. All he did, he would say, was merely to restitute this value to its rightful Proprietor. Certainly, pears are exemplary of any creature that owes everything in its being to the divine source of beauty and goodness. In their unremarkable way, they stand for much more than mere fruits. Aside from creation as a whole, it is possible to discern in them the image of human seductiveness—a veiled allusion to Augustine's sexual exploits and his reveling in the pleasures of the flesh, which is without value other than serving as a space of inscription for the universal brand, "Made by God." That is why, instead of venturing into the dirty aspects of his sexual yearnings, Augustine makes an abrupt transition from "the thorns of lust rose above my head, and there was no hand to root them out" (II.iii.6) to the narrative of thieving. The clothing of lust in vegetal metaphors, as the thorns that grow higher than the very seat of reason ("my head"), holds a clue to the figuration of fruit in terms of sexuality. In the end, Augustine steals more than the literal fruit and its intrinsic value; he also divests the reader of the anticipated perverse pleasure of learning about and vicariously participating in the protagonist's sexual depravities.

The Sheer Impossibility of Enjoying Fruit

A one-dimensional reconstruction of Augustinian thought is blinded by the enormous influence the writings of Plotinus exercised over him. Simply replace the Plotinian One with Augustine's God and you will be initiated into the philosophy of this naughty Father of the Church! (Or so the argument goes.) Yet this mechanical recipe for understanding ignores the ramifications of the Christianization of Plotinus. The devaluation of the body, for example, is a part of the Plotinian legacy, refined not only in theory but also in the austere practical guidelines for a monastic life, which should be ideally free of pride and sensuous pleasures, be they as seemingly innocuous as the pleasure of quenching thirst and satisfying hunger. What Augustine adds to the Plotinian program of pursuing spiritual at the expense of bodily reality is the segregation of use from enjoyment, *uti* from *frui*, which are the attitudes befitting the human relation to the world and to God, respectively. Whereas our appetites are driven by the objects that provide the means for their satisfaction, the good is sought for its own sake, as an end in itself, inappropriate for usage and suited for enjoyment. Since God alone is the supreme good, *summum bonum*, only He merits pure enjoyment devoid of use. Everything else in His creation may be justifiably converted into the means for external ends. Hence, Augustine's ostensibly outlandish addresses to God in *Confessions*, "I have sought a way to obtain strength enough to enjoy [*fruor*] you" (VII.xviii.24).

A thinker who has paid close attention to this dichotomy is Hannah Arendt, the author of a 1929 dissertation *Love and Saint Augustine*. While she regards Augustinian enjoyment as a precursor to the ethics of Immanuel Kant, Arendt highlights the inadequacy of "the opposition between use and enjoyment" to the love, which is neither a physical craving nor a longing for the divine. "What is beside and next to me," she writes, "I-myself and my neighbor, is neither to be 'used' nor to be 'enjoyed.'" Sure: my bodily aspect is no different from a pear, "a mere 'thing' to be used for the true life to come,"[4] but the soul is relatively autonomous from the logic of instrumentality. The image of God discernable in "I-myself and my neighbor" exempts both of us from the realm of divinely sanctioned exploitation and raises the question of a third, intermediary category between *uti* and *frui*.

An unexpected hint regarding this "missing third" lies in the etymology of enjoyment. The Latin verb *fruor* (to enjoy)—essential to the human relation to God as Augustine envisages it—is itself drawn from the natural world or, more specifically, from the world of vegetation. It is not an idle curiosity that "enjoyment" shares its grammatical root with "fruit." Something (like a pear) unequivocally handed over to unlimited usage confers meaning, from the outside, onto the order of enjoyment. As a skilled, professional rhetorician Augustine is well aware of this potential Babel of meaning. In the eleventh book of *The City of God*, he remarks: "I do not overlook the fact that, properly speaking, fruit is what one enjoys," even though "we are said to enjoy that which delights us in itself. Nonetheless, in speech as it is customarily used, we both use fruits and enjoy practices. For we quite properly speak of the 'fruits' of the field, even though these are temporal things of which we all make use" (XI, 26). What redeems this inexactitude of language is the identification of the fruit with the end of the reproductive process in a plant and its spiritualization that converts it into the embodiment of good works. Still unavailable for sheer enjoyment, the fruit as an end, both of a plant and metaphorically of a good Christian practice, is located in the excluded middle, between the mundane *uti* and the holy *frui*.

The nobility of the fruit, compared to the flower, is that it is much more than a pretty, albeit vacuous, piece of distraction. Augustine need not spell out the premise that flower religions are, without exception, pagan, absorbed as they are in the ephemeral beauty of the object of their worship and its implied sexual licentiousness. Understandably, in *The City of God*, he rails against the ancient cult of the goddess Flora, who presided over everything that bloomed and in whose honor shameless *ludi florales*, or floral games, were held annually. The worship of such deities Augustine calls "wholly wanton, impure, immodest, wicked, and unclean" (II, 27). If, as Arendt has proposed, for ethical reasons human relations do not fit either the mold of pure use or that of pure enjoyment, then flowers and the cults that flourish around them fall beneath this distinction altogether. They are utterly useless and often harmful, or else they parody an end in itself accessible in aesthetic contemplation. People who tie their fates to flowers are well on their way to perdition.

Augustine finds everything about the floral world abhorrent. To "the gentle odor of flowers and ointments and perfumes" he prefers the spiritual and highly mystical sense of smell attuned to the divine, "a perfume which no breeze disperses" (*Confessions* X.vi.8). Over the uncertainty of a flower that may fall from the tree without producing anything, he favors the consummation of the reproductive process in a fruit. The plant may be castrated, Augustine suggests, when its flowers are culled, like the vegetal god Attis, who in a fit of madness tore off his sexual organs, died, and was reincarnated as a pine tree, with violets springing from his blood. "But when that flower was lost," he writes, "there was no subsequent fruit; rather, barrenness followed. What, then, is the meaning of this remnant—of whatever remained after his mutilation?" (*The City of God* VII, 25). A mystifying accusation, to wit, as it comes from someone who has given a vow of abstinence, exchanging physical reproduction for the fruit of spiritual works!

What does the association of good works with fruit symbolize, if not yet another exchange of material riches for the wealth of spirit? To be rich in good works, according to Augustine, is not to own earthly possessions but to entrust oneself to and to be owned by God.[5] The strategy of spiritualization is that of inversion: from owning to being owned, and from eating or digesting actual fruit to being digested into God, who vociferates, through Augustine's confessional discourse, "I am the food of the fully grown; grow and you will feed on me. And you will not change me into you, like the food your flesh eats, but you will be changed into me" (*Confessions* VII.x.16). Along with the fruit itself, the activity of the ancient vegetal soul, responsible for the assimilation of nourishment, is upturned so that the "fully grown" creature, who has grown past the confines of earthly life, is incorporated into the divine Other. To feed on the body of God is to be fed into it. What, in this case, would spiritual excretion look like? Or, does being digested into (and re-membered within) God preclude any sort of waste, let alone an escape route from divine immanence?

When Augustine imagines memory as "the stomach of the mind" (*Confessions* X.xiv.21), he promotes the spiritualization of digestion by elevating it into the psychic realm, even as he inadvertently gives credence to a crucial intuition of plant-thinking, namely, that vegetal, physiological processes are sublimated into higher cognitive functions. Following his lead, Nietzsche will treat too-much-history, or an excess of memory, as a case of mental indigestion. Assuming that we are swallowed into or remembered by God, however, we become the causes of divine indigestion: kept safe within Him, remembered without the possibility of being forgotten, we are stored in the divine stomach for eternity. Philosophies of finitude play the welcome role of a laxative here.

The uncoupling of vegetal processes from the actual plants, of life from continuous growth, and of physiological activities from the mortal organism interferes with their vitality. A fruit that does not rot in the guise of a good work and a memory that, held within God, is not subject to forgetting are the theologico-metaphysical fantasies that ruin the body of the metaphor, which carries them.

This inversion is only a tip of the iceberg that is the spiritualization of fruit in good works. It would appear, at first glance, that the works are the tangible outcomes of just acts or, at a minimum, the acts themselves born of good intentions. At times, Augustine seems to corroborate this view. Offering his take on the creation story of Genesis, he asserts that the "fruit of the earth are to be allegorically interpreted as meaning works of mercy, which are offered for the necessities of life from the fruit-bearing earth" (*Confessions* XIII.xxvi.38). (With this, he hands us the hermeneutical key to the pears episode, where the stealing of fruit militates against divine mercy itself.) Or, giving a sermon on "the eight beatitudes of the gospel," he expresses his hope that his words would "bring forth fruit in your habits and conduct."[6] Nonetheless, Augustine remains unsatisfied, seeing that this interpretation is beholden to outward actions (the legacy of Judaism). The process of spiritualization is incomplete without a definitive relegation of the fruit to the sphere of psychic interiority: "But in those who provide the food, the fruit lies not in what they give but the spirit with which they give it" (*Confessions* XIII.

xxvi.39). In the rarified field of *Confessions*, the metaphorical fruit is not the act itself but the intention that animates it, the spirit of giving. For "fruit is the good and right will of the giver" (XIII.xxvi.41).

Thus, while we are in God, digested into Him, the spiritual seed and fruit are in us in the form of a good will and good works. Digested inside out, twice, we are in God and a trace of God is in us. But what of the opposition between *uti* and *frui*? Does it not become irrelevant as soon as the exteriority of means and the interiority of ends are impregnated with each other? The spiritualization of the fruit results in the permeation of use by enjoyment and the redemption of instrumentality through the powers of mercy and love. And all this comes to pass at the expense of the literal pears and the mortal body they symbolize. Augustine has no second thoughts on the subject: we should be ready at any moment to sacrifice both to the dream of eternal and incorruptible life. The slightest hesitation undermining such readiness will be summarily dismissed and an ethics of bodies or plants declared ludicrous.

Antivegetal Ethics: Repressing a Weeping Fig Tree

Augustine's tortuous journey to the event of the conversion was also a struggle against the Manichaeism that had overshadowed his early thinking. A formidable rival to early Western Christianity, the religion inspired by the writings of the Persian prophet Mani was a syncretistic amalgam of Zoroastrianism, Buddhism, Babylonian mythology, and the Christian tradition. Thanks to Manichaeism's emphasis on dualism and its view of the world as divided into two substances, good and evil, the movement's name has survived nowadays in the pejorative expression, "the Manichean split." It is, however, the relation of Mani's teaching to the split in Augustine's own biography that concerns us here.

The City of God bears the secondary title *Against the Pagans*, and much in Augustine's mature philosophy was formulated against the Manicheans, who, despite their Christian leanings, were grouped in that category. One bone of contention between the rivaling religious worldviews was the ethics of the natural world and, specifically, human treatment of plants and animals. Manicheans often accused Christians of their unwillingness to support vegetarianism and blamed them for their lack of sensitivity to the suffering of all living beings. This acrimonious debate shaped, in large part, Augustinian ethics.

We have already spotted Augustine weeping under a fig tree at a crucial point in his conversion. We've also noticed the symbolic import of this particular plant: it evoked the primordial sin and Adam, in whom humans are born for death. Augustine's farewell to a life of passions was equally an *adieu* to Adam, symbolized by the tree, and a rebirth in Jesus, through whom believers are destined to eternal life. But that was already the second mention of the fig in the *Confessions*. The first, having to do less with Christological symbolism and more with the trees themselves, had cropped up early on in the book.

In an open polemic against the Manicheans, Augustine writes:

> Gradually and unconsciously I was led to the absurd trivialities of believing
> that a fig weeps when it is picked, and that the fig tree, its mother, sheds
> milky tears. Yet if some [Manichee] saint ate it ... then he would digest it in
> his stomach and breathe out angels.... And I in my pathetic state believed
> that more mercy should be shown to the fruits of the earth than to human
> beings for whose sake the fruits came to be.
>
> (III.x.18)

The rewriting of this passage in the conversion scene should not fail to impress us, given how thoroughly Augustine renounces his previous beliefs, all the while leaving them visible as mere traces. The tears of the fig metamorphose into his abundant tears; the "milky tears" of the mother tree morph into the weeping of Augustine's own mother, Monica, pleading with God for his conversion. Saintly digestion of the fruit into spiritual beings is reinterpreted as the safekeeping of believers in divine memory (the ethereal stomach) and their incorporation into the body of God . . . Be this as it may, Augustine repents for having entertained the possibility of plant ethics and, as a result, is ever more entrenched in an instrumentalizing approach toward vegetation. No mercy can be shown to "fruits of the earth" because they stand for the paradigm case of utility, created as they were for the sake of humans. To mark a clear break in his intellectual and spiritual life, Augustine, therefore, swings to the other extreme: from a valorization of plants over humans to a cold dismissal of any meaningful duties we may have toward plants. Had

Augustine not adhered to Manichaeism prior to the conversion, would his ethical views have been more balanced, and would he have exhibited more compassion to nonhuman creatures?

All speculations aside, an intense and intensely negative reaction to Manichaeism is not the only roadblock on the way to an early Christian plant ethics. If Augustine's signature philosophical gestures are those of spiritualization, interiorization, and allegorization, then his ethics, though seeking legitimation from the discourse of natural law, depends on an unmistakable denaturing of both meaning and life. The strangest facet of this denaturing, with its fascinating inversions and paradoxes, was the spiritual digestion of believers into the body of God and of the Church. And the same tactic, the same hermeneutical machinery, is at work in the interpretations of commandments from the Old Testament scattered throughout Augustine's oeuvre.

Let's take, for example, "Thou shalt not kill." Read literally, it advocates absolute nonviolence, a prohibition to terminate the life of any creature. This is, in fact, how the Manicheans received the injunction, easily reconciling it with the tenets of Buddhism. Augustine is quick to object to the erroneousness of the literal take on the meaning of killing: "Some persons endeavor to extend this commandment to beasts and cattle, and maintain that it is not lawful to kill any of them either. Why, therefore, not also include plants and whatever else is rooted in the soil and fed by it? For things of this kind also are said to live, even though they have no sensations. By the same token, they can also die" (*The City of God* I, 20). Augustine ridicules vegetarians, clobbering them with the same inane slippery-slope type of arguments that have not lost their appeal today, sixteen hundred years after the composition of *The City of God*. Those who assume that the objective of "Thou shalt not kill" is to protect the lives of humans and animals do not have at their disposal a sound reason for excluding other living things, say, plants. For Augustine, this ratiocination is the product of "the most senseless error of the Manicheans" ("Do we, then, when we hear 'Thou shalt not kill,' for this reason conclude that it is wicked to pull up a weed, and acquiesce in the most senseless error of the Manicheans?" [I, 20]). The "senseless error" in question mirrors the very plant life they defend, a life lived in the absence of sensation. Above all, this error is the result of a failure to raise the theologico-philosophical question of who or what is truly *killable* and, conversely, whose life may be terminated with little or no negative consequences, as though it were but an annoying weed.

Between the lines, the weed is conceived, loosely, as a life that is not killable and that consequently does not fall under the scope of the commandment. A *planta sacra*, more abject still than Giorgio Agamben's *homo sacer*, it can be destroyed with perfect impunity, as we shall see in the chapter on the palm tree of Maimonides. From this standpoint, all plants are weeds, and so are animals; uproot them or slash their throats, and nothing unlawful would happen. How does Augustine substantiate this judgment? By detaching life (that is to say, a worthy and killable life) from its botanical and biological underpinnings. The denaturing of life relies on the traditional philosophical preference for human reason over the nonrationality of animal existence and the nonsentience of plants. A killable life is part and parcel of spirit, religion, and ethics. The commandment, which no being other than human can obey, applies exclusively "to man" and is semantically restricted "to mean [thou shalt kill] 'neither another nor thyself'; for he who kills himself kills what is no other than a man" (*The City of God* I, 20). Killing and letting live are sovereign actions and attitudes that concern one's relation to oneself and to the other, which is why it would also be nonsensical, in Augustine's opinion, to forge meaningful relations with animals and plants. If that is so, how much more puerile, then, would it be to include them under the banner of "killable life"!

When it comes to devaluing a form of life, a never-failing strategy is just this: to deny that a creature can really die or be killed. In the twentieth century, Martin Heidegger faithfully repeated the lesson of Augustine, indulging in the same refusal to confer the dignity of death and dying on plant and animal "perishing." (More on this later.) An ethical catastrophe is brewing in the refusal to admit *that* certain kinds of life are killable because it precludes the debate on *how* they can be killed. Donna Haraway challenges meat eaters and vegans alike to think about this "how." "Outside Eden," she writes, "eating means also killing, directly or indirectly, and killing well is an obligation akin to eating well. This applies to a vegan as much as to a human carnivore. The devil is, as usual, in the details."[7] The devil is in the details, and so are the angels that spring up from the saintly digestion of figs by the Manicheans, whom Augustine derides. It takes great intellectual honesty to acknowledge both the violence we cause to plants and animals and the inevitability of subsisting at least on a fruit and vegetable diet. Manicheans killed well and ate well: they viscerally sensed the fig's weeping the moment it was plucked and endeavored to turn themselves into the outlets for its spiritualization (eating figs and breathing out angels as a result). Enchanted and naïve as this belief might have been, it undoubtedly occupied a higher moral ground than Augustine's restriction of killing to humans alone.

While it is not far-fetched to think that "thou shalt not kill" cannot be addressed to any being other than human, surely "be fruitful and multiply" must apply to the whole of creation! Isn't even the wording of this blessing/commandment relevant to plants, in that it brings the capacity for reproduction back to its vegetal source (fruitfulness)? Augustine begs to differ. First, he erases all vegetal traces from the blessing, rewriting it as a tautology, "Increase and multiply." Second, he draws our attention to the fact that although the divine blessing given to Adam and Eve should have applied to all living beings, it did not: "I might further say that this blessing, had I found it bestowed upon trees and plans and land animals, belongs to those kinds which are propagated by reproduction; but for plants and trees and beasts and serpents, there is no mention of 'Increase and multiply'" (*Confessions* XIII.xxiv.35). So what accounts for this omission in the biblical narrative? Augustine, of course, does not deem it an omission. Following his hermeneutical program opposed to the immediacy of both biological life and literal meaning, he stands by the interpretation that what ought to increase are "the works of mercy." Clearly, plants and trees and beasts and serpents are not capable of performing these, which is why they do not receive the divine blessing. Like digestion and death, reproduction is denatured and spiritualized, unhinged from its biological and, indeed, botanical base.

If Augustine fuels his hermeneutical machinery with phenomena related to nourishment, decay, and reproduction, it is not only because they bespeak the materiality and finitude of life but also because they are the signature activities and "movements" of the Aristotelian vegetal soul. Now, these are the same activities that Augustine wants to suppress. With Plotinus, he joins forces in the travail of uprooting the plant in us, not the least by discarding the literal and material vegetal processes that flow on within human bodies and psyches. To the extent that the crudest manifestations of life are spiritualized, the Augustinian subject is filled with the intensely nihilistic hatred of material existence, notably of everything humans share with other forms of life. As he puts this with maximum crispness and honesty in one of his sermons: "Let this be the first clause of your agreement with the word of God, that you begin by first of all hating yourself as you are. When you too have begun to hate yourself as you are, just as God hates that version of you, then you are already beginning to love God himself as he is."[8] To hate yourself as you are, you must despise the vegetal and animal part of your physical constitution. This hatred, Augustine implies, will direct you toward an ideal self free of its biological heritage. The terms of the agreement are clear: via the odium of finite existence in all its manifestations, you will finally learn to love God.

Compared to the barefaced propaganda of hatred toward life as it is, a failure to enunciate plant ethics is a minor blip on the screen of thought. But pervasive nihilism does not, in any shape or form, diminish the consequences of this failure. Repressing the plant within, Augustine excludes the actual green plants from the purview of moral considerability. Despite the concession that the fruit of the earth allegorically represents works of mercy, a merciful approach is ruled inappropriate to plants. Those who love plants and animals, as Augustine himself did under the Manichean sway, live in a "pathetic state." It is up to us, latecomers on the historical scene and firsthand eyewitnesses of extreme environmental degradation, to redeem this pathos in the twenty-first century.

Matter Spiritualized: The Wood of the Cross, Divine Order, and Rustling Leaves

Even if it is judged by its own measure, the success of the Augustinian enterprise is, at the same time, its failure. The spiritualization of nourishment and reproduction engrains these processes and the finitude they portend in our immortal souls. The plant regerminates in us, as us. Indomitable matter returns to haunt the world of spirit. And it does so in the guise of the wood of the cross, on which Jesus was crucified.

Versed in ancient philosophy, Augustine knew that the Aristotelian "matter" carried the semantic trace of the Greek *hylē*, meaning wood. For his part, he reinvented this concept for the world of spirit by transposing it onto the most prominent symbol of Christianity, the cross. If mundane life with its temptations is akin to a stormy sea, then a boat constructed from the wood of the cross holds the hope for traversing these marine abysses: "So it's essential we should stay in the boat, that is, that we should be carried on wood, to be enabled to cross this sea. Now this wood, on which our feebleness is carried, is the Lord's cross, with which we are stamped and reclaimed from submersion in this world."[9]

The wood of the cross is light matter, the matter that, instead of sinking like a stone, floats, as though lifted by spirit. The feebleness carried on the cross is none other than the finite, fragile, and temptation-beset human body raised above the sea of worldly existence in a desperate struggle against itself. No longer a part of a living tree, wood seems to be little more than dead matter. Not only a human body but also wood is resurrected by and on the cross, promising a more secure life than that of any creature, including the tree from which it came into existence. A smidgeon of the organic world, from which it has been set apart and hence consecrated, the wood of the cross contrasts with the inorganic, inflexible, stony nature of Judaic law ("It's stones, you see, who are throwing stones, rock-hard men who are stoning you. They [the Jews] received the law on stone, and they throw stones").[10] Because, on it, external law was swapped for love (the law of the heart), the wood of the cross retains its lightness and thus carries humans who are not rock hard and who do not drop down like stones burdened with the weight of corporeal desire.

The relevance of the aquatic metaphor (frequently associated with the feminine in the scheme of sexual difference) to our embodied condition does not fade in the other sermons, either. Referring to procreation and eating as the "works of the flesh," Augustine notes: "You see, there are two works of the flesh which keep the human race going; holy and prudent people lower themselves to these works out of duty, the foolish plunge into them through greed."[11] Duty now takes the place of the wood of the cross, as it fulfills the same function of keeping the righteous afloat in a sea of carnality and temptations. Rather than plunge to the watery depths of sin, people who deserve to be called "holy" submerge themselves just enough to ensure the maintenance of the organism and of the species. Fasts and periods of abstinence are recommended to prevent a downright capitulation before the works of the flesh, harkening back, in both instances, to the excellences of plant soul. Kept in check by the "prudent," or rational, part of the psyche, sexual and gastronomic appetites ought to be brought to a bare minimum while censuring vegetal desire burning in us.

Save for a couple of rare passages in *The City of God*, Augustine has little to say about the desire of the plants themselves. There he accepts the Greek view that everything that lives "desire[s] to exist" and that trees do so "by putting down roots into the earth so that they may draw nourishment from it" and by putting forth "healthy branches into the air" (XI, 27). Further, he concedes that, though they are insentient, the "nourishment and generation [of trees] have some resemblance to sensation" (XI, 27). And he sums up his views in saying that, although not emotionally moved by anything, they "desire, as it were, that by which they might become more abundantly and bountifully fruitful" (XI, 28).

The above observations are not motivated by Augustine's botanical curiosity. They form the negative pretext for the discussion of a true love of existence, which is also the love of true existence, expressed in the human soul's cleaving to God, in whose image it was created. We betray that image as soon as we succumb to the biological attachment to life and, as a consequence, become ontologically indistinguishable from trees. Vegetal desire bespeaks, simultaneously, the centrality of love in all of creation (inanimate things also share in this attitude, as seen in their tendency to be attracted to the place where they fall, "for the weight of bodies is, as it were, their love" [*The City of God* XI, 28]) and the kind of feeling humans should repress in themselves if they are to attain to the true love of God. Pointing beyond itself, the plant is more than a sign and a symbol; it is an example of creaturely life and a counterexample of the form of life humans should avoid.

Not surprisingly, Augustine displays virtually no interest in plants themselves. After all, he treats them, along with all other creatures, as translucent screens through which something else (i.e., divine order) is visible. Things as trivial as "leaves driven by the wind, or floating over water" and giving "some resistance to the forces acting on them . . . teach something to men."[12] What do they teach? That even "things like the fluttering of leaves and the insignificant patter of house-mice [are] as necessary as the written book. Everything would belong to the same order."[13] While Socrates found that the trees and the countryside had nothing to teach him, Augustine is eager to receive the teaching of the leaves that comprise the Book of Nature, composed by God. They, too, point beyond themselves to the divinely instituted order of which they are a part. How to "read" these tree leaves, as though they were pages in God's great Book? What can we learn about the hermeneutics of creation, framed in vegetal terms?

The teaching of the leaves does not promote theoretical knowledge; it reinforces the three pillars of religion: faith, love, and hope. When we track the creatures, as so many threads leading back to their Creator, empirical information about them is as dispensable as knowledge claims about God are absurd. There is nothing capable of illuminating the nature of God, who, in His infinite wisdom, dwarfs Plato's sun and lights up the world. Finite beings silently invoke this "wisdom which governs the world down to the leaves that tremble on the trees" (*Confessions* VII. vi.8), without seeking a reason for the Reason of the world's existence. Loading the dice in favor of faith, they testify to the harmony and goodness of divine order, which, as a totality, envelops even the tiniest aspects of creation.

Augustine deflates the value of knowledge claims, precisely, with regard to a tree. In his axiological system, a "man who knows that he owns a tree and gives thanks to you [to God] for the use of it, even though he does not know exactly how many cubits high it is ... is better than the man who measures it and counts all its branches but does not own it, nor knows and loves its Creator" (*Confessions* V.iv.7). The tree, ready to be used and available for ownership, represents an object in general. These modes of relating to the tree-object are preferable to a thorough knowledge of its empirical features, so long as we concede that God is its real owner, who has authorized the consumption of His possession by us. Higher than the familiarity with the object's attributes is the trust we are requested to put in its essence as a part of God's creation, determining its place in the divine order of things.

If Augustine's philosophy is to remain pertinent to today's concerns, it will be necessary to extract an ethical kernel from the shell of its theological dismissal of the world. A good place to start is plant ethics, which will thrive once we dispense with the figurative meaning of vegetation and return to the literal fruits that have made enjoyment (*frui*) meaningful. Accepted as the gifts of nature, they would no longer be handed over for unlimited use but would elicit the sort of gratitude commensurate with use-less enjoyment, or with what in religious terms is known as "grace." And, since fruits are symbolic of worldly existence in general, the same ethical literalization may be extended to everything else in the world, not to mention to the world as a whole.

In the Augustinian universe, the love of the world was misdirected and nearsighted at best. It represented a diversion from the love of God, a dispersion of enjoyment in numerous, insecurely possessed things, and, hence, a renunciation of full and ideal being. The repudiation of finitude made sense against the background of faith in the existence of perfection above this world—the ideal against which the world was measured (failing, of course, to measure up to it) and to which it could be sacrificed as a whole in the hope of salvation. Once the transcendent absolute is no longer immune to questioning, however, the certainty that the world exists for the sake of something outside itself also crumbles. That we have not yet caught up with this momentous event is evident in the continuing treatment of the world as a collection of utilizable objects containing nothing that would merit our use-less enjoyment. What we urgently need to learn in the process of mourning the loss of absolutes is the sense of a modified Augustinian motto, *Mundo frui!* Enjoy the world!

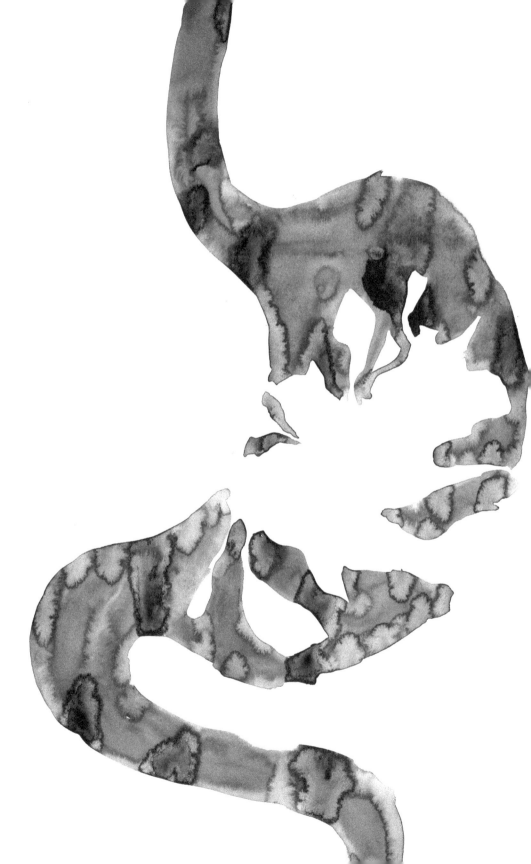

5 AVICENNA'S CELERY

Immoderate Philosophers, Excessive Plants

A Persian wunderkind born in the tenth century AD, Avicenna (the Latinized version of the name ibn Sīnā) knew a thing or two about plants. In addition to his enviable expertise in mathematics and physics, philosophy and astronomy, geology and Islamic theology, Avicenna was a practicing physician and the author of a five-volume *Qanun, The Canon of Medicine*.

For centuries after its composition, *The Canon* continued to be revered as the gold standard of the medical profession in Europe and outside its confines. This medieval state-of-the-art manual dealt with plants as the components of a human diet and, numbering in the hundreds, as remedies for sundry ailments. So essential were they to the Avicennian medical system that the book's English editors decided to preface the text with an excerpt from *One Thousand and One Nights*, where Scheherazade sings praises of the sage of Duban—the prototype of our sage—"conversant with the virtues of every plant, dried and fresh, the baneful and the useful."[1]

Dietwise, and contrary to what we might expect, Avicenna did not consider the consumption of fruits to be beneficial for human health. "Fresh fruits," he categorically stated, "are only good for those who carry out hard work, or take much exercise . . . for they render the blood too watery, and so it is apt to ferment."[2] Intense physical activity was recommended as an antidote meant to counterbalance their adverse effects by purging the blood of vegetal "crude humours" and lightening the burden these imposed on the human organism. Shockingly for us, about one thousand years prior to the "Five-a-Day" program implemented by the U.S. Department of Agriculture (USDA), fruits were seen as much more detrimental to human well-being than meat and wine.

The curative property of plants was another focal point of *The Canon* and, at the same time, a point of convergence for Avicenna's theoretical knowledge and some of the ill-fated events in his biography. Take, for instance, celery. The philosopher-physician deemed this plant suitable for improving digestion and liberally prescribed its seeds as a diuretic remedy.[3] When he, too, experienced the very digestive symptoms he had described, Avicenna did not hesitate to self-medicate in what he believed to be the strictest adherence to his own manuscript's guidelines. But things did not turn out the way he had expected.

Shortly before his death, Avicenna accompanied the prince of Isfahan on a military campaign. Seized by a colic attack and apprehensive that he would be left behind, he administered eight enemas to himself, causing intestinal lacerations.[4] Thereafter, he ordered an injection of two *danāqs* of celery seeds—a dose that was exceeded at least tenfold when, ignoring explicit instructions, five *dirhams* of the extract were dispensed.[5] To make matters worse, having determined that he should take opium for the alleviation of epileptic symptoms, Avicenna received an overdose of the drug from servants who used the occasion to rob their master.[6] Amazingly, these incidents, sufficient to debilitate the average person, failed to slow him down. The sage continued to indulge in the dietary and sexual excesses, for which he was infamous, preferring to measure the days (and the nights) of his life in breadth, rather than in length.[7]

Evidently, Avicenna learned a great deal from Aristotle, save for the patently Aristotelian virtue of moderation, that is, of finding an optimal middle course between surfeits and deficiencies. If we are to trust his biographers (and the accuracy of their assertions is currently under dispute),[8] the real cause of Avicenna's death was vegetal excess: various overdoses of herbal medications, overeating, and, according to the disciple Al-Juzajani, extremely frequent sexual intercourse. Besides the actual celery and poppy seeds—the source of opium—directly implicated in the philosopher's death, the two hyperactive dimensions of his vegetal soul—the nutritive and the reproductive—also had a hand in his demise.

When pressed about the pitfalls of such a hectic lifestyle, Avicenna responded: "God, Who is exalted, has been generous concerning my external and internal faculties, so I use every faculty as it should be used."[9] In reflecting on his life, he did not seem to give much thought to the inner conflict among the faculties, nor did he reckon that some of them had to be controlled by other, more rational regions of the psyche. Much different, as we shall discover, is Avicenna's theoretical view of the soul, whose parts, organized in rigidly hierarchical and quasi-feudal relations, owe obedience or reign supreme depending on their respective positions in the psychic edifice.

The immoderations of the philosopher's life, pointing in one way or another toward the vegetal sphere, parallel his view of plants as the placeholders of ontological excess. In their basic constitution, Avicennian plants are so chaotic and unstable that they are barely fit for receiving a soul. According to his cosmogony (a theory of the origination of the universe), the elements of earth, fire, water, and air must come together in more or less balanced proportions to furnish matter capable of receiving a form (which is another word for a soul). Plants have something of this harmonious mix: "When the elements are mixed together in a more harmonious way ... other beings also come into existence out of them due to the powers of the heavenly bodies. The first of these are plants."[10] Closer to the state of equilibrium than minerals, plant matter is "disposed for receiving the vegetal soul."[11]

Regardless of the thesis that plant matter is a definite advance on the crudeness of stones, it is the least balanced substratum of the living. The subaltern position of plants at the bottom of the metaphysical hierarchy stays unchanged throughout the philosophical tradition; what varies is the justification of their presumed inferiority. As Avicenna would have it, of all kinds of creatures, plants exhibit the greatest deviation from the mean. If an animal comes "after the plant," it is because the former "emerges from a compound of elements whose organic nature is much nearer to the mean ... and is therefore prepared to receive the animal soul, having passed through the stage of the vegetable soul."[12] On its progress from chaos and disharmony toward perfection, the soul must shed its vegetal shape, which Avicenna significantly calls "natural," *taby'yat*.[13]

Animal and human forms are, in comparison to those of plants, denaturalized. So, does the association of the vegetal with the natural

bestow upon this stratum of existence a modicum of normality we usually attribute to nature? Not at all. With reference to the measurements
of pulse, Avicenna clarifies that the natural is, above all, that which is
exceptionally strong and vigorous, "excessive as to strength."[14] Faithful
to the Greeks in one respect, he parts company with them in another.
As in ancient Greek philosophy, nature is still metonymically expressed
in the plant, and it is for this reason that the faculties of the vegetal
soul are designated as "natural." But Avicenna's nature is not exactly the
total movement of self-generation and harmonious growth that it was
for the ancients; it denotes excessive vigor in exercising a function *or*
the disequilibrium of elements still lacking the cohesive force and form
of the soul. The philosopher's replica concerning the use of his faculties
is, undoubtedly, tied to the first signification of the natural: nature as
vigorous excess in him *and* in the plant . . . But such "cherry picking" is
untenable, since the two definitions of nature (hence, of vegetation) go
together. That is why the vigorous use of the philosopher's reproductive
and nutritive faculties led to his ruination.

The excesses integral to plants do not foil their search for perfection.
Growth, for instance, strives toward perfection when it augments the
bodily extension of growing beings in a balanced manner: "Growth implies an increase in all directions in the proper proportion. To become fat
or obese with advancing years, after being slim, is not growth. It is not
growth unless the increase is in all directions and in natural proportions,
so as to culminate in a state of perfection of growth."[15] Yet the plants'
striving toward perfection is easily thwarted thanks to their exposure to
externalities that obstruct their development and growth. The example
Avicenna cites in *The Metaphysics of* The Healing is "the cold's freezing
of plants, afflicting them at the time ripe for their perfection, so that
[their] proper preparedness and what is consequent on it become cor-
rupted."[16] Provided that plant matter is inherently unbalanced, external
disturbances have a greater impact upon it than upon the animals, who
are better suited to resisting environmental contingencies. Avicenna
does not know that plants, as a rule, do not resist but adapt to and work
with the environment by changing their physiological and morphological states. For him, plants are defenseless. Too weak to overcome whatever hinders their striving toward perfection, they persist in the state of

unrealized preparedness, breathing with the promise of form that is far from being actualized. But, then, so do human thought and existence!

The Feudal Order of the Vegetal Soul, or Aristotelianism with a Twist

The poverty of nature in Avicennian thought is astonishing. Although the philosopher tends to refer to the vegetal soul as the "natural faculty," in his understanding, nature is still more deficient than the plant that exhibits the first and shakiest union of matter and psychic form. Taken in isolation, nature is impotent, "unable to originate a souled body in one stroke" and "in want of a power by which she can fabricate a living body by the promotion of growth."[17] To generate anything, nature requires the assistance of Divine Providence, which is the unquestioned source of the soul, from the simplest vegetal to the most complex human varieties. We might say that Avicenna anticipates the modern reductive view of nature as a conjunction of mathematizable and mechanically driven processes. To be sure, in contrast to modern naturalism, his mechanized nature is made tolerable by the deus ex machina of the soul. But, subtract this "soulful supplement" from his philosophy, and you will end up with a world uncannily resembling the Newtonian universe of efficient causes and effects.

So, what belongs within the realm of nature, properly so called? In addition to the classical elements, Avicenna includes under this heading four forces: "the attracting, the holding, the digesting, and the excreting (repelling) [jādhiba, māsika, hādima, dāfi'a]."[18] Intimately related to the nourishing, growing, and reproductive faculties of plant soul, the four forces of nature are inferior to these self-organizing—in contemporary parlance, autopoietic—capacities. Their inferiority allows plant soul to establish its tenuous mastery over nature. Vegetal life is, as Avicenna has it, "sub-served" by the forces of nature.[19]

The relations of mastery and vassalage binding together the living plant and the inorganic world give us an accurate snapshot of the socioeconomic relations in the times of Avicenna. Whereas the plant may be a feudal lord over the elements, it is still reduced to the serf of the animal and the human. What is more, since its soul does not subsist as a simple unity, its different faculties enter into relations of mastery and subservience among themselves. The hierarchical (political) economy of plant soul is the cynosure of Avicenna's "Aristotelianism with a twist."

With recourse to elementary logical deduction, we conclude that when Avicenna defines vegetal soul as "natural" (*taby'yat*), he obliquely ascribes to it the deficiency of nature and an unstable form of life verging on death. The plant's proximity to the mechanical forces of nature is especially evident in the nourishing part of its soul that strings together the attracting, the holding, the digesting, and the excreting. The nutritive faculty, *ghāzīa*, is "that whereby the aliments are transformed into the likeness of the thing nourished, thereby replacing the loss incidental to the process of life."[20] To transform the nourishing other (for the plant: sunlight, water, minerals, etc.) into the nourished same, this faculty must engage directly with the four forces of nature, adding to them the practical notions of difference and identity. Avicenna stresses that *ghāzīa* is not to be confused with the digestive power "in its service"[21] precisely because the nutritive faculty is above and beyond mere digestion and introduces relations that are no longer only physical but crudely spiritual, that is, difference and identity. At the same time, this faculty is comprehended as the lowest stratum of the lowest kind of soul as a result of its near immersion in the realm of nature. Actively mastering the attracting, the holding, the digesting, and the excreting, the nutritive faculty passively submits to the "augmentative faculty" of growth, *nāmīa*.[22] Why?

In *A Compendium on the Soul*, Avicenna distinguishes two types of movement: that according to the element and that against the element. The first type is completely natural, such as a heavy body that strives downward, toward its proper element, the earth. The second type is, for a lack of a better term, spiritual; it betrays the existence of a soul that drives the ensouled body away from its physical element, as does "a flying bird's motion with its heavy body high up through the sky."[23] Growth is akin to the avian flight, in that it also destines the relatively heavy body of the plant, pertaining at once to the earth and to water, to the airy expanses above. The augmentative faculty operates *contra natura*, which is why it earns the standing above its nutritive counterpart. Not only does it organize the forces of nature, but it also opposes these forces, attesting to the interference of something that comes from the outside and remains inexplicable within the mechanical ordering of the elements. This external interference is, for Avicenna, an indelible imprint of the soul, thanks to which the excessive matter that comprises the plant submits to the impositions of form.

Nāmīa, or the faculty of augmentation, stands higher on the ladder of the vegetal soul for yet another reason: it sets its sights on perfection. We have already seen that growth entails an increase in bodily dimension *in the right proportion*, and it is this measured and balanced augmentation that would permit it "to achieve perfection."[24] Now, balance and proportionality are indicative of matter's refinement, just as disorder and excess are the barometers of its unpreparedness for the reception of form. Insofar as growth abides by the teleological ideal of perfect proportionality, it (1) moderates the excessive ontology of plants and (2) boosts the formative drive of the soul at the expense of crude matter. Yet the conceptual limit of growth is that, along with nutrition, it serves a mortal individual growing being, not the species as a whole. Even if it strives toward the end of perfection, it is but a means for the higher ends of the generative faculty. Indeed, growth is a sort of go-between, bridging the lowest and the highest layers of plant soul,[25] much like the plant itself in its capacity of an intermediary between the inorganic and the organic worlds.

The generative faculty (*mawallida*) houses a spark of divine, creative, form-bestowing force: "The reproductive faculty gives the matter the form of the thing."[26] Rather than replace "the loss incidental to the process of life" within an organism, it substitutes the whole creature with another like it. While the nutritive faculty transforms difference (nourishment) into sameness (the nourished), and while the faculty of growth augments the same (bodily extension) in the right proportion, *mawallida* articulates sameness and difference in a more complex constellation.

First, the reproductive faculty is the home of potential similarity, which can be actualized through its mixture with other bodies.[27] Second, swerving away from the other two faculties shared equally by all nourished-growing beings, *mawallida* is unique to each self-reproducing species, not to mention the fact that it is split between sexual and asexual reproduction. As Avicenna writes: "We find them [living beings], beside having the obtaining of nourishment in common, to have growth also in common, but to differ in the propagation (of offspring), since there are, among growing things, such as do not beget."[28] On the one hand, asexual reproduction falls under the category of growth, because it is conceptually indistinguishable from the continuation of existing matter.

True "begetting," on the other hand, bears a new form, which potentially resides in the begetter. For these reasons, difference and identity cohabit in the generative faculty of the vegetal soul.

None of the above renders the formative capacity of plants commensurate with the souls of animals, let alone those of humans. "The animal faculties in their entirety," Avicenna concludes, "are served by the vegetable faculties, of which the reproductive is the first in rank and the highest one."[29] Just as the mechanical forces of nature are the vassals of the vegetal soul, and just as within this soul there is another hierarchy based on feudal relations of superiority and subordination, so the plant kingdom and the vegetal faculties are the instruments of animals and of other souls moved by the power of volition. At this point, the historico-political analogy exhausts itself. In a feudal society, vassals exchanged their obedience for protection by powerful lords, a benefit squarely denied to plants. When it comes to the feudalism of the soul, what do the vegetal faculties—particularly those pertaining to the plants themselves—gain from their subservience to the animal principle?

Today, pioneering authors, including Michael Pollan, contend that we've got the instrumentalization of plants by animals and humans all wrong.[30] What if, they ask, we are actually used by plants to spread their progeny worldwide? Where would a humble potato be if it weren't exported from southern Peru and northwestern Bolivia to the farthest corners of the world? What would the fate of celery be, had humans not carried its seeds from the Mediterranean basin where it had originated to the Americas and beyond? Do plants and their "psychic faculties" put up a pretense of obeying the animal and human masters, whom they secretly use for their own reproductive ends? Or are plants, perhaps, neither subservient nor superior to animals and humans but deserving of an equal status in the republic of the living?

Under no circumstances would Avicenna respond to these questions in the affirmative. But he does inadvertently throw the fastidiously constructed hierarchy of the soul into disarray by pointing out a matter of profound "agreement" between plants and animals. It turns out that the two kinds of creatures share "the power of impulsion ... more widely embracing than the power of perception."[31] The will of the animal corresponds to the plant's "adaptation for attracting such foods as are useful and pushing off such that are harmful and incompatible,"[32] except that the former resorts to motion, aided by perception, as a means of pursuing its interests and fleeing from danger. The absence of locomotion does not prevent plants from being impelled toward their goals without perception, which is one among many tools in the arsenal of the living for attaining their aims.

So far, so good. But Avicenna makes an unwarranted logical leap as soon as he classifies plants in a paradoxical group of insensate living beings. He suppresses the idea that perception through animal sense organs is not identical to sensation as such. Let us assume that the so-called distance senses of vision, hearing, and so on are germane solely to those animals that are able to dash in an instant toward a far-off source of food or run away from a predator. Still, other kinds of sensitivity would be indispensible both to sessile animals and to plants, if they are to determine whether or not they have reached the target toward which (or away from which) they are impelled. It is folly to think that being sensate is the function of the nervous system alone. "Insensate living beings" is a contradiction in terms, because the life of the living requires a high degree of discernment to preserve and promote itself.

Avicenna's correct intuition about the plant's power of impulsion should have prompted him to explore the murky terrain of vegetal sensitivity. It did not. Instead, the philosopher was forced to concede an unsettling similarity between the plants and the stars, which were also negatively defined as "insensate living beings": "As for the starry firmament and plants, the feeling power and the imagining power have not been imparted unto them, even though each one of them has a soul and though it has life: the firmament has not these powers, because of its loftiness; plants have them not, because of their abasement in comparison to it."[33] Replicating the Aristotelian "beasts and gods" who lead an essentially apolitical life, Avicenna's plants and planets live without sensation below and above the thresholds of animal and human existence, respectively. Only those beings do not need the powers of feeling and imagination that are either too deficient or too self-sufficient to pursue their goals. The uppermost and the lowest strata in the hierarchy of the living come together in the region of life scarcely comprehensible from the human point of view and, as a result, are showcased in negative terms: "insensate." So much so, that the insensate life of plants is just one of two exceptional cases where Avicenna accepts a constitutively negative definition as entirely satisfactory.[34]

Another wrench stuck in the Avicennian hierarchical machinery makes the plants' inferior status and their real capacities less and less compatible. What I have in mind are the correlates of the vegetal faculties in the spheres of perception and thinking. In *The Canon*, Avicenna likens the "natural forces" organized by the nutritive faculty, as well as the augmentative and generative faculties, to mental processes. To wit, the force of attraction is equivalent to perception, retention is memory, transformative power refers to cogitation, the force of expulsion corresponds to expression, the augmentative faculty is translatable into the acquisition of knowledge, and the generative faculty is tied to inventiveness and creativity.[35] Such is Avicenna's plant-thinking in a nutshell. Well in advance of Spinoza's *Ethics*, physical processes and the tendencies of "the lowest" soul are interpreted as modes of thinking wholly under the sway of matter, unfiltered through the purifying form of (abstract) thought. By absorbing and retaining water and solar radiation, the plant "perceives" and "remembers" the liquid and sunlight; by growing, it acquires the "knowledge" of its environment, exploring the locale's most beneficial, resource-rich niches; by reproducing itself, it invents, each time anew, its genus . . .

And, vice versa, humans "think" by way of eating, drinking, and expelling the byproducts of nourishing substances, by growing and by having children, though the more rarified forms of thought are available to them, as well. Avicenna is certainly not alone among the philosophers in attaching a negative value judgment to these material modes of thinking. But we would be amiss if we were to disregard his emphasis on medicine with its concern for adjusting the material conditions of life, being, and thought so as to promote healing and individual well-being. In a markedly Plotinian language, we might say that Avicenna's medical corpus is the place where abstract thinking cares for its material corollary, or where the rational soul worries about the vegetal soul within the human. It is not that, page after page in *The Canon*, the mind tries to cure the body. In this magisterial, albeit often flawed book, human thinking endeavors to optimize plant-thinking within us.

Despite this optimistic vision of collaboration among the different kinds of psyche, hierarchical classifications reassert themselves both within and between plant, animal, and human souls. Much revolves here around the extent of materiality's predominance: the soul of plants is the lowest because almost completely enmeshed with matter, while the soul of humans is constituted by more formal structures and processes. But this simple bifurcation too is deceptive, since materiality creeps into human thinking, whereas formalism potentiates the generative aspects of plant-thinking. Within the mental faculties *proper* some—notably, perception—are engrossed in material reality, and others (inventiveness, creativity) facilitate the play, recombination, and emergence of forms. The hierarchy of the vegetal soul infinitely mirrors and is mirrored by an equally striated arrangement of the human psyche, with perception ranked below knowledge acquisition and inventiveness. For centuries after Avicenna this gradation of knowledge will be unquestioned; it is kept virtually intact as late as in Hegel's phenomenology of Spirit, which commences with perception as the lowest and most vacuous form of knowing. And, in many quarters, it is still alive now, in the twenty-first century.

It appears, on the face of it, that the division of the psyche in Avicenna is Aristotelian through and through. But his is, in the best of cases, "Aristotelianism with a twist." Or, more precisely, with twists. Quite blatantly, Avicenna begs to differ from his ancient Greek forerunner on the subject of plant soul's simplicity—the thesis that it is the indivisible origin (the geometrical point) of life. In Avicenna's thought, what Aristotle called *to threptikon* brings together four disparate forces of nature that do not, as such, possess a soul. Furthermore, for the medieval thinker, vegetal soul in its totality is irreducible to one fundamental capacity to obtain nourishment, of which the rest would be more or less elaborate variations.[36] Nor does Aristotle contend, as Avicenna does, that the soul penetrates the body from elsewhere, having originated outside the creatures it animates.[37] Ernst Bloch's praise of Avicenna's "naturalism"[38] sounds particularly suspect in this regard.

One of the twists in the philosophical plot that represents Avicenna as an Aristotelian has to do with the differences and divisions the former spliced into the vegetal soul. In the aftermath of Avicenna's transformative reading of the Philosopher, the primordial level of the psyche is no longer imaginable as a pure and simple source equivalent to the geometrico-metaphysical point, which cannot be further subdivided into component parts. At the origin, there is no coherent unity—the ideal of all metaphysical philosophy. It's a pity that while undermining a fundamental tenet of metaphysics the medieval thinker commits yet another cardinal sin. Organizing differences into hierarchical conglomerates, he sanctions the enduring oppression of the vegetal (as much as of nature) both within and outside of the human.

What Do Plants Love?

After learning that Avicenna conceptualized plants as insensate living substances, readers will greet with understandable suspicion the revelation that he deigned to include these creatures devoid of "the power of feeling" in his *Treatise on Love*. How is it possible for plants to love anything, if they are so deficient as to lack the entire emotive layer of the soul?

We should backtrack a little in our argument thus far, to pick up a clue to the nature of plant love. Recall that Avicenna has established the existence of the vegetal "impulsion," presaging the will of animals, albeit acting without the assistance of perception. Plants are driven toward their goals and, finally, toward perfection by an impulsion that expresses their love, *'ishq*, a state much broader in scope than emotional attraction and attachment. In the words of Avicenna, "Every type of love has as object either something already attained or something which is still to be attained. Whenever the goodness of a thing increases, the merit of the object of its love increases also, and so does the love for the good."[39] It follows that the objects of vegetal love are life-sustaining nutrients, self-augmentation in growth, and the renewal of the genus through reproduction. Without either perceiving or understanding these objects (as a matter of fact, without relating to them qua objects), plants strive toward them, loving them with a love that is literally blind.

There might be more than one grain of truth in saying that plants are "water loving" or "sun loving" since these are things they strive to attain as nutrients guaranteeing the physical conditions for their existence. But the sense of love Avicenna alludes to is considerably broader than the colloquial phraseology would imply. Each faculty of the vegetal soul has its distinct goal, a unique perfection, and a peculiar kind of love. The plant is moisture and light loving inasmuch as it is reduced to its nutritive faculty, which is "the source of its desire for the presence of food in accordance with the need of matter for it."[40] We would not be off the mark were we to put this idea side by side with the Platonic, Plotinian, and Augustinian formulations of vegetal desire discussed previously. The gist of Avicenna's *Treatise on Love* is, indeed, Neo-Platonic, as every brook, creek, and stream of creaturely love gushes into the great river of loving the pure good.[41] But what plants have to offer to this great cosmic rush toward being and the good is not limited to a desire for nourishment. Their augmentative and generative faculties each contribute something to the meaning of love within the general *ordo amoris*.

The type of love "specific to the faculty of growth" is the plant's "desire for the increase fitting the proportions of the body which is nourished."[42] Presumably excessive in their constitution, plants must practically discover a bodily equilibrium indispensible for the living. The love inherent in their growth affirms what is already in being and strives toward perfection, tied to the proportionality of the growing body. It is, therefore, compatible with the love of beauty in the sense of proportionality and with the love of existence wherein that entity which manages to strike the right physical balance within itself and with its environment conserves itself for the duration of its finite life. (An apt example of this from early modern philosophy is the Spinozan *conatus*.)

Whenever Avicenna writes about love, he presents a scenario where an imperfect being tends toward perfection, beauty, the good, incorruptible being, God ... Nutritive and augmentative kinds of love cling to the finite creaturely existence of the vegetal, animal, and human lovers in the hopes of participating in that being which always is. Procreation, conventionally paired with love, fosters a more secure participation in the eternal, in that it no longer bets on the futile self-preservation of the living just as they are. The generative faculty responds to the need for the renewal of an organism not in itself but in another that issues from it. To this faculty is attached still another kind of love—"the desire to produce a new principle similar to the one from which it [a living creature] derives itself."[43] Generative love is the desire of the finite for infinity, or for a potentially infinite regeneration of the wellspring of its own life in another creature akin to the progenitor. What is reproduced is not just another celery plant that will germinate from a seed but a new principle, a fresh beginning, through which the same (genes, genus, and so forth) rejuvenates in a material substratum resembling that of the parent. The love of the generative soul emphatically says "yes" to being (ergo, to the good) by recommencing finite life *after* death, to which it denies the honor of having the last and decisive word.

All this is not to say that the three vegetal variations on love furnish a proof of exceptional plant agency. In Avicenna's thought, love is not foreign even to inanimate objects, where matter yearns to receive form so as to "shy away from absolute non-being."[44] It is not limited to an affect experienced by living creatures; in the first and in the last instances, everything and everyone—including natural forces, vegetal, animal, and human powers—seek the Necessary Existent, or God, as the absolute good.[45] The *how* of love, not the fact *that* it is experienced, is of the essence. The difference between modes of being is indexed to the diverse modes of loving the good.

If the *how* of loving matches the *how* of living (not to omit the inorganic kinds of being), then the loves of plants should be as excessive as their lives. According to Avicenna, in their aspiration to perfection, which ignites love, beings imitate the First Cause, the absolute good, the Necessary Existent, or God. By resisting nonbeing and staying at rest once they have been reunited with their proper elements, natural bodies, for instance, imitate the ideal immobility that typifies the object of their love. Now, plants emulate the First Cause in aiming to preserve the individuals and the species, "even though, in their beginnings, aims such as sexual intercourse and nutrition have no resemblance to It."[46] Like all other creatures, they imitate the Necessary Existent "in the *aims* of their activities but not in the *origins*,"[47] but, contrary to other creatures, plants, as the first bearers of the generative faculty, ensconce the problematic of origination (generativity) in the aims of their activities. Blurring the distinction between the aims and the origins, they imitate the First Cause excessively, mimicking it in what it is not.

In Avicenna's Platonic Aristotelianism, living creatures as well as inanimate objects are not impelled by a force emanating from the past of their origins but are moved from the future of their aims that invariably point the way to the good. All roads lead to Rome. Avicenna's masterful fusion of Aristotle's notion of the unmoved mover and Plato's doctrine of love culminates in the observation that "that which moves the mover without undergoing change through intent and desire is the end and the objective toward which the mover aims. It is the object of love. And the object of love, inasmuch as it is the object of love, is the good for the lover."[48] Plants, too, love what is good for them and, therefore, in our terms, pursue their interests: to maintain themselves in being, individually and through their progeny. Seeing that Avicenna accepts the ancient equations of being with the good and nothingness with the privation of being (evil), the love of existence in everything that lives connotes a love of the good and a resistance to evil. When plants grow toward the light of the sun, they are moved from the outside, in parallel to the good that animates its lovers from a certain "end" of their activity, in Avicenna as well as in Plato. In other words, when plants are said to love light and moisture, the real objects of their love are being and the good. And we, humans, cannot help but recognize bits of ourselves in their conduct and *love this vegetal love*.

As I've mentioned, for Avicenna, neither plants nor other creatures are the exclusive subjects of ontological love. Inanimate entities also cling to being, resisting entropy and yearning to find rest in their respective elements. This caveat should not be used to deprive plants of their claim to moral considerability. If anything, it makes Avicenna-inspired environmental ethics capacious enough to encompass entire ecosystems, such as rivers rushing to be reunited with the watery element, which they love, in the sea. That inanimate objects also love being after their own fashion does not detract from the love of eternity and of existence that permeates all three layers of plant soul.

In one of the most poignant moments in the *Treatise on Love*, Avicenna construes the human propensity to kiss and embrace as our affirmation of the loving proximity to and the desire for a union with one another.[49] "Tree-huggers" are generally derided for inappropriately transferring these affective gestures onto the flora and the environment as a whole. But the kiss and the hug need not be literal. Our drawing near the environment, whether in experiencing concern for its future or in understanding its constituents as so many imitations of and loving approximations to the good, amounts to a virtual embrace of the world. "What do plants love?" is much more than a question; it is a symbolic kiss and hug given to the being of plants.

The Aporia of Knowing Ourselves (as Plants)

At the opening of *A Compendium on the Soul*, Avicenna exhorts his reader to pursue with the utmost rigor the ancient injunction to "know thyself." Avicennian self-knowledge is, in effect, tinged with a medieval flavor, in that it is sought not for its own sake but with the view to gaining insight into the nature of God, whose traces we are. Between faith and knowledge, there is, in this regard, a phenomenal consensus: "wise men and pious saints" proclaim, in a single voice, "Whoso Knoweth himself, Knoweth his Lord."[50]

What form does knowing oneself take in a soul, whose parts are lined up in a hierarchical chain of command? If humans are the composites of vegetal, animal, and rational (speaking) capacities, then the awareness of all these, working in concert, is indispensable for their genuine self-knowledge and, by extension, for the knowledge of God. But is it really possible to know how the nourishing, growing, and generative capacities set themselves to work in our everyday life? Can we ever be fully alert to the way the plant in us grows, flourishes, and withers away? To know ourselves, we must pay heed to the physiology of the body and to the unconscious—those vegetal dimensions of our existence that dodge our senses and conscious grasp. It could well be that Avicenna's scrupulous medical researches were, at bottom, ways to grapple with these most difficult aspects of self-knowledge. Even so, no investigation—no matter how painstaking—is in a position to expose the complete workings of the vegetal soul without losing track of their unconscious character. Hence, the aporia (the roadblock) of the simultaneous necessity and impossibility of knowing our "vegetal" self at the extreme limits of self-knowledge.

The aporetic situation into which plant soul has forced Avicenna and us goes from bad to worse, seeing that the true destination of self-knowledge is not this very self, but God. So, if God is ultimately unknowable, it is not only because His infinity overwhelms our finite minds but also because we cannot fully comprehend ourselves: the vegetal part of our psyche orchestrates our growth, the processing of nutrients, and sexual maturation largely unbeknownst to us. Conversely, what we do grasp about the operations of the vegetal soul feeds directly into our knowledge of the divine. Medical research is, therefore, replete both with psychological and theological overtones. Avicenna himself alludes to this odd conceptual knot of medicine, philosophy, and theology on the pages of *A Compendium*:

> I have also read that this saying ["Know thyself," etc.] was engraved in the façade of the temple of Aesculapius, who is known ... as one of the prophets

and whose most famous miracle is that he was wont to heal the sick by mere loud supplication; and so did all priests who performed sacerdotal functions in his temple. From him have philosophers got the science of medicine.[51]

The essential incompleteness of our self-understanding has been already foretold in *The Canon*, especially in the comparison it makes between the augmentative faculty of growth and acquisition of knowledge. On the one hand, thanks to the hindsight afforded by the Age of Enlightenment that stretches between Avicenna and us, this analogy seems to support a belief in unbridled progress. The sky is the limit to vegetal growth and to knowledge acquisition, soaring up to airy realms on the wings of spirit ... (Lest we get carried away with this protoidealism, the analogy also suggests that our systems of knowledge are plantlike, in that they can wither away, die, and serve as fertilizers for subsequent generations, which is the fate of all growing things.) On the other hand, and more accurately, both growth and knowledge extend toward their ends, the sun and the good, without ever reaching these objects of their love. Rather than instigate the march of progress, their incompletion foregrounds an unbridgeable distance, the abyss between growing-knowing beings and that toward which they grow or that which they wish to grasp knowingly. It measures the degrees of separation between plants and the sun, us and the good, us and God, us and ourselves.

In defiance of the laws of physics, persistent growth and knowledge seeking actually increase these various distances, not so much by laying bare what we do not yet know as by situating the conditions of possibility (which are, at the same time, the final objects) of growing and knowing outside the ambit of these activities. Knowing that we are, among other things and in our innermost depths, plants is knowing that we will never know ourselves (and God) absolutely. No system of psychological knowledge, however exhaustive, will fill these gaps. "Know thyself!" will not even be heard properly unless it is accompanied by the Socratic profession of not-knowing—an aporia, all over again. The plant in us is our opaqueness to ourselves, our distance from God, our unconscious, if you will. And it is, at the same time, what is exceedingly near: our body, love, and being on the hither side of abstract knowing.

MAIMONIDES' PALM TREE

Arbor Sacra

Rabbi Moses Ben Maimon (abbreviated as Rambam and known in the Western world under the name Maimonides) performed for Judaism the same invaluable service as Aristotle rendered to ancient Greek philosophy. The classical philosopher presented a unified worldview, one both building on and disputing the theories of his predecessors; the rabbi from Cordoba systematized disparate religious laws into a colossal fourteen-tome *Code* titled *Mishneh Torah*, or *Repetition of the Torah*. For this reason, the disciples of Maimonides nicknamed him *ha-nesher ha-gadol'*, "the great eagle," as a tribute to the panoramic vision of the Law he bequeathed to future generations.

Maimonides also did not hesitate to descend from the heights of the Law to the minutiae of the everyday, proffering answers to the most obscure problems. He stipulated what was and was not permitted to the observers of Sabbath (the day of rest), came up with principles for resolving property disputes between neighbors and applied them to singular cases, and discussed the merits of boiling food in fruit juices. In light of his impressive macro- and microvision of the world, we may ask: What do plants look like from the perspective of the eagle, that is to say, from the eagle's-eye view of that teaching which purports to repeat the teaching of the Torah? And when zeroing in on any given plant species or a family of plants—say, *Arecaceae*, palm trees—what does Maimonides see from his preferred theological and philosophical vantage points?

The Book of Acquisition (*Qinyan*), contained within the fourteen-volume *Code*, details the rules governing sales and gifts as well as the rightful enjoyment and utilization of property. There Maimonides wants to ensure what we now call "sustainability," the chance for tree groves purchased specifically for felling to regenerate. So he requires that the buyer of olive trees leave untouched at least a stump and two shoots growing close to the ground. But "in the case of palm trees," he writes, the buyer "may dig and root them out because their stumps do not grow anew."[1] Palm trees are subject to absolute appropriation, which would leave no trace of their existence, except a hollow in the ground, once the felling operation is over. In stripping them of all legal protections, Maimonides thus exposes these trees to unlimited violence.

The Italian philosopher Giorgio Agamben coined the term *homo sacer* to refer to a human being reduced to the state of "bare life," exposed to unlimited violence, and handed over to the possibility of being killed with impunity (though not sacrificed).[2] Similarly, a palm tree in *The Book of Acquisitions* takes on the features of what we might call *arbor sacra*, a creature that is either barely alive or not deemed alive at all and that at any moment may be chopped down without care for the future. Palm trees grow in a permanent state of exception and, as we will soon realize, stand for all other trees and plants, excluded by Maimonides from the sphere of the living. They occupy the *"zone of indistinction between nature and right,"*[3] between life and death, between legal limits (within which they are nonetheless caught up) and unlimited violence.

The sentence by Maimonides I've quoted above is not the only mention of palm trees in laws regulating sales and other acquisitions. In those cases where the owner of the land and of the trees that grow on it is not one and the same person, the subterranean part of plants is said to belong to the proprietor of the field, while the aboveground portions pertain to the owner of the trees. But the rule is not applicable to palm trees, whose "owner does not receive any of the wood because the trunk of a palm tree does not bring forth shoots."[4] What is the justification for this reasoning? Bereft of generative power in their trunks, palm trees are nothing but extensions of their roots and, as such, legally belong to the owner of the land. In addition to being—like all other plants—deprived of life, they are poor in the distinctively vegetable capacity of growth. Doubly marginalized, the palm is, for Maimonides, a deficient tree, barely reminiscent of the miracle of Creation, the memory of which is preserved in the generative power of vegetation, time and again, renewing and reaffirming this singular event.

It is this power, in fact, that converts plants from appropriated objects into the means of appropriation. Like classical Liberals after him, Maimonides believes that the act of possession is not sealed until the possessor's labor is mixed with the property: a field is plowed, seeds are sowed, fruits are gathered, and so on.[5] But the activity of nature itself (*natura naturans*) is equally admissible as grounds for appropriation. So how and when do trees act as justifications for legitimate land claims? And does this usage mitigate their objectification?

Consider the following two stipulations. (1) When a vendee purchases three trees, he receives, along with them, the ground necessary for them to grow.[6] (2) When the titleholder of a plot sells it excluding the trees that grow there, he thereby retains half of the land.[7] The foundation for these judgments is a simple form of appropriation by occupation,[8] where the occupying agent may be a plant, not a human subject. But the agency of this agent is perplexing, as it is denied the status of a living being and thus rendered uprootable either unconditionally, as in the case of a palm tree, or provided that minimal conditions are satisfied, as in the case of an olive tree.

The exceptionality of *arbor sacra* extends so far as to absolve a potential violator of the Sabbath of responsibility and deflect accusations of wrongdoing. In *The Book of Seasons* (*Zemanim*), Maimonides states that "if one hurls a stone or shoots an arrow, intending to kill another human or an animal, and the missile does not kill but instead uproots a tree in the course of its flight, he is exempt."[9] Although he does not specify what happens when, aiming to uproot a tree, one actually kills a human or an animal, it is not hard to guess that the exemption would not apply. If the unintended nature of the outcome frees the shooter of liability, it is because the "victim" of the action is not a victim at all but *arbor sacra* prone to unrestrained violence. In contrast to Christianity, intentions are not as weighty as the unintended practical outcomes of human behavior that, only seemingly arbitrary, emanate from God's sovereign and recondite will. One uprooted tree is a small price to pay for absolving a potential violator of the Sabbath through a direct (and sovereign) divine intervention in the sublunary realm.

Any residual doubts on the value of plant life in the work of Maimonides immediately dissipate when we chance upon the other law of the Sabbath, prohibiting work to "promote the growth of plants." Whether one "sows seeds, or plants trees, or layers trees, or grafts or prunes them,"[10] one shows disregard not only for the day of rest itself but also for the divine act of Creation it reminds us of. What is salient in the juxtaposition of the two laws is that the unintended termination of a plant's existence does not break the Sabbath, but the intended care for plants does. (The case of the intentional uprooting of a plant during the Sabbath is more nuanced: such activity is sternly prohibited and classified with other instances of "gathering.") This is a perfect example of what, centuries later, Nietzsche would consider as the inverted, "life-stunting values" of both Judaism and Christianity, consistent with their overall nihilistic weltanschauung. Were a virtual dialogue to ensue between the two thinkers, Maimonides would have certainly contended that plants did not really live and, therefore, that, *stricto sensu*, there was no plant life to be either valued or violated. But this rejoinder does not change the fact that a theological-metaphysical hierarchy, which takes shape in the *Code*, prioritizes God's sovereign will over human intention (*kavanah*)— and human intention over the rest of the world. A palm tree, much like all other trees and plants, can be demoted to the condition of *arbor sacra* thanks to its identification with mere matter, whereupon human intentions and divine will are stamped.

The Maimonidean palm, indeed, betokens the destructible materiality of everything in the sublunary world, as opposed to the indestructibility of heavens:

> There are no contraries in heaven. That thesis is correct. However, we have not claimed that the heavens have been generated as the horse and palm tree are. Nor have we claimed that their being composite renders necessary their passing-away as is the case with plants and animals because of the contraries that subsist in them.[11]

The tree may be destroyed with impunity because it is thoroughly *destructible*—to do so is to bring out its finite nature and to activate the clash of the contraries it contains *in nuce*, the contraries ready to erupt at some point in time, rendering the tree's existence no longer logically possible. The composite nature of plants and animals, represented by the palm and the horse, is radically distinct from the metaphysical simplicity of heavens. It matters, of course, in which context we facilitate the passing away of plants and animals, that is, whether this is done in a ritually correct way and at an appropriate time (i.e., not on the Sabbath). But from the ethical standpoint informed by the thought of Maimonides, there is nothing inherently wrong in terminating the existence of a given plant or animal, seeing that this possibility is anticipated in their *genesis*, the mode of their generation. Harboring contraries, they contain the seeds of their own destruction.

At the same time, it is misleading to talk about the place of "plants and animals" in the philosophy of Maimonides. Exemplary of the plant as such, the palm tree grows in the space of a permanent exception from the ethical order of being. Within this order, if "the Universe does not exist for man's sake, but . . . each being exists for its own sake, and not because of some other thing,"[12] it would be reasonable to assume that plants, too, have an intrinsic value and an inherent worth. This ethical principle is a part of the admirable vein in Maimonidean thought that resists the immaturity of anthropocentrism and anthropomorphism both when it comes to the contemplation of God's essence and to our relation to the world around us.[13] His statement "man has an erroneous idea of himself, and believes the whole world exists only for his sake"[14] could very well be the rallying cry in today's struggles against human domination of nature.

The problem is that "each being," deserving of life and respect in its own right, does not include plants! Already on the next page of the same text, Maimonides emphasizes that "God gave the plants to man and other living beings" and that "plants exist only for the benefit of the animals, since the latter cannot live without food."[15] Far from a logical contradiction, the exclusion of plants from the ethical base of Creation is tantamount to their exclusion from the realm of being. Assuming that "each being exists for its own sake," the plant, which exists only for the sake of animals and humans, does not exist for its own sake and, therefore, is not a being. As *arbor sacra*, it is suspended between being and nothingness, in yet another Agambenian "zone of indistinction." The ban on vegetable ontology and on plant ethics, legible between these lines, is further reinforced by the negation of plant vitality. Whether Maimonides can, in practice, sustain the scandalous argument that plants are not exactly alive remains to be seen.

"A Plant or a Mineral" or God

The Guide for the Perplexed, Maimonides' major philosophical work, composed in Arabic as a three-volume letter to his student Rabbi Joseph ben Judah of Ceuta, is both clear and austere on the subject of plants. Rather than group them together with animals, the author of *The Guide* prefers to lump plants together with inorganic matter. Explaining the idea of "negative attributes" that characterize a thing as what it is *not*, he suggests those who see a living being from a distance first grasp "that the object is not a plant or a mineral."[16] Whence this categorical denial of plant vitality? What is the reason for the plant's closer proximity to minerals than to the animal kingdom?

In the first instance, departing from the Aristotelian tradition, Maimonides associates the Hebrew terms *nefesh* (soul) and *khai* (living) with sentience. He particularly emphasizes the homonymy of soul and blood, which is also denoted by the word *nefesh* in Deuteronomy.[17] Evidently, then, since plants are insentient and bloodless, they cannot be said to live. Second, locomotion is "one of the distinguishing characteristics of living beings, and is indispensable for them in their progress toward perfection."[18] In consequence of this assertion, the plants' immobility disqualifies them from participating in the realm of the living as well. The Maimonidean verdict sounds irreversible. But is it really so? To get a full picture, let us take a closer look at some of the wrinkles and ambivalences in this ostensibly smooth theoretical narrative.[19]

Maimonides is adamant about the absolute difference between the life of sentient creatures and that of God. Ordinary language fails us; we take it upon ourselves to describe the existence of God based on our own measure and, in so doing, commit a series of blunders when we attribute to Him an enormous body, all-detecting perception, and the aptitude for moving voluntarily from place to place. Counseling his readers on the sense of biblical anthropomorphisms, Maimonides warns them against the insidious prejudices that creep into a common conception of life. In contrast to the "ordinary man's"[20] idea of life, which would certainly be inapplicable to divine existence, he recommends resorting to the negative attributes of God's vitality, namely the insight that "God exists without possessing the attribute of existence." "Similarly," Maimonides continues, "He lives, without possessing the attribute of life; knows, without possessing the attribute of knowledge. . . . "[21] His life is not an accident superadded to His essence but *is* this very essence, and the same holds for His oneness, knowledge, and power. The issue is that humans are rarely, if ever, contented with empty and abstract negative descriptions alone, which is why they help themselves to an analogical understanding of God's movement, organs of perception, and bodily extension. But what if our epistemic relation to plants were comparable to that of God? What if, in other words, we made a basic error when we tried to comprehend their life through the lens of animal (and human) existence?

It is imperative today to decouple plant life from animal vitality and to reiterate the critique Maimonides launched against those who understood biblical anthropomorphisms literally, this time with regard to plant existence and intelligence. For plants, too, know otherwise, insofar as they "see," "smell," "feel" pressure, and perhaps "hear" in the absence of readily recognizable organs of perception. They also move differently: not by dislocating themselves in space but by reaching out with their roots to the mineral resources in the soil and with their branches and leaves turned to the light of the sun. Maimonides is correct in his assessment of locomotion, which, he observes, allows animals "to approach that which is good for them and in harmony with their nature, and to escape from what is injurious and contrary to their nature."[22] The claim that God moves in space is as absurd as the assertion that He requires food and drink for His sustenance, given that all three modes of behavior are the results of a certain need or lack. Animal perfection, transposed onto divinity, mutates into "the highest degree of imperfection."[23] And the same goes for plants: they approach what is good for them in a manner different from animal motion and, though they are unable to flee, react to dangerous stimuli by changing their physiological states. Maimonides did not pursue to the full extent the implications of his critique of this narrow-minded view of life. But he did supply us with a formidable rule of thumb, namely to keep in mind the relevance of each activity and mode of behavior to the being that acts.

Still, the Aristotelian heritage of medieval philosophy is too weighty for the notion of plant soul, *tō threptikon*, to fall by the wayside in the writings of Maimonides. In *Eight Chapters*, included in his *Commentary on the Mishnah*, the Jewish thinker objects to the ascription of the same nutritive soul to everything that lives. Consistent with his relativizing of "perfections," this faculty of the soul varies along with the kind of being it animates, such that "the man's nutritive part, for example, is not the same as the nutritive part belonging to a donkey or a horse."[24] Plants are absent from this discussion, albeit not for long. Already in the next sentence, a palm tree makes an appearance alongside animals and humans. And this time it is not entirely soulless: "For man is nourished by the nutritive part of the human soul, a donkey is nourished by a nutritive part of the donkey's soul, and a palm tree is nourished by the nutritive part of its soul."[25] The point is that the faculties of the soul do not find exact equivalents in other species and are not divisible as parts of the body are. What Aristotle treated as the most common, "shared" kind of psyche is, in Maimonides, a soul specific to each creature. The question is why Maimonides is so invested in proving that Aristotle went astray on this point. My hypothesis is that, lurking behind this laudable avowal of difference by the medieval thinker, is the general rule of noncontamination—avoiding mixes of the pure and the impure, as well as one class of beings and another—which is the ontological and ethical lynchpin for the entirety of Maimonidean philosophy and theology.

The indivisibility of the soul, unaffected by its specialization into individual faculties, is, for Maimonides, the ground for all phenomena of life. He grasps life as the property of the whole organism, buttressed by the fact that "when parts of a living being are cut off they cease to live."[26] Plants, on the other hand, disprove this proposition, in that their shoots continue to live when they are detached from a loose assemblage that constitutes the "whole" plant. It is, most likely, this transgression of the borders that separate part and whole (not to mention life and death) that prompted Maimonides to divorce the concept of the plant from that of life. But if plants do not properly live, then what is the alternative principle of their existence? What motivates their growth?

To grasp the logic guiding the exclusion of plants from the realm of the living in the Maimonidean system, it is necessary to touch upon his "theory of spheres." The unity of the universe is a simple fourfold of spheres that (1) effect "the mixture and the composition of the elements," (2) supply "every growing thing with its vegetative functions," (3) give "each living being its vitality," and (4) endow "rational beings with intellect."[27] The movements of the spheres trigger the motions of the souls that correspond to them. It is noteworthy, for our purposes, that the vegetative force is distinguished from the power that imparts vitality to the living. Plants are animated by the first two spheres, without attaining to the life of sentient beings, let alone to the intellect of the rational ones. Humans, conversely, combine all four spheres in their existence and thus microcosmically embody the entire universe, the unity of which reflects the Oneness of its Creator.[28] In this scheme of things, plant-thinking is an abomination, as it mixes the elements of the second and the fourth spheres.

Even so, Maimonides is not unaware of the biblical and Talmudic passages where the nutritive appears to be conflated with the rational. He does not condemn these texts but vindicates them as "figurative." (Let it be said, in passing, that, despite all appearances, the hermeneutical stance of Maimonides is quite different from that of Augustine, who did his best to spiritualize meaning as a part of a larger process of transitioning from the literalness of Jewish Law to the inwardness of Christian Love. Maimonides, in turn, is more pragmatic: he terms those meanings figurative that do not accord either with the insights of reason or with the articles of faith that prohibit the attribution of a physical, or human, body to God.) The *Guide*'s section devoted to a scrupulous analysis of homonyms in the Bible, for example, clarifies why the verb "to eat" may be linked to "acquisition of wisdom" and "learning." Intellectual perceptions, Maimonides states, "preserve the human form (intellect) constantly in the most perfect manner, in the same way as food preserves the body in its best condition."[29] Nutrition is the all-important vegetative function, reluctantly admitted as a template for the assimilation of knowledge.

The semantic contamination of thinking with the intake of food does not violate the principle of nutritive souls unique to each class of beings or species. If pressed for a further explanation, Maimonides would argue that the association of eating with the acquisition of wisdom is attributable to the peculiar makeup of the human nutritive soul, which is a biological capacity in a being gifted with intellect. This unstated premise works as the invisible prosthesis propping up the parallel between the preservation of intellectual and bodily forms through the incorporation of knowledge and food, respectively.

Now, the sphere regulating vegetative functions was, like all the others, set into motion by God. That, Maimonides corroborates, was the first cause of the growth of plants: "Our Sages have already explained that the herbs and trees, which God caused to spring forth from the ground, were caused by God to grow, after He had sent down rain upon them...."[30] Whenever seeds germinate and sprout, we are reminded about the act of Creation. The Maimonidean plant may not live as animals do, but each time it returns to the earth as a seed or reconnects with the soil through its roots, it renews and reaffirms the Creator's will. So much so that the plant's bond to the earth, while still unbroken, immunizes it against any sort of uncleanness or impurity. Replaying the exceptional time of Creation on the mundane timescale of the seasons, plants restore the judgment of God about the result of His work, "that it was good."

Rituals of Purification:
The Plant, the Ground, and a Perforated Pot

On several occasions, *The Book of Cleanness* (*Taharah*) praises the purifying properties of the ground, or, more precisely, of the plant's undisturbed attachment to the soil. Paragraph 19 in the chapter on "Uncleanness of Foodstuffs" reads, "If unclean seeds are sown, what sprouts from them is clean, even if it is something whose seed does not perish, provided that the seed has sent out roots; but if they have not yet sent out roots, they remain unclean, even if it is something whose seed perishes."[31] Along the same lines, "roots which are left in the ground ... and all roots usually chopped off whenever they are pulled up with the edible part" do not "contract uncleanness nor convey uncleanness."[32] And, finally, "foodstuffs which grow from the ground can contract uncleanness only after they are uprooted: so long as they are attached to the ground by but the smallest root from which they are able to live, they cannot contract uncleanness."[33] What is behind this quasi-miraculous, purifying influence of the soil? What does it dispense to the plant, in addition to the water, minerals, and physical support they draw from it?

Their reversion back to the earth retrieves not just the biological but also the theometaphysical origin of plants in the act of Creation. The genesis of creatures, of course, must be pure; to hold otherwise is to teeter dangerously on the precipice of blasphemy, blaming imperfection and impurity on God. So the defect does not lie in the plant itself, which is why even the weakest of the root's attachment to the soil exonerates the entire lettuce rooted in it. The flaws and blemishes are in how humans handle produce, rendering it impure by bringing it into proximity with a dead body, for instance. Regardless of seed contamination, their sprouts are purified, once they give off roots, reviving their primordial connection to the divine origin of existence. Humans who transgress the Law are impotent to undo the work of Creation, which is vigorously repeated in each germinating seed.

As always, Maimonides stays attentive to the nitty-gritty details of everyday life that complicate the unconditional purity of natural growth. What if a plant is grown in a pot? Although rooted in the soil, would it not be closer to a product of human industry than to a spontaneously sprouting thing of nature? This question reverberates across the entire Maimonidean legal corpus. In *The Book of Seasons*, where to "pick something growing is a species of reaping" and is thus prohibited on the Sabbath, an exemption from liability is granted to anyone who "picks a plant from a pot without a hole . . . because the plant is not in its natural place of growth." "On the other hand," Maimonides adds, "a pot with a hole large enough for a small root is subject to the same rule as the ground, and if one plucks a plant from it, he is liable."[34] *The Book of Acquisitions* relates that seeds planted in a perforated pot no longer fall under the category "movables"—these seeds are, rather, deemed to be "planted in the ground, and whatever is attached to the land is like the land."[35] *The Book of Cleanness* validates this idea: "If a plant pot has a hole big enough for a small root to come out through it, it counts as the ground, and what is planted is not susceptible to uncleanness."[36]

Anxiety about such seemingly meaningless details is symptomatic of a deeper source of worry for Maimonides. The plants' uncontrollable growth, above and below ground level, threatens to destabilize the rigid boundaries set by the Law. Rootlets growing through the perforation of a pot muddle the difference between natural and artificial environments. The roots of a tree in a field disrespect private property lines and extend to neighboring territory (in this case, if, while digging a well, one encounters the roots of a neighbor's tree, one is legally allowed to cut through them).[37] Giving rise to new plants, contaminated seeds cause an upheaval in the distinction between the pure and the impure. What plant growth thus compromises is the very integrity of the Law, which is built on the premise that the boundaries it has drawn would ensure, with the greatest precision possible, the conceptual, categorial, and practical segregation of various types of beings, spheres, and activities. In traversing distinct fields—both agricultural and ontological—plants thwart nothing less than the spirit or the *animus* of the Law. The philosopher's worry about them is, at bottom, a worry about the limits of the Law and its finite capacity to institute a perfectly immutable world-system (or, better yet, to reiterate and subscribe to the one already created by God).

The philosophical dimension of this anxiety is discernable in the Maimonidean ratiocination that the nutritive and imaginative faculties of the soul are completely unrelated to the Law. Besides their incapacity to follow the commandments, they are powerless even to transgress legal precepts because "there is no obedience or disobedience in the nutritive or imaginative parts."[38] While it is not a carbon copy of the vegetal soul in Aristotle, the nutritive part of our soul is equally heedless to the voice of reason crystallized in the Law. Along with imagination, it cannot act otherwise than it does, being totally oblivious to the distinctions spelled out in *Mishneh Torah* and elsewhere. As a result, the nutritive and the imaginative parts of the soul potentially imperil the entire systematic project of Maimonides.

Since legal frames cannot contain the activity of the nutritive soul within and outside of us, Maimonides resorts to the purity of the species in order to keep the vegetal excess in check. He prohibits grafting, which violates species boundaries and rouses idolatry and raw sexuality, the two crucial components of fertility rituals. Maimonides actually singles out grafting for its orgiastic and ritualistic connotations. Appalled by the rites of the Sabaeans, who in the beginning of the first millennium BC founded a kingdom in the area of contemporary Yemen and the southern tip of the Arabian Peninsula, he describes how "when one species is grafted [by the Sabaeans] upon another, the branch which is to be grafted must be in the hand of a beautiful damsel, whilst a male person has disgraceful and unnatural sexual intercourse with her; during that intercourse the woman grafts the branch into the tree."[39] To Maimonides, grafting is offensive both for its public display of raw vegetal and human sexuality and for the mixing of species. But, above all, it is a perversion of Creation, where the divine decree caused plants to spring forth from the ground, not from other plants. Whereas the return of the seed to the soil purifies the shoots that germinate from it, the technical operation of grafting, imbricated with the "unnatural" sexual intercourse prominently featured in the ritual, is a sign of heresy and contamination.

It bears repeating that the plants themselves are not blameworthy, as they are a priori freed from responsibility for their activity. Without further ado, Maimonides assumes that their growth is indifferent to the outcome, whether it reconnects the plant with the ground from which it is separated by a perforated pot or fastens it to another tree as a graft. It is up to humans to prevent vegetable miscegenation by taking precautions, for example, not to "sow any two kinds of seed together or near each other."[40] The Law is entrusted with the mission of policing the conceptual and physical borders between species, domains, and categories. The proscription of growing different crops together is but the tip of the iceberg in the *Book of Agriculture*, with its detailed prohibitions of seed (*zeraim*) mixtures. Here, the root ceases to play a purifying role; au contraire, "mixed" grains and fruit become hallowed when sowing is successful and when they take root.[41] For all intents and purposes, seed mixtures and grafts are indistinguishable in their negative effect on the legally instituted order.

So extreme is the demand for noncontamination—and, at times, so foreign to the modern sensibility—that it prescribes the purification of urban spaces of trees that do not properly belong in the city. "A tree," Maimonides writes, "may not be grown within a distance of twenty-five cubits [about eleven meters or thirty-eight feet] from the town, or fifty cubits if it is a carob or a sycamore tree, in order to preserve the beauty of a town."[42] After we get a chance to catch our collective breath upon reading this admittedly outlandish rule, its logic becomes relatively clear. The beauty of urban space lies in its purity—a formal purity, in Kantian vernacular—that does not tolerate any admixtures of elements drawn from the natural environment. The ban on planting trees within and immediately outside the city limits resurrects the figure of *arbor sacra* for aesthetic reasons, themselves deeply rooted in the concerns with what is sacred, that is, separated and set apart. From the perspective of a city dweller, the tree is relegated to a permanent state of exception, which is congruent with our alienation from nature.

Against a Talking Tree, or the Unfinished Work of Disenchantment

Vis-à-vis polytheism and idol worship, the nonmystical strands of Judaism present themselves as the champions of disenchantment. Despite operating within a religious context, "rational" Judaism ridicules those who see wondrous, if not miraculous, features in the creaturely existence of animals, plants, and certain aspects of inorganic nature. The ban on grafting needs to be set within this broader context, much like Maimonides' scathing critique of fertility cults that mention "a tree which in its root resembles a human being, utters a loud sound, and speaks a word or words."[43] The fables about the wonders of plants are just that—mere fables. But they carry a grain of truth, which we are only now beginning to discover in plant signaling and communication studies. Certainly, plants do not speak in a human voice, but they do send complex biochemical messages to other plants and insects. The roots of corn seedlings, for instance, produce acoustic emissions, for a yet unknown reason.[44] What Maimonides pejoratively dubs "those days of darkness" might well be more in tune with the future of botany than the reductionist view of plants to which the Jewish sage adhered.

With his unwavering commitment to science and to a reconciliation of faith and reason, Maimonides conducted his own botanical researches, assembled in his treatise *Medicinal Plants*, a book that falls within the tradition of Aristotle and Dioscorides.[45] In the context of this commitment, his denial of plant vitality is itself an effect of his earnest desire to "disenchant the world," as Max Weber once put it. To speculate a little, Maimonides must have thought that to grant plants the status of the living is to indulge in the excesses of animism, separated by a hair's breadth from the myths of talking trees and other fabular, fabulous, wondrous things. Determined to purge the Bible of anything reminiscent of the premonotheistic worldview, he advances a figurative reading of those sacred textual fragments that are ostensibly inconsistent with the precepts of reason. The rational form of religion demands this sacrifice of literalness; only on the condition that the text announce something other than what it actually says does the holy writ gain the right of admission into a "reconciled" conglomeration of faith and reason.

Along these lines, the Maimonidean hermeneutical machine processes two striking passages from Isaiah: "The mountains and the hills shall break forth in song before you, and all the trees of the wood clap their hands" and "The fir-trees rejoice at thee." Animated or emotive vegetation is, on this reading, "clearly and evidently" a rhetorical device.[46] With a great dose of sobriety, Maimonides insinuates that anthropomorphic descriptions of nonhuman beings and of God are symptomatic of the immaturity of mythic thinking. He holds that myths are much more than childish stories; they are also the narrative dressing of our hubris, which begins by placing the human at the center of the universe and culminates with anthropomorphizing the entire world— and, alongside the world, its Creator. Read without the patience they deserve, prophetic visions can pass for mythic fragments in an otherwise rationally defensible text. So what differentiates them from myth? Why are Isaiah's rejoicing fir trees admissible while the talking roots of the Sabaeans aren't?

Maimonides perceives the glaring difference between mythic thinking and prophetic allegory as dependent not on the usual contrast between dream and reality but on a distinction between a dream that does not know itself as such and a dream conscious of itself. Psychoanalytically speaking, prophesies are procured from unconscious material already elevated to the level of conscious analysis. As such, they are aware of their indirect meaning and dreamlike, associational structure.[47] Prophets yearn for the interpretation of the vision (khazon: also meaning "dream"), the deep meaning of which is often foreclosed to them at the beginning. Myths, conversely, are entirely submerged in unconscious life, where ideas are not represented but embodied in objects, both animate and inanimate. They do not move past the belief that a talking tree, qua tree, is the dwelling place of a spirit that communicates to us. Abstractly put, myths do not contend with the meaning of meaning, starting with a metarealization that, in addition to being itself, the tree is a cipher for something else.

There is much to be said in defense of literalness, which, to be sure, is not as entrenched in mythic thinking as Maimonides makes it out to be. A literal reading may, in effect, be more ethical than its allegorical counterpart. Prophetic visions see past the trees themselves but myopically miss the forest; myths give vegetal life its due, in that they do not ask (at least, not openly so) whatever else this life signifies. However contrived it may be, the literalness of myth resonates with the literal meaning spatially expressed by the plants themselves and contained in their every shoot, branch, and leaf.

For a proponent of allegorical sense, the plant itself, in the bareness of its existence, is meaningless. This axiom is the cornerstone of the paradoxical hermeneutic construction of *arbor sacra*. Nowhere is this meaninglessness as pronounced as in the processes of vegetal decay, because what does not truly live cannot really die. (A coming attraction: Heidegger's take on the exclusion of plants from the sphere of death in chapter 10.) Whereas germination is a symbol reaffirming the continuity of Creation, the death of plants and the loss of their parts are downright inconsequential. As mere chance occurrences in nature, they are too paltry to be subject to God's decision-making power ("For I do not believe that it is through the interference of Divine Providence that a certain leaf drops [from a tree]"),[48] which judges humans alone the epicenters of free will.[49] The nonmechanistic complexity of humans plays itself out at the expense of the machine-like simplicity of nature. It is this complexity that gives us depth and makes us interesting, perhaps even for God Himself. In the great *theatrum mundi*, God and, in a different sense, the humans are actors; the rest is a series of props and decorations. Worse still, the plants' exclusion from the category "living beings" in Maimonides relegates them to the background of the background, the mostly unobtrusive green milieu, a stage set for a stage set.

Forlorn by the ideally omnipotent God, the plant is entrusted to the blind routines of mechanical causality *and* chance. But in this state of abandon lies the promise of freedom. Plants are trivial and, therefore, unworthy of divine interest—that is how they manage to slip away from God's untiring vigilance and potency. They delineate the edges of direct divine engagement in the world and drop off the radar of God's (and "the great eagle's") totalizing, panoramic gaze. A chain reaction ensues: plants are neglected, left to their own devices, and subsequently grow all the more mysterious. Their freedom is still more radical than that inherent in human free will. Incidentally, this last notion is a metaphysical fiction that creeps into Maimonides' dream of a disenchanted, purely rational religion. The work of disenchantment is unfinished and will remain so until the last tree is uprooted and the final bit of unconscious material taken up in conscious analysis.

PART III

MODERN PLANT-IMAGES

7   LEIBNIZ'S BLADES OF GRASS

In the Bushes of a Royal Garden

The year: 1685. The place: the gardens of Herrenhausen, the Electoral Palace of Princess Sophie in Hanover. A frantic search is under way, led by the distinguished courtier Carl August von Alvensleben. No, the ladies and gentlemen of the Hanover court were not looking for a lost earring of Princess Sophie. The object of their quest was much more prosaic than that; they were trying to find two leaves that were exactly alike. Why this sudden obsession with the plants growing in an undeniably magnificent Baroque garden, the most emblematic of its kind in Europe? The answer thrusts us into the thickets of Gottfried Wilhelm Leibniz's philosophy and introduces one of its pivotal principles, which von Alvensleben sought to refute in the crudest empirical way imaginable.

A later date: June 2, 1716. In a letter addressed to the English philosopher Samuel Clarke, Leibniz recalls the garden episode in connection to his famous principle of the identity of indiscernibles, or, simply put, "Leibniz's Law":

> There is no such thing as two individuals indiscernible from each other. An ingenious gentleman of my acquaintance, discoursing with me in the presence of Her Electoral Highness, the Princess Sophia, in the garden of Herrenhausen, thought that he could find two leaves perfectly alike. The princess defied him to do it, and he ran all over the garden a long time to look for some; but it was to no purpose.[1]

The futile search casts in the limelight a metaphysical principle that extends to the least element of nature, such as green leaves or blades of grass. If no two entities are exactly the same in all respects, then they all bear a stamp of uniqueness and individuality, ultimately harkening back to the wisdom of the Creator. Since God does not do anything randomly but always for a sufficient reason and following the laws He instituted, there would be no point for Him to place two exactly identical beings in different places. Each being and every corner of the material world are matchless and irreplaceable. The ethical consequences of this ontological axiom are obvious: to destroy a leaf, let alone an entire plant, is to do away with something that will not regrow in exactly the same shape ever again. While Leibniz will stop short of drawing this implication of his basic principle, it is safe to say that never has a metaphysical intuition been as conducive to ethical reasoning and practice as that pertaining to the identity of indiscernibles.

The incident at the royal gardens is notorious in the history of Western philosophy. In his *Logic*, Hegel could not resist the temptation to make fun of the search for an empirical counterproof to a metaphysical law of difference: "As regards the principle of Leibniz, difference must be understood to mean not an external and indifferent diversity merely, but difference essential. Hence the very nature of things implies that they must be different."[2] For all the time one dedicates to the study of concrete leaves or blades of grass, with all their finite differences, one will never get to the bottom of the issue, namely to "difference essential," one that makes things what they are, bestowing identity upon them. (This, by the way, was a maxim Hegel adopted in his own dialectical thinking, where it functioned at one of the lowest levels of Spirit's phenomenology, that is, perception attuned to the world of things as the world of constitutive difference.)

A garden-variety metaphysics, which isolates the principles of difference and identity from the concrete examples we find in our life-world, comes to a head with and mocks the forgetting of metaphysics in the royal garden. The diversity of leaves and blades of grass is "external and indifferent," that is to say, trifling, when inspected from the heights of metaphysics. Actual differences are but effects of the intangible wellspring of things. But, if real distinctions and unique traits of plants do not matter, then the ethical implications of Leibniz's Law are also nullified, since the destruction of an empirically unique tree does not affect in the least that difference which Hegel calls "essential." The return of metaphysics clashes with the ethics oriented toward the finite in its finitude.

But what if neither von Alvensleben nor Hegel got Leibniz right? When, later on in the present chapter, we touch upon the Leibnizian doctrine of expression, we will realize that, for him, discernment and indiscernibility are neither purely empirical nor absolutely metaphysical categories. The differences among living beings (and even among parts of these beings) of the same kind are not the ontological be-all and end-all. Even less are they something entirely external to the essence of these beings. Rather, they stand for the differences *within* God, expressing an infinite number of His perspectives on the world. If there are many species of plants, and if each species includes an untold number of sub-species, it is because all these must exist so as to actualize the immense possibilities of God's self-expression. The brute fact of biodiversity and a mindboggling empirical variation within a given species are awash with theological and ethical underpinnings. The apparently neutral statement to the effect that any two leaves growing on the same bush are materially distinct suggests that their actual differences, far from being "external and indifferent," contribute to the fullest (and best) possible actualization of divine essence in existence. In turn, the loss of biodiversity detracts from nothing less than the wealth of expressions God finds in the world.

A year after the garden episode, Leibniz revisits the identity of indiscernibles in an essay on "Primary Truths." Divulging that the source of this principle is St. Thomas's "separated intelligences," "which, he [St. Thomas] said, never differ by number alone," Leibniz contends that the same is true for any and all material objects: "Never do we find two eggs or two leaves or two blades of grass in a garden that are perfectly similar. And thus, perfect similarity is found only in incomplete and abstract notions."[3] Only mathematical or geometrical notions differ in magnitude and in no other respect; matter, on the other hand, presupposes a predifferentiation and non-numeric determination well in advance of its concretization in things. At the threshold of the modern era, the garden is converted into the arena of valiant philosophical resistance to the mathematization of the world, where everything can be assigned its corresponding quantitative value on a uniform spatiotemporal grid of coordinates.[4] And plants, despite being historically understood as incomplete or deficient things, are at the forefront of this struggle against the incompleteness of philosophical and mathematical abstractions.

In a polemic against John Locke and the empiricists, Leibniz elaborates on the materialist corollaries to his influential law. Acceptance of the conclusion that "no two individual things could be perfectly alike," he argues, "puts an end to the blank tablets of the soul, a soul without thought, a substance without action, empty space, atoms, and even to portions of matter which are not actually divided," among other things.[5] The Leibnizian universe, much like his writing,[6] resembles a Baroque garden or a Baroque painting, wherein space is saturated to the maximum, in an intricate imitation of vegetal excess. Emptiness and nondifferentiation—the mind as a blank slate—have no place there; their true home is the sterile sphere of mathematics and of modernity's desire to force reality into quantitative molds.

In protest against the pretentious universal perspective without perspective that goes under the name of objectivity, Leibniz celebrates the inimitable point of view of each living creature: "Two souls of the same species, human or otherwise, never leave the hands of the Creator perfectly alike, each of them having its own inherent relationship to the point of view which it will have in the universe."[7] Each blade of grass has its point of view on the world relative to the distinct place it occupies, its particular exposure to sunlight, its proximity to other types of vegetation, and so forth. Forget for a moment the next step of the argument that will reconcile all these perspectives under the umbrella of God's self-expression. Absent such reconciliation, what remains is a phenomenology of various life forms, not the least of which is the phenomenology of vegetal life, or, in my terms, *phytophenomenology*.[8]

In brief, phytophenomenology may be encapsulated in the thesis that plants have their own take on life and on the world, their growth and reproduction being the lived and enacted processes of interpretation. The multilevel approach of this theory takes into account the fact that each species has its unique perspective, as does each individual specimen comprising the species and each part of any given plant. The difference between two blades of grass boils down to a divergence, however negligible, between embodied orientations to and lived interpretations of the environment. The world, moreover, is nothing outside of a nonmathematical sum, or a confluence of these differences. Assuming that two blades of grass were completely identical, they would have represented one perspective, one life, one piece of being, one blade of grass ... In that case, the world would be poorer—or, better yet, it would *not be*— since it flourishes only in and as the variance among the beings that comprise it. Difference is at the origin of the world: it "worlds."

This is what the Leibnizian universe looks like when God is out of the picture. And, dare we say, it is doubtful that the universe would look any different were He to make a miraculous comeback. The God of Leibniz embraces all the perspectives on the world, irreducible to one totalizing outlook that would be somehow separate from those of His creatures. He is, to borrow an expression of the Portuguese writer José Saramago, "all the names" that cannot be distilled in one Name. In contrast to the impersonality and facelessness of modern reality, He "views all the faces of the world in all ways possible."[9] Even two nearly identical (though not quite!) blades of grass present two faces of the world; they are the actual variations on the theme of a possible blade of grass, which, in and of itself, is abstract and incomplete, lacking in realization. The backbone of Leibniz's monadology is this wedge of difference, responsible for the separation among perspectives on the world. Hence the erroneousness of the ancient idea of the "world soul, diffused through the world, which, like the air in pneumatic pipe organs, produces different sounds in different pipes."[10] The dignity of the living (plants included) hinges on their relative independence from the all-devouring Spirit or the one substance into which they can be dissolved as so many superfluous "accidents." Each blade of grass has its sufficient reason, elucidating the necessity of its existence just the way it is, despite the inexhaustible array of possibilities for it being otherwise.

The origin of Leibniz's family name suggests an apt postscript to the garden episode and the subsequent inclusion of blades of grass as examples of "the identity of indiscernibles." A derivative of the Slavic *lipnice*, "Leibniz" is evocative of "a certain kind of grass that grows in river bottoms."[11] We have seen how Plato inscribed his proper name in the plane tree that overshadows *Phaedrus*. It was also not uncommon for thinkers of the early modern period to encrypt their proper names in their philosophical writings. Spinoza finishes his *Ethics* with the praise of blessedness, *beatitudo*—Proposition 42: "*Blessedness is not the reward of virtue, but virtue itself . . .* "[12]—which is pertinent to the translation both of his Hebrew (Baruch) and his Latin (Benedictus) names, meaning "blessed." For Spinoza to say that blessedness is virtue itself is an act of self-affirmation consistent with his thinking. But why does Leibniz add blades of grass to the examples of a law that has become associated with his name? Doesn't he thereby assert, whether consciously or not, his own individuality and uniqueness, arguing, to a large extent contra Spinoza, that we are not a series of interchangeable avatars of the one substance?

A Garden Within a Garden: The Labyrinths of Vegetal Infinity

Once we enter the Leibnizian garden, we find ourselves trapped in its labyrinths. From the actual gardens of Herrenhausen, the philosopher guides us to the allegorical garden depicting his understanding of matter. In *Monadology*'s Proposition 67, he urges us to conceive of "every bit of matter" as "a garden full of plants or a pond full of fish. But each branch of the plant, each member of the animal, each drop of its bodily fluids, is also such a garden or such a pond."[13] Every portion of matter is, in accordance with this image, a garden within a garden within a garden—and so on to infinity. Much in the same vein, Baroque theater frequently employed the device of "a play within a play," the most prominent instance of which was Shakespeare's *Hamlet* with its staging of *The Mousetrap* in scene 2 of act III. In theater, this technique often opened the space for self-reflection right within the texture of the original play. But what is the philosophical import of a device that, roughly, implies an intricate folding of a concept unto itself?

To appreciate Leibniz's ingenious definition of matter, we ought to examine the propositions immediately preceding and following the figure of a garden within a garden. Propositions 65 and 66 advance the theory of the infinite divisibility of matter, which is "actually endlessly subdivided, every piece into further pieces, each of which has some motion of its own" and contains "a whole world of creatures."[14] Against the atomists, Leibniz puts forth the thesis of interminable differentiation—not into the smallest possible and ultimately homogeneous components of reality but into entire worlds that fit within the barely perceptible portions of the universe. Or, as Jonathan Swift put it a little more humorously with reference to animals instead of plants: "So naturalists observe, a flea / Has smaller fleas that on him prey; / And these have smaller still to bite 'em; / And so proceed *ad infinitum*."[15]

For Leibniz, the bodies of the living are "divine machines"[16] within which other machines are nestled like a series of Russian dolls or Chinese boxes. It follows that the distinction between the whole and a part, as well as between the one and the many, becomes meaningless, and it does so precisely with reference to vegetation. If each branch of a plant is a new garden, it is because each plant is inherently many: "each branch of a tree is a plant which is separately capable of bearing fruit."[17] Plants are indeed the archetypes of matter even though, unlike in Aristotle, their exemplary status is explained not with reference to the passivity of *hylē* but to the ease with which plants house difference, divisibility, and new wholes within their parts.

Anyone who has ever cultivated strawberries will quickly understand how a plant within a plant works. As they grow, strawberries send runners sideways, which then develop roots and leaves, finally producing a new plant. Thereupon, runners can be removed and replanted, a part producing a new whole and, potentially, an entire strawberry garden. Of course, Leibniz's Law still holds: divinely created body-machines do not produce facsimile copies of themselves but reproduce with the difference engrained in each of the corporeal subdivisions. It is this tireless exercise of their generative capacities that fashions plants and gardens into the vanguard of matter as a *plenum*—the bastion of abundance.

Leibniz's theory of materiality stands at the watershed between the premodern and the modern outlooks. At the same time that he opts for a modern machine metaphor, the philosopher reacts against the ancient *horror vacui*, which we have already diagnosed in Plotinus. This terror before the void prompted Baroque painters to fill every square inch of their works with elaborate details. In Leibniz's thought, matter is likewise bursting with gardens within gardens and machines within machines. What better image than a plant to encapsulate this excess? *Monadology*'s Proposition 68 continues the work of destroying the identity of matter, which began in the preceding paragraphs that made a rigorous opposition of parts to the whole and of the one to the many nonviable: "And though the earth and the air emplaced between plants of the garden or the water emplaced between the fish of the pond are certainly neither plant nor fish, they contain yet more of them, though mostly of a minuteness imperceptible to us."[18] Exteriority is folded into interiority; the space between plants is composed of innumerable miniature plants; the zones outside the garden pertain to a multiplicity of gardens. Translated into formal philosophical terms, if a garden is X, then not-X is still X; in fact, it is X to the *nth* degree.

According to Leibniz's own criteria, the vegetal configuration of matter as—let us say succinctly—the plant *within* and *in between*, clashes with his definition of a "clear idea" that "enables one to recognize the thing and distinguish it from other things."[19] What exactly do we recognize on the road to such clarity? Nothing other than identity! Curiously, Leibniz will give the example of a plant to substantiate the practical outcomes of recognition: "If I have a clear idea of a plant, I shall pick it out from others which are close to it—if I cannot, the idea is obscure."[20] A clear idea depends on a distinct memory of differences embedded in the system of classification and aided by extreme attention to detail. The best test for it is pragmatic: having picked out the right plant, distinguished from all those that are similar to it, serves as a practical piece of evidence for the clarity of cogitation.

On closer examination, however, Leibniz's example thwarts what it was supposed to exemplify. First, the identity of a plant and its status as a monad are far from certain—more on this later. Second, the labyrinths of vegetal infinity throw into disarray all those taxonomic systems and classifications that are tasked with pinning down the genera and species of living beings. And, often, they do so for contingent, historical reasons. Just "when we think we have thoroughly described a plant, someone may bring from the Indies a plant which exactly fits everything we put in our description and which nevertheless can be seen to belong to a different species. So we can never perfectly determine *species infimae*—lowest species."[21] The exteriority of the colonies (the Indies) bursts forth in the shape of a plant grown there and explodes the molds of identities constructed in Europe. Instead of being folded into the immanence of vegetal matter, the colonial plant disrupts old ontological and epistemological constructions. The infinity heralded by vegetation is now transposed onto infinite variation at the level of the lowest species, where it is unclear whether minute distinctions are meaningful enough to define a new species or whether they may be accommodated on the terms of a more general category. Around the edges of "clear ideas" things get somewhat blurry: plants break through the straightjacket of imposed identity, while matter, conceptually sculpted in their image, overflows all conceivable limits.

The lack of fixity in the lowest species is a variation on the theme of infinity, which is more open-ended than the Russian-doll-like self-reflection of matter. Leibniz concurs that "we can indeed go on *endlessly* varying them [lowest species], as is illustrated by the many varieties of oranges, limes and lemons which expert people can name and tell apart. The same thing happened with tulips and carnations when these flowers were in fashion."[22] Notice that the philosopher's choice of flowers is far from arbitrary: citing the varieties of tulips that used to be "in fashion," he is referring to the infamous "tulip mania," the first instance of a speculative economic bubble that peaked in Holland around 1637. Here we have another historical contingency, changing the field of botanical knowledge. When, in the 1630s, a tulip bulb cost more than ten times a skilled laborer's annual wage, specialists registered previously disregarded differences among its lowest species. The emergence of new varieties is a matter of attention, a scrutiny that can always, for whatever reason, intensify without reaching an inherent closure. The take-home lesson, then, is that there are no discrete identities, whether of plants or other creatures, sharply differentiated from the neighboring categories.

Leibniz christens this principle of infinite subdivision the Law of Continuity: "The *Law of Continuity* states that nature leaves no gaps in the orderings which she follows."[23] Potential breaches in the order of nature are filled with intermediate categories, and these are interspersed with other intermediate terms, ad infinitum. Whereas the principle of the identity of indiscernibles churned up the example of leaves and blades of grass, the Law of Continuity extracts another pattern from the world of vegetation—that of flower varieties. It is this law that explains why "modern botanists believe that distinctions drawn from the forms of flowers come closest to the natural order," even though it "would be wise not to rest one's comparisons and rankings entirely on a single foundation, such as the one drawn from flowers."[24]

The natural order, which knows no gaps, breaks, or leaps, is most faithfully portrayed in a perpetual parade of living forms, such as those of flowers. Yet it would have been imprudent to base our delineation of the entire system of nature on one criterion alone: were we to do so, in keeping with the law of continuity, we would have had to rely on imperceptible differences in form that would make further biological comparisons impossible. To avoid falling into self-contradiction, other markers of difference would have to be stressed as supplements to the preferred foundation for botanical taxonomies. As soon as plants replace the principle of sameness with that of difference, we quickly come to realize that there is no master difference wielding the same explanatory force as identity. A "single foundation" is not so much shattered as forced to branch out into a mesh of differences.

It goes without saying that the image of a garden within a garden insinuates itself into the dynamics of the lowest species and their endless subdivision, permitting no gaps and knowing no original foundation. Admittedly, a garden does not thrust us into the untamed nature of a forest, let alone a jungle; to the contrary, it is the quintessence of verdant nature fit for human (aesthetic) consumption, carefully landscaped and cultivated. Does the domesticated vegetation of a garden therefore contradict both the thrust of Leibniz's plenism and my analysis of it? A reference to the Baroque "play within a play" may, once again, prove helpful. The redoubling of play, its folding unto itself, provokes an intense self-reflection by giving the viewers a chance to experience an overdose of artificiality. Leibniz, for his part, is wary of a commonplace dichotomy of the natural and the artificial. For him, the things of nature are more machine-like than human-made machines are. Disassemble a product of human artifice, he suggests, and at the most basic level you will no longer recognize it as a machine—only as pieces of brass. Not so when it comes to the "natural automaton," which is a machine all the way down, in line with the concept of matter. "It is this that constitutes the difference between nature and artifice, that is, between divine artifice and ours."[25] Technicity, as the contemporary philosopher Bernard Stiegler argues, is originary: it stands at the origin of life.

All this is not to deny that Leibniz was extremely partial to cultivation. Tying this activity to progress, he believed that the universe "always proceeds to a greater development [*cultus*], just as a large portion of our world is now cultivated [*cultura*] and will be more and more so."[26] Cultivation, awakening, and enlightenment are terms that are synonymous, if not interchangeable: "There are always parts asleep in the abyss of things, yet to be roused and yet to be advanced to greater and better things, advanced, in a word, to greater cultivation."[27] In other words, matter is not the force of dumb and passive resistance to the noble endeavors of form-giving spirit, and neither is the plant within a plant that epitomizes matter. With proper cultivation—first and foremost of our attitude toward it—the Leibnizian plant too can awaken, giving free reign to its vegetal mind. Such awakening of what lies asleep "in the abyss of things" will activate new modes of expression, where God, human and nonhuman minds, and the world commune.

What Does a Plant Express?

"Expression" is the glue that holds the disparate constituents of Leibniz's philosophy together. Formally, it inaugurates the division of labor between minds, on the one hand, and substances, on the other: whereas the former express God, the latter express the world.[28] Leibniz proceeds to build a value hierarchy on the bedrock of this division that positions minds, made in the image of God, above the world. As he blatantly states: "A single mind is worth a whole world, since it does not merely express the world but also knows it and governs it after the fashion of God."[29] But what, in the first place, is the sense of expression in general, prior to its partitioning between minds and other substances?

Be it a mind or another substance, the entity that expresses something does so without exerting any special effort. It signifies, pointing beyond itself, simply in virtue of being itself. A mind need not hunger for theological knowledge to express God; in acting as minds do—that is, knowingly and self-knowingly, in a manner foreclosed, in Leibniz's opinion, to animals[30]—it repeats on a smaller scale the perfectly rational activity of the Creator. The same goes for other substances. In being what they are, they express the entire world from the ontological perspectives appropriate to them. Crucially, minds and substances alike give a voice to realities incomparably greater than they themselves are, so much so that the entire universe "is epitomized, though always from a different point of view, in each of its parts and even in each of its substantial entities."[31] The universe is essentially made of a plurality of expressions, with each part embodying the whole, from a unique and equally indispensable perspective. This is what, in his book on Leibniz, Gilles Deleuze calls "a fold," *le pli*, or, more precisely, a Baroque fold within a fold of parts at once included in the whole and including this whole.[32] The vegetal shape of the Leibnizian fold is already quite familiar to us as the garden within a garden.

The plant is not only a sessile living being but also, at the same time, a mode of expressing the world from the vegetal point of view. It is a non-verbal sign for an incomparably greater reality. The tiniest blade of grass epitomizes the universe as a growing whole, though it is not an exhaustive epitome, just one of a myriad views God has of the world.[33] And, like any other creature, it is a dynamic point at which possibility passes into actuality without a trace of randomness. For Leibniz, each blade of grass must be exactly the way it is, because its actualization (its "straining toward existence") is the necessary expression of its essence. "The one that exists," he contends, "is the one through which the most essence or possibility is brought into existence."[34] Besides channeling moisture and nutrients from its roots to the tip, a blade of grass translates bits of essence into existence, such that "the most essence" is concentrated in its actual being. In the Leibnizian vernacular, it thus obeys the principle of sufficient reason. (The inexorable striving of essence to existence was, by the way, Leibniz's response to the vexed questions, "Why is there something rather than nothing?" or "Why does the world exist?" recently revisited by Jim Holt.)[35]

To sum up, the plant expresses (a) the world, (b) God's vegetal perspective on (a), and (c) essence as it actualizes its possibilities. In the capacity of a nonverbal sign, it is oversignified, too charged with meaning, entrusted with carrying the weight of the theological and metaphysical entities revealed, in part, through it. How to respond to this barrage of significations?

To avoid lapsing into the other extreme, with its insistence on the meaninglessness of plants, it behooves us to survey their meaning in the absence of theologico-metaphysical superimpositions. In phenomenology, the existing phenomena by no means express the inaccessible essence of things, a Platonic world behind or above the world here below. When phenomena do point beyond themselves, they refer to other phenomena, creating chains of material, spatial, "thingly" signification. Plants, too, are living signs that articulate the sense of place free of displacement, gathering together the mineral and the organic, not to mention the animals (and the humans) they attract. Their meaning lies in the finitude of existence that expresses itself, not in an invisible essence. The mere being of plants is reason enough: their *raison d'être* is the vegetal *être* (being) itself. Existence is self-grounded, that is to say, based on itself alone and, hence, metaphysically speaking, on *nothing*. Existential self-grounding and self-expression are the manifestations of what metaphysics rejects as nihilistic groundlessness, which is, at bottom, a singularity more singular still than the one Leibniz defends. A blade of grass is a singular sign of itself and a unique point of intersection for the organic and the inorganic worlds.

Judged against the background of Leibniz's philosophy, the formal division of labor between the expression of minds and that of substances is highly suspect. For one, it contradicts the law of continuity in nature, which "never makes leaps,"[36] including those that skip from a nonrational substance to a mind. If the law is theoretically upheld, then it will require a continuity of expression, as well. The difference between minds expressing God and the other substances expressing the world will be one of degree, not of kind, with a vast continuum of intermediate forms stretching between them. As a result, the sacrifice of the whole world for a single mind will become ethically unjustifiable.

Between the lines of *New Essays on Human Understanding*, Leibniz accepts the theory of intermediate forms. In a tongue-in-cheek attack on empiricism, he admits to treating animals as "sheer empirics," whose thought sequences jump from image to image, adding up to little more than "a shadow of reasoning."[37] An insult to the empiricists, this statement is nonetheless a compliment to animals, who in this light are said to possess the powers of reasoning (albeit weak) and immortal souls.[38] Nonhuman forms of life are not the playthings of reason they are made out to be in *Theodicy*[39] but are the centers of meaning that irradiates from them, or from the divine perspective they express. In addition to being made sense of by us, they make sense of the world they inhabit.

Now, if animals exhibit "a shadow of reasoning," then plants display a shadow of this shadow. In his *Essays on Human Understanding*, Locke confirms that "there is some small dull perception" even in oysters and cockles. Responding to the British empiricist in his *New Essays*, Leibniz quips: "Very good, and I believe that almost the same could be said about plants."[40] The law of continuity thus covers the differences among biological kingdoms. Sessile organisms, be they animals or plants, share a basic orientation to the world that moves *around* them. Neither oysters nor plants need "the quickness of sensation"[41] advantageous to fast-moving animals. It is this peculiarity of their lifestyle that invalidates the hierarchical arrangement of perceptions from the sharpest to the smallest and dullest. The opening of a sessile organism to the environment is adapted to its world, with which it coevolves, or which, following Leibniz, it expresses from an inimitable divine perspective. To posit the standard of clear reasoning and sharp perception, in relation to which the rest would be but a shadow and a shadow of a shadow, is to pour scorn on the God-sanctioned pluralism of existences and their expressions.

The Plant as Monad: A Theoretical Conundrum

The powers of perception at the disposal of plants testify to the fact that they are ensouled entities and, therefore, monads. "The great analogy," Leibniz writes, "which exists between plants and animals makes me believe that there is some perception and appetite even in plants; and if there is a vegetal soul, as is generally thought, then it must have perception."[42] But the treatment of vegetal soul in a "great analogy" to that of animals raises fresh problems, which the philosopher leaves largely unacknowledged. The soul, for Leibniz, is the place—a withdrawn place that occupies as little volume as possible—where the infinite series of divisions into body-machines comes to an end. Lacking extension, it is "a simple substance or 'monad,' "[43] which preserves the identity of the entity it animates[44] and ensures "the real unity"[45] of the organism. Is this monadological description adequate to plants?

The answer is a resounding *No*. Plant monads are a contradiction in terms, because each "individual" plant is a loose assemblage of other, semiautonomous plants that do not persist in the state of real unity. Consequently, we may conjecture *either* that plants are, despite Leibniz's vigorous objections, to be banned from the domain of psychic life *or* that they have a material, extended, divisible soul figured in nonmonadological terms. If the second, more provocative, conclusion holds, then vegetal souls will be freed from the yoke of metaphysical identity, self-enclosure, individuality, and originality. No longer will it be the case that "if plants and brutes have no souls, then their identity is only apparent, but if they do have souls their identity is strictly genuine."[46] Rather, in plants we will discover souls shorn of identity, the souls whose restlessness and disquietude express the vivaciousness of life itself (in the guises of growth, spatial movement, thought . . .). Living is incongruent with the monadic self-enclosure of organisms, with the *stasis* of identity, and with the "real unity" of a "simple substance." We would be more faithful to the spirit of Leibniz's thought than Leibniz himself were we to locate essential difference not only in the body-machines of all forms of life—vegetal, animal, and human—but also within their respective souls or modes of subjectivity.

Leibniz is not entirely oblivious to psychic differentiation, which he grants in Proposition 70 of his *Monadology*: "Every living body has a dominant entelechy, which in an animal is the soul. But the members of this living body are themselves full of other organisms—plants or animals—each of which also has its own entelechy or dominant soul."[47] Let us go over this difficult passage slowly and methodically. Entelechy is, certainly, an Aristotelian word meaning "the actualization of the merely potential," and it accounts for the process whereby the soul enlivens the body. Leibniz complicates this one-to-one relation between the body and the soul with reference to the multiplicity of organisms comprising each living being, organisms with the bodies and souls of their own. Extending to the lowest microscopic levels of being, the chain of entelechies infinitely defers the moment when a monad, as a simple and indivisible substance, would make its entrance on the philosophical scene. At any rate, the souls already articulated with bodies do not correspond to the ideal of a monad, as they are inhabited by other, more basic vegetal and animal souls that consistently defer their monadological closure.

The levels of entelechy emulate the infinity of matter, conceived as a garden within a garden. Nonetheless, as a payoff for this materialist conception of the embodied soul, we are required to give up the radical immanence of the fold. The souls that animate body-machines are lined up in structures of dominance and subordination, that is to say, in hierarchies. At the top of the hierarchy is an easily recognizable individual identity, the dominant entelechy of the animal. Less individualized are the smaller plant and animal organisms comprising its living body. Although these also have their "dominant souls," they are neither readily identifiable nor do they feature distinct identities. Shrinking back from the anarchy of proliferating differences befitting a plant, Leibniz leans toward a rigidly hierarchical order of entelechies.

By privileging the unity of dominant wholes over the aggregate of multiplicities devoid of real identity, Leibniz implicitly chooses the animal model of the soul over its plant counterpart. And, in responding to the Italian philosopher Michel Angelo Fardella in 1690, he reveals just how zoocentric and ultimately metaphysical this prejudice is: "Hence, it seems probably that animals, which are indeed analogous to us, and similarly plants, which correspond to animals in many ways, are not composed of body alone, but also of soul, by which the animal or plant, the single indivisible substance, the permanent subject of its actions, is controlled."[48] We can only applaud the daring proposition that the plant is not a passive object available for human and animal manipulation but a subject capable of acting. The flaw, however, lies in the double comparison of animals to humans and of plants to animals. The standard, to which all other living beings are supposed to measure up, is incorrigibly anthropocentric, as it implies that animals are the less perfect humans and plants the less perfect animals. Supporting this problematic conclusion is the indexing of perfection to sensibility in Leibniz's thought; the souls of living beings range "from more to less sensible, from more perfect to less perfect, or the reverse."[49] The more individualized a creature, the more sensible it is, the more it embodies the real unity of the soul, the principle of identity, and, indeed, self-identity. And thus an ancient metaphysical bias creeps into a philosophical system that has boldly put forth the plant-based idea of infinite matter and the expressive singularity of every leaf and each blade of grass.

8 KANT'S TULIP

A Flower Against the System

Just two marginal references, en passant and without any apparent significance. That is what Kant's tulip boils down to in his *Critique of Judgment*. The first mention is nothing more than a footnote, where the tulip is cited as an example of a beautiful flower, "beautiful, because we meet with a certain finality in its perception, which, in our estimate of it, is not referred to any end whatever."[1] The second time a tulip germinates on the pages of the same book, it is charged with the task of substantiating the difference between the logical judgment "All tulips are beautiful," on the one hand, and the judgment of taste that delights in "an individual given tulip," on the other.[2]

The tulip is useless and singular, much like Kant's references to it. But it is not altogether innocent: planted on the text's margins, in its exemplary capacity, it both illuminates and threatens to dislocate the philosophical system, which is barely able to accommodate it. The tulip's "flower power," not unrelated to the slogan of the American counterculture movement of the late 1960s and early 1970s, will be the centerpiece of the present chapter. But let us not run ahead of ourselves. It still remains to be seen why Kant was so fixated on flowers. And what attracted him to tulips, of all things?

The tulip that blossoms on the margins of the *Critique of Judgment* is actually not native to this text. It has been transplanted there from a book by the founder of alpinism, Horace-Bénédict de Saussure, whom the German thinker admired. Without exaggeration, we might say that the Kantian tulip germinates already as a dry specimen in an intellectual herbarium, not as a flower Kant himself would have experienced "in the wild." In his *Journey in the Alps*, de Saussure reports having sighted a "wild tulip"—"I found, in the woods above the hermitage, the wild tulip I had never seen before"[3]—which is the referent of Kant's famous example. Most likely, the voyager made a taxonomic error, as tulips are not wildflowers and, moreover, are not indigenous to Europe, even if they had been crossbred, cultivated, and traded on the continent for centuries before de Saussure's journey.[4] The specimen deposited in the intellectual herbarium appears to be mislabeled, though that inaccuracy did not prevent the flower from striking Kant as an exotic instance of singular beauty, a rare variety thriving in the Alps, far away from Königsberg, the hometown he never left.

More generally speaking, devotion to matters aesthetic must have been an upshot, in part, of Kant's marked *Galanterie*. His biographer Manfred Kuehn tells us that, in his dressing style, Kant "always followed the ... 'maxim' that the color of one's dress should follow the flowers." "Accordingly," Kuehn continues, "a brown coat required a yellow vest."[5] The maxim *Follow the flowers!* is not a bad place to start learning not only about the details of Kant's wardrobe but also about the finer points of his aesthetic philosophy. Besides using them as standards for matching the colors of his coat and vest, how does the German thinker follow the flowers—and tulips, above all? Here are three possible leads:

A In his penchant for abstraction, Kant reduces flowers to instances of pure color, and that of tulips seems to be the purest of them all. In the notes on aesthetics, we read in the author's shorthand: "A pure color; the distribution of colors for charm (tulips, pheasants). . . . All pure colors are beautiful, because art is already indicated in their being unmixed."[6] Although the emphasis on the colors being "unmixed" presupposes their material purity (for instance, an intense red without a trace of any other tonalities), what Kant is really after is the purity of form, which resonates not in the object itself but in its subjective appreciation. While following the flowers with their beautiful pure colors, we ultimately return to ourselves and to the aesthetic enjoyment they provoke in us.

B The tulip is a no-frills flower, if there ever was one. Its simple shape does not distract us from the beauty of its pure color and, in this, it fits perfectly the austerity of Kant's philosophy and the strict splendor of his aesthetic thought. Even if it is a mere adornment, the tulip itself is unadorned, its ascetic form opening directly onto the beautiful. A singular passage into the universality of beauty, it does not exactly bedazzle the spectator, does not strike the gaze with baroque petal arrangements or color contrasts. Its calm, almost self-effacing grace is what gives beauty a chance to shine forth.

C Unlike the nourishing fruit, flowers are completely useless and utterly super-fluous (at least for humans, albeit not so much for the bees). They do not sat-isfy an immediate physiological need but symbolize the luxury of excess, our desire for adornment when the cravings of hunger and thirst are pacified. That is why, the anthropologist Jack Goody notes, in African cultures flowers are virtually absent from religious and social rituals; they play a negligible part "in the domain of design or the creative arts," and, whenever they are mentioned, it is exclusively in anticipation of the fruit they will metamor-phose into.[7] And that is why, more pertinently, Kant treats tulips as examples of finality "not referred to any end," where by "end" he means those practical goals that are associated with economic activity broadly understood. They are the concrete images of freedom from necessity and of the desire for the superfluous—ingrained in aesthetic pleasure and withheld from those lan-guishing under the tyranny of need—that makes us human.

That tulips came to be the symbols of noneconomic superfluity at the time of Kant's Third Critique testifies to a short span of cultural memory. As the previous chapter has related, a mere century and a half prior to the publication of Kant's work, Europe (and especially Holland) was in the grip of a tulip mania, the first speculative economic bubble in world history. At the time, the assertion that tulips were the bench-marks of finality without any practical end would have been laughable, as a year's wage could be exchanged for a single bulb of the flower. It makes little difference whether the joke is on Kant and his inability to historicize his abstract transcendental arguments or whether the irony is carefully built into the text. The take-home message is that the role of a flower cannot be pinpointed outside its historical and cultural con-text, wherein it is economically prized, aesthetically enjoyed, or entirely unnoticed. Once this premise is admitted, we begin to hear the abstract system of thought, which has presumably freed itself from all contextual constraints, cracking at the seams. And, strangely enough, the culprit in the system's undoing is not a still more powerfully armed conceptual apparatus but a single flower.

To be fair to Kant, neither the flower nor anything else receives one immutable meaning in his philosophical universe. His *critical* project is one that delimits the domains of human knowledge, practice, and aesthetic contemplation, setting each of them within their proper bounds. Theoretical understanding, for one, cannot extend its reach indefinitely, as it is hemmed in on different sides by what our finite reason cannot grasp (e.g., the nature of God) and by the nontheoretical facets of our existence. Etymologically traceable to the Greek word *krinein*, which implies "separation" or "division," Kantian critique sets distinct domains of inquiry and practice apart both from one another and from what is absolutely inaccessible to humans. There are three such domains, corresponding to the three Critiques: that of pure reason or theoretical understanding, that of practical reason or ethics, and that of aesthetic judgment.

The meaning and, indeed, the being of a tulip varies depending on the domain, in which we encounter it as a natural object of study and scientific investigation, an object of utility piquing our practical interest, or an alluring incarnation of the beautiful. There is, however, no one approach that could assemble all three significations of the tulip into a coherent whole. The tulip of a scientist, of a commercial flower grower, and of a spectator at the annual Canadian Tulip Festival in Ottawa are not one and the same thing. For a scientist, this flower is a specimen, a sample derived from the species and the genus it belongs to. It is a network of vessels, plant tissues, and organs—quantifiable and objectively measurable. For a commercial flower grower, it is also convertible into a numeric value, however this time the number corresponds to the price per bulb that can be reasonably set on the market. For festival spectators, it is an opportunity to feast their eyes on the flashes of red or yellow or another color on the vast flower beds of the Ottawa-Gatineau region in May. ("Flower beds have a charm," Kant reminds us from his aesthetic perspective, "because they give us occasion to involve ourselves in fantastical representations of carefreeness and leisure.")[8] These general, if not generic, contexts are indispensible for making sense of Kantian philosophy.

Kant's "Copernican turn," referring to a shift of emphasis from the object of knowledge to its subject, is easy to grasp, provided that we keep in mind the virtually irreconcilable perspectives of the three Critiques. While a premodern ontological inquiry would be inclined to ask "What is a tulip?", Kant would concentrate on the diverse human dealings with the flower, outside which not the least bit of information about it would have been revealed. Within the conceptual architecture of the *Critique of Pure Reason*, the question would thus be, "How is it possible for me to know the tulip?" The *Critique of Practical Reason* would demand to know, "What can (or should) I do with the tulip?" And the *Critique of Judgment* would ask, "What can a tulip do to me, so that through the contemplation of its singularity I would get in touch with universal beauty?" We may, as well, forget about unearthing the flower *itself*, above and beyond a potentially measurable organism, a placeholder of economic value, or a narrow passage toward the beautiful. The tulip itself is a thing-in-itself, unknowable and thus disengaged from the critical apparatus of Kantianism.

But the story of the tulip does not end there, in the Third Critique's relatively marginal invocations of the flower. Kant's tulip has been leading a veritable posthumous existence in some of the most influential writings on aesthetics in the twentieth century. Exempted from the "natural order" of reproduction and from the considerations of utility alike, it has persistently reproduced itself on the pages of philosophical treatises. More than that, the tulip's posthumous life has been anything but peaceful. It incited a clash of interpretations as to whether the critical system can stomach the tulip's disruptive potential.

On the one hand, the refrain of Jacques Derrida's reading of the tulip episode in *The Truth in Painting* is that aestheticization is made possible by "the *sans* ["without": a French homonym of *sang*, "blood"] of a pure cut." The flower is cut off not only from the logic of means and ends and from its biological functions but also from all meaning- and sense-making activity.[9] It would be shortsighted to associate this "without" and this cut with lack and negativity, as they augur that freedom which remains inaccessible to the conceptual and practical transactions with the tulip. Still, Derrida contends, the aesthetic resistance of the flower to its being appropriated, understood, or utilized is in vain. Kant's system of thought has the last word, in that "the whole system which has its sights on that beauty supplies the course, determines the vagueness (as lack) and gives sense and direction back to errancy: its destiny and its destination."[10] Flower power is subservient to critical philosophy's conceptual police authorities; a beautiful revolt of the beautiful against the system ends in a disappointment, lending a hand to the very thing it had opposed.

On the other hand, Jay Bernstein in *The Fate of Art* bets on the radical singularity of the tulip, of aesthetic judgment, and of the claims of beauty, taking them to be "interruptions in what the critical system intends."[11] At issue are, precisely, the status of the singular and the limits of what the system can bear: whether aesthetic singularity is an undigestible remainder, if not an open wound, within the Kantian critical project or whether it is neutralized upon contact with the motivating drive of this very project. True: for someone like a scientist, who operates exclusively within the limits of understanding, an error in the classification of a flower (say, the tulip) makes a tremendous difference. Not so for an artist or a spectator making or enjoying a drawing of the same flower. (Clearly, Kant received de Saussure's book in the spirit of aesthetics, not that of science, which is why he did not question the discovery of a previously unseen wild tulip referenced there.) The singular experience of beauty makes the general idea of the flower irrelevant.

Indeed—as Bernstein himself admits—the truth or falsity of propositions still holds sway in the aesthetic sphere. How do we carry on the work of interpretation when meaning is lost (for, after all, interpretation, "which requires judgment, is a discourse of truth, of restitution")?[12] Is aesthetic autonomy an illusion, provided that the critique of judgment borrows so heavily from the critique of reason, with its discourse of truth? Is the extraconceptual singularity of the tulip wholly outside the concept, or does it, as Derrida and perhaps even Bernstein's intellectual hero, the critical theorist Theodor Adorno, would say, form an outside inside the conceptual totality?

It is not my ambition to resolve this conflict of interpretations. In many ways, the disagreement is reminiscent of the dilemmas faced by social- and political-protest movements in parliamentary democracies. An intended disruption of liberal capitalism can be easily made complicit with what it intends to disrupt, and, at the extreme, it can be cited as an example of the system's "openness" or "tolerance" of dissent. George Sorel's anarchosyndicalist argument that a general workers' strike poses the threat of a radical interruption is, on the contrary, equivalent to the claim that aesthetic singularity cannot be appropriated by the philosophical system it ruptures. The test for these competing claims might as well be pragmatic or outcome based: Does capitalism survive either its criticism or general strikes? Does the interpretation of the beautiful still make sense on the playing field delineated by the dominant discourses of meaning and truth?

In the grand scheme of things, Kant assigned to the faculty of judgment a middling place in his philosophical system and a function of mediating between theoretical understanding and practical reason.[13] The very singularity, which presumably breaks with the system, plays a lead role in integrating the realm of necessity and that of freedom, the theoretical philosophy of nature and the practical philosophy of morals.[14] A critical project worthy of the name tolerates no integration other than the one that is itself dis-integrated and that leaves intact the separations, fissures, and divisions constitutive of critique. Aesthetics is the groundless ground of Kant's philosophy; on this extraordinary soil, the tulip blossoms.

What Can We Know About Plants?

Skeptical readers will have their misgivings about philosophers being the right people to ask, "What can we know about plants?" Wouldn't specialists in botany, molecular biology, biochemistry, and the related sciences be more qualified to take up this query?

Before trivializing the philosophers' credentials, let's take a look at the precise form of the question—neither "What *do* we know about plants?" nor "What *might* we know about them in the future?" The modal auxiliary verb "can" is a codeword for what Kant terms the *conditions of possibility for knowing* that are distinct from the content of what is (was or will be ever) known, that is, from the empirical information about our subject matter. Such conditions of possibility map out the field of knowledge before populating it with facts and the research outcomes of scientific investigations. As they precede whatever is known about

X, these conditions are called "a priori," that is, prior to any information we might be able to procure, and "transcendental," that is, in excess of the experience they enable. Besides providing a general theoretical framework for scientific discoveries, philosophers therefore establish the parameters for knowing within the limits of the humanly possible.

Kant's theoretical generalization from what was empirically known about plants in his day and age shores up the idea that their biological organization resists the drive toward systematization. In his unfinished final work, *Opus Postumum*, he deduces that plants are "aggregates without a system" from the fact that they "permit grafts."[15] Since, as Kant notes in the same manuscript, transcendental philosophy is "the philosophical system of knowledge" or "the system of ideas in an absolute whole,"[16] the biological peculiarity of plants is that they do not follow the outlines of such a philosophy. Within the system of understanding, they signal a breach, a leeway that, if explored with all the care it deserves, enables us to escape from the suffocating limits of the system. To follow the plants in this respect is to envision, with valuable input from Kantian transcendental imagination, alternative modes of human social and political organization, which might prompt us to cohabit in anarchic "aggregates without a system," as well.

Defiance of systematization in plant and human collectivities does not mean that their participants (leaves or branches, human individuals or groups) are independent of one another. The exact opposite is the case: mutual interdependence is increased when the predominance of the "whole" over its constituents diminishes. As Kant puts it in the section of the *Critique of Judgment* dedicated to "teleological judgments,"

> a part of a tree also generates itself in such a way that the preservation of one part is reciprocally dependent on the preservation of the other parts. An eye taken from the sprig of one tree and set in the branch of another produces the alien stock of growth of its own species, and similarly a scion grafted on the body of a different tree. Hence even in the case of the same tree each branch or leaf may be regarded as engrafted or inoculated into it, and, consequently, as a tree with a separate existence of its own, and only attaching itself to another and living parasitically on it.[17]

In decentralized, nonsystemic plant and human communities, the model of coexistence does not posit the subservience of parts to the whole but the interdependence of relatively autonomous parts. This, for Kant, is a matter of life and death, survival, and self-preservation. Observing the plant, we can get a preview of anarchic togetherness in diversity, of an "alien" stock flourishing together with a dynamic aggregate of members, none of them more essential than the others. Kant is steadfast in his commitment to the nonsystemic view of the plant, where, rather than a unified whole, the same ("the same tree") is a conglomerate of differences, of parts grafted onto one another. Despite attaching the label "parasitism" to this kind of a community, the German philosopher cannot help but admire the plasticity of a living plant aggregate. Plants can cope with injuries much better than an animal organism, and that feature rightfully belongs "among the most wonderful properties of the forms of organic life."[18]

The production and reproduction of difference within the same plant for the purpose of its self-preservation is, according to Kant, the third and final variation on the idea of "physical ends" governing vegetal life. If we are to know anything whatsoever, we must rely on ideas that, at the theoretical level, are not tied to experience and that can serve to regulate "the orientation of the understanding with respect to the totality of knowledge."[19] To understand plants as objects of knowledge, we must search for the ends or purposes built into their existence. In addition to the end of preservation, with its principle of mutual interdependence, Kant lists two further goals of vegetal existence: the self-reproduction of the genus and the self-production of the individual plant or tree.

Highly indebted to the nutritive and reproductive faculties of the plant soul in Aristotle, Kant's formulations of "physical ends" aim to capture every activity observable in the world of plants. When a tree gives rise to another of the same species, it "preserves itself generically,"[20] lending itself as a vehicle for the continuation of the genus to which it belongs. But when a tree grows, it produces itself individually, as this particular specimen. Kant, in fact, forewarns his readers against conflating growth with an automatic "increase according to mechanical laws." Imbued with a fair share of freedom, growth is an outcome of the plant's own activity, roughly analogous to human labor, whereby the plant "first prepares the matter that it assimilates . . . and develops itself by means of a material, which, in its composite character, is its own product."[21] Like the legendary Baron Munchausen, plants pull themselves up by their own bootstraps. Consider, for instance, how they thrive on com-post, itself made up of other decomposing plants and parts of the same plant—say, the leaves and acorns that have, over the years, rotted around the roots of an oak. Just as humans live on the products of their own laboring activity as well as that of the past generations, so plants grow thanks to the nutritional assimilation of the products of their (and other plants') past growth.

The idea of the plants' physical ends is regulative, in the sense that it determines their actual life processes, as though it were their blueprint. Not only do ideas make human reasoning, with its search for "true cau-sality," possible, but they also "become efficient causes (of actions and their objects), namely in morality, but also in regard to nature itself."[22] In the continuation of this passage, Kant cites with approval Plato's the-ory of ideas, adding that a "plant, an animal, the regular arrangement of the world's structure . . . —these show clearly that they are possible only according to ideas; although no individual creature, under the individual conditions of its existence, is congruent with the idea."[23] The incongru-ence of the actual tulip with the idea of the tulip is the best proof that Kant does not confound ideas and ideals, where "ideal" means a "repre-sentation of an individual existence as adequate to an idea."[24] There are no perfect plants, animals, or humans because none of them coincides with their respective pregiven representations. In this sense, Kant's phi-losophy is not idealist, regardless of how it burdens ideas with formal and efficient, epistemological and ontological causality. In the absence of a prefabricated model or a perfect ideal, a beautiful flower is seen each time for the first time.

So is it really justifiable to retain plants in the list of beings possi-ble "according to ideas"? Is there anything generic in the arrangement of these aggregates without a system? A regular mold for irregularity? Don't the creativity and the plasticity of plant life hinge precisely on its propensity to experiment with its morphological and physiological givens?

A freestanding idea is too scarce a condition of possibility to know any-thing about the plant. Take an environmental stressor, such as drought. In response to such adversity, plants will virtually reconstitute them-selves, activating stress-inducible genes—*rd* (responsive to dehydration) or *erd* (early responsive to dehydration)—in what botanists call "transcriptional reprogramming," or adaptation based on targeted genetic al-terations.[25] Unless a tree is of a shade-loving variety, its crown will be more extensive on the sunnier side and, without exception, its roots will be denser around resource-rich soil patches and in close proximity to plants of other species. These external factors are neither transcendental nor a priori and they surpass the idea of the plant in determining its individual existence. The environmental niche (read: the repressed "con-text" of growth) molds the plant's physical look and is, itself, molded by the communities of plants that inhabit it.

In his personal notes from the 1760s, Kant stands by the thesis that a "plant is possible only in accordance with an idea," defining the latter in terms of "the a priori cognition of the understanding, through which the object becomes possible."[26] Cognitions a priori precede the data of expe-rience, seeing that the experience of an object is based on a preexistent idea of that object. In distinguishing ideas from ideals, Kant left enough conceptual space for the deviations of everything that exists from its corresponding idea. Plants, however, are still more resistant to idealiza-tion than animals and humans because they are less prone to obeying the authority of an idea. Their intimate connection to the physical context of their growth allows material "accidents" to shape them in a way that is qualitatively different from animal and human dependence on their environments. With this, Kant's decontextual philosophy arrives at the (uncritical) limit of its potential to engage with vegetation, for which the outside world is of the essence.

What Can We Do with Plants?

What, in Kant's view, can we do with plants—that is, how should we treat them? Where do plants fit in a moral philosophy obsessed with duties and founded on respect?

The Metaphysics of Morals draws a sharp contrast between love, inter-preted as the power of attraction, and respect, understood as the force of repulsion. "The principle of mutual love," Kant writes, "admonishes them [human beings] to *come closer* to one another; that of the respect they owe one another, to keep themselves *at a distance* from one an-other."[27] In the *Critique of Practical Reason*, too, respect is not an emotion similar to love but a feeling that arises immediately from practical reason itself and is spurred by the moral law that commands: "So act that the maxim of your will could always hold at the same time as a principle in a giving of universal law."[28] What is respectable, moreover, is not the fragile, embodied, finite condition of humans but their capacity to abide by this principle and to will, in their particular actions, the universal good. In respecting the other, I respect her as a subject of practical reason (the so-called transcendental subject) as opposed to a living being with physical needs and wants (the so-called empirical subject). The distance of respect depends on the incomplete overlap of these two subjectivities in the same human being.

While the material facets of human existence are not, in Kant's eyes, worthy of respect, even less so are nonhuman animals and plants that do not have a share in the rationality of transcendental subjects. "Respect for the environment" would have been an oxymoron, were we to continue playing by the rules of this practical philosophy. There is but one opportunity to include plants and animals under the umbrella of Kantian respect, and, in an exquisitely circuitous way, it has to do with human *self*-respect. To respect oneself is to pay heed to one's own transcendental subjectivity and the capacity freely to follow the moral law that resides in the self-respecting individual. This, for Kant, is the sine qua non of moral duty: a human "must have respect for the law within himself in order even to think of any duty whatsoever."[29] The question is: Would a self-respecting individual inflict irreversible damage on the environment? If the maxim underlying a harmful action were to turn into "a principle in giving a universal law," would this law be consistent with practical reason? Evidently, it would not! The hope is that respect would, so to speak, trickle down from the incontrovertibly respectable subjects to those that, though they are not in themselves deserving of respect, should be protected as a consequence of rationally based actions.

A more straightforward Kantian formula of respect is that it "is always directed only to persons, never to things."[30] In the list of examples that follow, Kant puts horses and dogs on the same footing as a sea or a volcano—the objects of our fear or love, as the case may be, albeit never of respect. Yet plants and animals are neither persons nor things; from this "excluded middle," they trouble the traditional distinction between the respectable and the merely utilizable. Sorely missing from Kant's moral philosophy is an intermediate category, which would be appropriate to nonhuman forms of life.

One somewhat unsatisfactory solution is to loosen the limits of personhood so as to incorporate animals and plants within the definition of "persons." Matthew Hall's recent *Plants as Persons* moves in this very direction without, at the same time, spelling out the legal and philosophical overtones of this loaded term. Legally, personhood entails the right to own property and, therefore, is firmly entrenched in the crude binary that sets this category over and against inanimate things. Plants are, arguably, the least proprietary living agents on the planet, insofar as they act as passages for the elements, which they welcome and transform.[31] Philosophically, too, personhood is a purely formal and abstract stratum of subjectivity, an empty shell that recalls the Latin word *persona*, or mask. This may certainly sound counterintuitive if you are used to the routine meaning of the term "personality," which admits everything that makes you unique and which is what you express in your clothing style and in other aspects of your external appearance and actions. The point is that plants are *not* persons *either* in the philosophical *or* the everyday sense of the word; to argue that they are is to impose an alien description onto them and to fail to do justice to their mode of life.

I do not think that we are doomed to a black-and-white choice between persons and things, especially because finite life overflows these seemingly contrasting but, in fact, equally inert death masks of identity. In a philosophy disconcerted by the elusiveness of life uncontainable by conceptual forms, the object of ethical concern is the fragility of the living and of the ecosystems they participate in, their finitude and exposure to violence. Although fragility is not within the purview of Kantian respect, the fundamentals of his philosophy cannot be left untouched by (in his jargon: be transcendentally indifferent to) the protracted wars, genocides, and ecocides of the twentieth and twenty-first centuries. In other words, we ought to confront Kant's thought with a host of possibilities it would not have entertained on its own.

To begin with, it is necessary to suspend the axiomatic status of the assertion that there is nothing meriting respect in the empirical subjectivity of humans, animals, or plants. As Judith Butler, relying on the work of the French philosopher Emmanuel Levinas, has pointed out, the most relevant focus of ethical concern is "precarious life," the fragility of embodied human existence and of the "structure of address" that binds us to others.[32] How much more precarious, then, is the life, or lives, of animals and plants who do not join us in a conversation! How much more exposed to violence are the bodies of creatures that are not admitted to the discursive domain as interlocutors and partners in the venture of living! Respect for the empirical subjectivity of fragile living bodies will goad us to experiment with new structures of address, where a life speaks to another life, unchained from the exigencies of theoretical and practical reason and from the requirement of vocalization. That is how a silent address of the plant, which communicates its distress otherwise, by means of biochemical signaling, will attract our ethically motivated attention to *its* precarious life.

Similar to respect for the environment mediated by human self-respect, our duties toward plants and animals are, Kant argues, indirect at best: "Even gratitude for the long service of an old horse or dog (just as if they were members of the household) belongs *indirectly* to a human being's duty *with regard to* these animals; considered as a *direct* duty, however, it is always only a duty of the human being *to* himself."[33] Since duty is the relation of every finite rational subject to the law,[34] it is direct only when our action immediately affects other finite rational subjects. In all other cases, duties are assumed by way of reflux, a return of human beings to themselves even there where the fate of animals and plants is at issue.

Conceivably, you may feel deep gratitude toward an old fig tree for the cool shade and sweet fruit it has gifted you with over the years. But Kant's gloss on our indirect duty toward plants does not contemplate this scenario. In a blatant violation of his own separation between the three Critiques, he relies on a mix of theoretical understanding of plants (the First Critique) and their aesthetic appreciation (the Third Critique). Defining plants as "matter organized for reproduction though still without sensation,"[35] Kant debases them to mere things or, in any event, "nonhuman objects" before which we have no obligations whatsoever. Framed in these terms, why would anyone respect insensitive, self-reproducing, green matter?

To Kant himself, the disenchanted scientific description (which, as we now know, is factually wrong, because plants have a sophisticated sensory apparatus) appears to be insufficient. Already in the subsequent paragraph of *The Metaphysics of Morals*, he marvels at "the indescribable beauty of plants," the destruction of which, along with that of any beautiful thing, "is opposed to a human being's duty to himself."[36] Make no mistake: this qualification does not relieve plants of their designation as *things*. It does not make the slightest difference whether beauty shines forth through a crystal or through a piece of vegetation; its purposeless purpose leaves such a powerful impression on humans that we owe it to ourselves to protect each beautiful phenomenon without worrying about its practical value or conceptual status. And, while beauty does not foster morality, it hones in us a "sensibility that greatly promotes morality or at least prepares the way for it: the disposition, namely to love something."[37] Both beautiful crystal formations and plants are showcased as the examples of beautiful, *lovable* things that awaken in us this disposition. To destroy them is to commit a moral crime against ourselves, that is to say, against the loving disposition that draws us close to the objects of our affection and primes us for a more detached moral attitude of respect.

Despite the exemption of beautiful plants from the framework of unlimited use, Kant prefers to treat vegetation as sheer material for human appropriation. A tree is a thing that may be claimed as my "exclusive possession" so long as I "perform the actions that designate what is mine, i.e., cut down the tree or make it into lumber."[38] In so doing, I can finally celebrate my absolute proprietorship over the tree once I deprive it of the life that did not sit well with its categorization as a thing. My appropriation of the tree is a self-fulfilling prophecy: I say that the tree is a thing, and, to prove that I mean business, I cut it down and really turn it into an inanimate object, a piece of wood. The singling out of beautiful plants is a poor consolation for the murderous effects of persons, who exert their will on what they deem to be (and transform into) inanimate vegetal things. So, to repeat our question, what can we do to plants? We can do almost anything, as long as the naturally beautiful specimens in their midst are set apart and reserved for our moral and aesthetic edification.

What Can Plants Do to Us?

I have commented, if all too briefly, on Kant's Copernican turn that shifted the spotlight from the independent being of an object of knowledge to the subjective conditions of possibility for approaching it. In the theoretical and practical domains of human activity, this strategy works well: the meaning of the scientist's and the flower vendor's tulip varies, depending on human intentions, frames of reference, and subjective constructions of the vegetal object. But something else altogether takes place in the realm of aesthetics. In an apparent violation of the Copernican turn, it is a beautiful object that orders us around by prescribing "universal delight" above and beyond individual differences of taste. Human spectators are the recipients of an injunction that speaks through a flower, whose "beauty is to be taken for a property of the flower itself which does not adapt itself to the diversity of heads and the individual senses of the multitude, but to which they must adapt themselves, if they are going to pass judgment upon it."[39] Instead of completing the Copernican turn, the flower makes our heads turn and forces us to bow to the universal beauty it instantiates. Before passing judgment upon it, we must heed and adapt to the injunction it issues, namely to see (and smell) past agreeable or disagreeable sensations in an effort to espy the universal and empirically unidentifiable property of beauty.

Against the relativism of individual sensory responses to the same aroma, which pleases one human subject but "gives another a headache," Kant brandishes the universality of the aesthetic judgment that, in saying "This flower is beautiful," lays "its own proper claim to the delight of every one."[40] In addition to their spatial and biochemical modes of expression, plants "speak" in the voice of universal beauty, so that the judgment I pass on a beautiful flower is nothing but a *repetition* of the claim this flower has already laid on me and on all other human subjects. Before I have a chance to appropriate it as a potentially useful thing, I am possessed by its beauty, which leaves no space for disagreement, just as the moral law and the laws of understanding tolerate no individual dissent. As soon as I step outside the field of conflicting opinions and differently processed sensations, I rise to the level of transcendental subjectivity, joining others in a detached appreciation of the flower. Unbreakable consensus reigns there where the universal property of the beautiful object corresponds to a universal subject who delights in it, quite apart from the interference of empirical peculiarities. Lingering and unresolved conflicts of opinion are, conversely, symptomatic of the failure to gain admission into the philosophical promised land of transcendental subjectivity.

Conflicts among people can be also extinguished in the pursuit of knowledge and of the good. Guided by pure theoretical reason, we accede to the universal laws of understanding that orient our knowledge of objects. Listening to the dictates of practical reason, we freely accept the universal moral law that regulates our relations to others. Mimicking the living and anarchic flower itself, the universality of beauty, however, is nonconceptual and lawless, in defiance of the founding principles that rightfully belong in the preceding Critiques of reason.[41] The mystique of the beautiful flower is that, in its singularity, it seizes upon the whole of beauty! And it manages to do so in a way that is literally immediate, free of conceptual and legal mediations that reconcile the universal and the particular in theory and in practice, respectively.

An idée fixe of Kant's aesthetic philosophy is to protect the beautiful from the encroaching categories housed in the other two Critiques. The project of demarcating an independent domain for aesthetic experience explains why many of the terms that describe it are negative: *dis*interested pleasure, concept*less* universality, purposiveness *without purpose* . . . (Hence Derrida's "*sans* of a pure cut" as a key reference to Kantian aesthetics.) Historically, plants have been also understood by negation, as insensitive organisms or living beings without a soul. Such conceptual resonance cannot be accidental: Kant selects a flower to exemplify the beautiful because both this tulip and the beauty shining through it are accessible to us exclusively through negation or withdrawal.

It's worth taking a closer look at how flowers resist the impositions of theoretical and practical reason in the *Critique of Judgment*. Like anything beautiful, flowers must be useless: they do not serve a definite purpose in fulfilling any physiological human need. They defy the utility of practical reason as much as they do the idea of physical ends sought by theoretical reason. Kant does not repudiate the notion that flowers are vital links in the chain of plant reproduction, through which the genus is preserved. But neither does he think that their beauty plays any role in this process, and, as a result, he can casually disregard the difference between natural and artificial flowers, an actual tulip and foliage represented on wallpaper.[42]

We know that, on this last point, Kant was amiss: the scents, shapes, and colors of flowers attract various pollinators that complete reproductive activity on their behalf. There is, however, a grain of truth in his assessment. Tulips cut loose from their roots and placed in a vase are unchained from the physical end and from their organic connection to the soil at the price of their immediate life. More often than not, in their "afterlife," they still serve the economic ends of florists, unless we are talking about wildflowers. Thanks to de Saussure's classification error, Kant's tulip was supposed to be precisely a wildflower and, hence, nothing instrumental. Its uncoupling from natural and cultural ends was complete.

In flowers and in aesthetics as a whole Kant sees a utopian prefiguration of human freedom. When he calls flowers "free beauties of nature,"[43] he has in mind their liberation from natural necessity and from conceptual understanding alike. Do symmetrical petal patterns contravene this freedom? Kantian aesthetics is distinctly modern in that it detests symmetry and regularity restricting the freedom of imagination and curtailing a free play of our mental faculties. Symmetry and regularity are objectively rulebound and thus are not the qualities of free beauty.[44] The orderly nature of a pepper garden bores the onlooker, since "it imposes and irksome constraint upon the imagination: whereas nature subject to no constraint of artificial rules, and lavish . . . in its luxuriant variety can supply constant food for his taste."[45] Thus, we are brought back, again, to the aesthetic valuation of the "wild" that was so important in the case of the mislabeled tulip. The problem resides in an artificial regularization and taming of wild nature, not in nature's innate diversity and luxuriance and certainly not in the symmetry of flower petals. An aesthetically astute landscaping technique would be one that strives to reproduce the free play of the wild. It is in this spirit that Kant offers a concrete suggestion that, when it comes to ornamental gardens, "regularity in the shape of constraint is to be avoided as far as possible."[46]

While flowers flash before our eyes an image of utopian freedom, they are not aesthetic ideals. Stricto sensu, Kant views ideality as the perfect coincidence of an idea and of a concrete entity it refers to. Yet, aesthetic objects are not reachable via ideas (theoretical reason), much less via the constructs of ideality. "An ideal of beautiful flowers, of a beautiful suit of furniture, or of a beautiful view, is unthinkable."[47] Why "unthinkable"? Because beauty is not an object of thought, nor of logical judgment, nor of purely pragmatic purposes. A beautiful flower may be too weak to take on the entire system of thought, which has slotted it within the structure of aesthetic judgment and harnessed it to the demands of purposiveness without purpose. Of one thing we can be nonetheless sure: it does not succumb to the sinister influence of idealization that performs a magical disappearing act, causing everything singular, imperfect, and concrete to dissolve in the mist of indifferent abstraction.

9 | HEGEL'S GRAPES

From Grapes to Spirit(s)

During his extensive travels throughout Europe, Hegel wrote letters to his wife, Marie, recounting what had happened in his voyages. On a pleasant afternoon of September 24, 1822, he found himself in the West Prussian town of Koblenz. We can imagine the great dialectician exactly the way he describes himself at the opening of the letter he composed on that day: sitting by the window, contemplating a splendid view of the Rhine, and "eating grapes—and what grapes! the sweetest and the tastiest in the world."[1] When time comes to bring the letter to a close, the grapes suddenly reappear on the page. Along with Marie, we learn that Hegel is tired after an arduous walk to the Ehrenbreitstein Fortress on the east bank of the Rhine, opposite Koblenz. Although his hunger has already been quelled by the delicious grapes, he will now have a real meal, to replenish his energy.[2] Just as writing the letter was a lovely spiritual intermezzo, so snacking on grapes was a welcome physical interlude between a vigorous exercise and a full dinner.

Quite independently of these *faits divers*, grapes are a felicitous example of a dialectical fruit. Grapes that are past their prime undergo fermentation; instead of simply rotting, they shed their initial form only to be reborn and, with a little assistance from humans, to metamorphose into wine. In the transition from grapes to wine, nature is dialectically transformed into culture, which is not coincidentally intimately tied to agriculture and, more specifically, to viniculture. Rather than signaling a separation from nature, culture is the cultivation and processing (here, the distillation) of nature's fruits. The domain of Spirit (*Geist*) becomes accessible through the production of spirits. Wine, to be sure, causes inebriation, seduces us, and leads us astray from the gravitas of work, which may be credited with having created the space for cultural activity. This inner contradictoriness, palpable in the clash between the "causes" and the effects of wine, is responsible for its conceptual allure, however: while laying the inroads into culture, it is also an escape route from what we call civilization. *In vino veritas* acquires its perversely dialectical sense of being, at once, the womb and the tomb of culture.

When we press grapes, we squeeze out of them more than their juice, along with which flows the very logic of the Hegelian dialectics. As Hegel construes it, dialectics is a tortuous journey through a series of negations inherent in the negated thing itself, negations that, at the same time, cancel out, preserve, and elevate the negated. The technical word for this process is sublation, or, in German, *Aufhebung*. In fermenting, grapes lose their natural shape and therefore are negated, even as their juicy essence gets preserved and elevated, both literally and metaphorically—in the form of spirits and Spirit. Realizing their sweet essence in the state of ripeness, they must abandon their identity as grapes to keep something of themselves intact. The natural immediacy of a plant is sacrificed for the sake of a cultural mediation.

Dialectically speaking, we find it challenging to recognize ourselves in what is external to us and, even more so, in what has sprung up independently of human cultivation—for instance, wild sagebrush. In *Phenomenology of Spirit*, Hegel states that a basic human and animal mode of confronting this foreign presence of an object is to eat it up. (No wonder that babies and puppies put in their mouths whatever they encounter in the vicinity!) Bridging the distance that separates us from material things, we eat (or drink) them up. This, in Hegel's words, is "the most elementary school of wisdom": students devour bread and wine following "the ancient Eleusinian Mysteries of Ceres and Bacchus," even though "they have still to learn the secret meaning of the eating of bread and the drinking of wine."[3] To eat and drink—emblematically bread and wine— is to behave as dialecticians do. How so?

In search for an answer, we might reflect a little further on the dialectical principle of negation. We make a thing our own and appropriate it all the better the more we negate its immediate givenness or the manner in which it stands over and against us: its mute and dumb material reality. A thorough act of appropriation is the one that destroys the appropriated object, morphing it into an integral part of the proprietor. Is this not what happens in digestion? Biting into grapes, we destroy them but do so productively, breaking them down into the glucose, vitamins, and minerals that nourish our bodies. The vegetal "other" becomes a part and parcel of the "same," the eater, who, in negating its otherness, elevates it to what Hegel would deem to be a higher end of sustaining a human body. The mystery of eating is, precisely, this event of establishing a hidden dialectical identity of the eater and the eaten: I am what I eat . . . "The most elementary school of wisdom" designates the lowest level of dialectics, where a sequence of negations and sublations is wholly physical and material, if not animalistic. "And all of Nature," Hegel adds, "like the animals, celebrates these open Mysteries which teach the truth about sensuous things."[4]

There is, certainly, a marked difference between the eating of grapes and the drinking of wine. In contrast to humans, animals do not engage in viniculture and do not prepare food for consumption, except for, in some cases, chewing and regurgitating it for their offspring. In the wine, the grape has already become other to itself; the beverage is, as it were, self-digested prior to its being broken down in our stomachs and livers. Cooking, too, accelerates the breakdown of foodstuffs (their own self-negation) by means of heat, mimicking temperature increases in the course of fermentation. This other "school of wisdom" is culinary!

Hegel, for his part, wants us to graduate from the relatively elementary schools to those esoteric circles where the "secret meaning" of bread eating and wine drinking is taught. You will have guessed that, here, the German dialectician gestures toward Christian symbolism, according to which bread is the body and wine the blood of Christ. How do we pass from Bacchus to Jesus? And what does this passage mean?

In the Eucharistic mystery, added onto and exceeding the mystery of digestion, wine is supposedly transubstantiated into divine blood. In other words, the other, whom we consume when we drink this substance, is not a vegetal but a divine other, not lower but higher than ourselves, the drinkers. The inversion is complete if, as Augustine once put it, we are eucharistically digested into Christ as soon as we partake of his flesh and blood. The higher other is, moreover, someone who has self-sacrificially given his blood and his earthly life for us. The Eucharist is both the bodily and the symbolic memory of this sacrifice, preserved in the memory of ripe grapes that lingers in the wine and in the traces of sunshine and the soil's chemical composition that persist in the grapes.

The transition from Bacchus to Jesus is a passage from physical to spiritual digestion. Above all, it is a crucial leap from consciousness to self-consciousness, from a confrontation with an external object of the senses (the eater and the grapes), in the first instance, to a conversion of consciousness itself into its own object (the eater and herself), in the second. Somewhat densely, Hegel writes:

> But what is disclosed to consciousness is still only absolute, i.e., abstract Spirit, which is this simple essence, not Spirit as it is in its own self; in other words, it is only *immediate* Spirit, the Spirit of Nature. Consequently, its self-conscious life is only the mystery of bread and wine, of Ceres and Bacchus, not of the other, strictly higher, gods whose individuality includes as an essential moment self-consciousness as such. Therefore, Spirit has not yet sacrificed itself as *self-conscious* Spirit to self-consciousness, and the mystery of bread and wine is not yet the mystery of flesh and blood.[5]

Bacchus and Ceres are, like the wine and the bread themselves, suspended between immediate nature and pure Spirit; they are the spirits *of* nature, incompletely released from its domineering clasp. To be so released, one would need to sacrifice oneself, giving up natural, biological existence for the sake of spiritual life. Dying to nature, one is reborn in Spirit. For Hegel, such a death, however symbolic, is indispensable to the formation of self-consciousness, where the confrontation with an external object gives way to a confrontation with oneself as other to oneself. Only after Spirit has attained consciousness of itself does the "mystery of bread and wine" turn into the "mystery of flesh and blood." Jesus's self-sacrifice provides Hegel with a standard for the formation of a free self-conscious subjectivity no longer separate from its objects because the object of self-consciousness is consciousness itself. That's why the bread and the wine, full of fermented spirits, are spiritualized as parts of the divine body. And that's why, partaking of these spiritual products, we actually consume *ourselves as other to ourselves*, metaphorically letting our subjectivity ferment and rise, like a gas, to the rank of self-consciousness.

Like everything dialectically negated, nature does not disappear as soon as Spirit consumes it but returns with the load of a new meaning, one adequate to self-consciousness. As a self-conscious subject, Spirit gets intoxicated with and full of itself, even when it uses the seemingly independent things of nature: "in the mystery of bread and wine, it appropriates this independence along with the meaning of the inner essence."[6] Fully mature self-consciousness realizes that, besides consciousness, everything else that appeared to belong to the outside "real world" constitutes its own internal object. The physiology of digestion destroys the grapes, the wine, and the bread as separate substances; the psychology of Spirit does away with the separateness of physical reality as a whole. The divine moment, the *kairos* of the reconciliation of nature and Spirit arrives when in bread and wine—as well as in other things it did not explicitly will—self-consciousness recognizes itself. By the time of this recognition, we will have left the elementary school of wisdom behind and enrolled at Hegel's university.

The achievement of Spirit capable of identifying itself in the pregiven objects of Nature does not imply that it should enslave itself to these objects. If "external reality" has been rid of the illusion of its independence, then art, as one of the highest activities of Spirit, should not bend before the things of nature in an attempt to reproduce them with the greatest accuracy. Hegel's conceptual illustration of this lesson is the story of the Greek painter Zeuxis, who lived in the fifth century BC: "The grapes painted by Zeuxis have from antiquity onward been styled a triumph of art and also of the principle of the imitation of nature, because living doves are supposed to have pecked at them."[7] The triumph of art is actually its defeat in the fallenness of Spirit that imitates nature, accepting the given just as it is given. What we could categorize as the nonviolence of the aesthetic appreciation of grapes is, for Hegel, the sign of an impotent refusal to destroy them creatively. Whereas wine stamped the pressed grapes with the insignia of Spirit, the painted grapes subjugated and devoured the very consciousness that reproduced them.

Having said that, the flesh-and-blood grapes and wine did not satisfy Hegel, much like the afternoon snack that he ate while composing the letter from Koblenz. Prone to graft philosophy onto plants and plant parts, the German thinker explained the plurality of philosophies by the impossibility of putting forth a metaphilosophy that would be independent of Spirit in its historical unfolding. In his *Encyclopedia of the Philosophical Sciences*, he allegorically compared various philosophies to fruit, asking: "Would anyone, who wished for fruit, reject cherries, pears, and grapes, on the ground that they were cherries, pears, or grapes, and not fruit? But when philosophy is in question, the excuse of many is that philosophies are so different, and none of them is the philosophy—that each is only a philosophy."[8] The point is that the universal (*the* fruit, *the* philosophy) is in each of the particular fruits and philosophies. Every historical epoch has its own philosophical worldview, which, despite its limited context, warrants access to the whole of philosophy, truth, and Spirit. But this is where Hegel is disingenuous: philosophies are incomparable to fruits because, unlike the former, the latter do not dialectically negate one another. Cherries are not negated in pears that are themselves not negated in grapes. Conversely, some philosophies are closer to realized Spirit than others: in ancient Greece (in contrast to Hegel's Germany) thought and reality, Spirit and Nature, were neither reconciled nor known as two complementary parts of the same Idea. According to his own rules of the game, our admiration for the diversity of fruit should be construed as the lowest level of consciousness, the sensory knowledge overwhelmed by the seemingly infinite variation in shapes, colors, flavors, and so on of its physical objects.[9] Surely, the historical array of philosophies would be a far cry from *that*... Or, is it the case that, presented in the guise of fruits that are laid out on the marketplace (of ideas), philosophies are humbled, brought down from the pedestal onto which Hegel's thought usually mounts them, and—God forbid!—compared to something that can easily rot without as much as fermenting?

Adventures in Vegetable Dialectics

In our analysis of Hegel's grapes thus far, we have not yet touched upon his explicit notion of the plant. Now is the time to fill in this gap by exploring his dialectical botany.

It was an innovation of Hegelian dialectics to consider various modes of life, institutional structures, and social processes as the avatars of Spirit at various stages of its march through the world. Plants are not exceptional in this respect; the vegetal world represents the first (and the most precarious) stage of Spirit's "being-for-self" and hence a "subjective

point of life."[10] Akin to the fermenting grapes, suspended between nature and culture, the plant is a dialectical point of transition. Although
it establishes minimal mastery over the inorganic world of minerals that
nourish it, the plant is a passive master, exposed to the elements and incapable of opposing itself to the milieu of its growth. This, for Hegel, is
a convincing justification for the total subordination of plants to animal
and human needs, in which Spirit has perfected its "being-for-self" and
has further individuated the subjective point of life.

In plant life, Spirit sees a shadow of itself. Just as plants spread on the
face of the earth, conquering the inorganic domain, so Reason (which *is*
Spirit before its reconciliation with material reality) begins to appropriate
the world: "While at first it [Reason] is only dimly aware of its presence in
the actual world, or only knows quite simply that this world is its own, it
strides forward in this belief to a general appropriation of its own assured
possessions, and plants the symbol of its sovereignty on every height and
in every depth."[11] The symbols it plants are, of course, the plants themselves, with their roots burrowing deep down into the earth's crust and
their branches soaring high above in the airy expanse. The depths probed
by the roots are the figures of understanding, which is not an end in itself
but an enabling factor for the continual growth of Spirit: "Reason digs
into the very entrails of things and opens every vein in them so that it
may gush forth to meet itself" in the guise of its other, that is, nature.[12]
What does this image convey to us about the subjectivity of plants?

Depending on how sympathetic you are to Hegel, you might adopt a
"glass-half-full" or a "glass-half-empty" approach to his construction of
plant life. On the positive side, plants are the vehicles of Spirit taking its
first steps on the path of organic life. As such, they are subjective beings,
not quasi-inanimate things. Hegel would not deny that plants are, to some
extent, aware of their surroundings, even though their awareness is "dim."
In them, a baseline of individuality has been reached, as the individuated
germ or seed testifies.[13] On the negative side, plants stay too close to the
inorganic realm they have superseded: they are the mere intermezzi between the inorganic and the organic that must, themselves, be overcome
for life to come into its own in the animal. Their proximity to the mineral
world is made evident in their resemblance to crystalline forms (e.g., in
the arrangement of flower petals) and in the outward movement of growth
that causes them to become "benumbed and rigid."[14] Their individuality is

still weak, as they do not oppose either their environment or one another and, consequently, are often not clearly demarcated from what they are *not*: another plant of the same or of a different species, for instance.

On balance, those inclined to criticize Hegel for his construction of plants as the figures of deficient Spirit have more reason to do so than those who prefer to praise his sensitivity to plant subjectivity. What tips the balance in favor of the "glass-half-empty" approach is that the Hegelian plant is a being-for-itself that is not self-related, that is to say, that does not make a full circle in a return to itself from the world outside it. Admittedly, it assimilates water, sunlight, and minerals in the nutritive process, but the "return-into-self in which assimilation terminates, does not have for result the *self* as inner, subjective universality over against externality, does not result in self-feeling."[15] Its principle of subjectivity is a bizarre soul devoid of interiority and essentially incomplete because of its interminable movement outward, detectable in growth. Elsewhere, Hegel will refer to the idea of such movement as "bad infinity," a series that does not reach any inherent closure but ends more or less abruptly, terminated by contingent and external factors. The plant, then, is literally stuck on the dialectical spiral, where "progress" entails, rather than a blind surge forward, a back-and-forth of venturing outside oneself and returning with the luggage of experience to the safe haven of interiority and "self-feeling." The only thing that will disrupt its fixation on the pure exteriority of growth is the process of reproduction, whereby the individual plant productively negates itself in generating another like it and, at the same time, outlives its purpose. I will take up this vein of the argument later on in this chapter.

Hegel associates the paradox of plant subjectivity, lacking the space of inner freedom and self-determination, with the "flower religions" (an Orientalist label) of the East. If the practitioners of these religions endorse "a selfless representation of the self,"[16] positing the ideals of purity, innocence, and peace, it is because they fashion themselves after the attributes of their worship, the flowers. Vegetative peacefulness is not the outcome of a laborious mediation and reconciliation of contradictions; it is, rather, attributable to the plant's inability to pull itself together, to muster enough force of resistance, and to oppose whatever it is not. Disintegrated, disorganized, not quite an organism but a quasi-inorganic life form, the plant lacks the necessary inner organization and self-relatedness that would have held its parts together as interdependent organs. "Strictly speaking," Hegel concludes, "the plant is an aggregate of a group of individuals which form a single individual, but one whose parts are completely self-subsistent. This self-subsistence of parts is the impotence of the plant; the animal, on the contrary, has viscera, members which are not self-subsistent, which can exist only and solely in unity with the whole."[17] The independent strength of individual parts is won at the expense of the power of the whole.

Earlier Kant had pointed out that plants were "aggregates without a system" and hence problematic elements neither within nor outside of the essentially systemic philosophical project. Hegel goes further than that: the nonorganismic anarchy of plant parts indifferent to the whole is responsible for the dialectical defeat of the plant, which at any rate does not have the means of self-defense at its disposal because it has no integrated "self" to defend. The failure of vegetal self-integration goes hand in hand with the absence of psychic interiority in plants and with their weakness, passivity, and exposure to the other.

Never mind that Hegel was not aware of the biochemical responses of plants to threats in their environment; he also overlooked the simplest vegetal defense mechanisms, such as thorns. Nor did he give enough thought to the "soft" power of plants, expressed, for example, in their plasticity, which promotes their alteration along with their environment and therefore helps them stand their ground otherwise than by means of organized resistance. More importantly still, Hegel is oblivious to the vegetal *and* nonvegetal modes of organization that favor a decentered network of communication channels over the elaboration of a coherent whole. This, in effect, is the case of plant signaling and communication,[18] made possible by molecular cell-to-cell transports (for instance, of calcium or potassium) and networks of hormonal transmission (ethylene, methyl jasmonate).[19] So, is the aggregate of individual plants, crisscrossed by multiple channels of communication, as loose as Hegel presents it? And where are we to locate Spirit within the open network of interacting, semi-independent tissues constituting a plant?

The "selfless" subjectivity of plants is objectivity reiterated in their nonorganismic constitution and in the generic nature of their parts, all of them derivatives of a leaf. Relying heavily on Goethe's *The Metamorphosis of Plants*, Hegel argues that "the whole growth [*Production*] of the plant shows the same uniformity and simple development; and this unity of form is the leaf."[20] The incomplete individuation of plant life, both on the subjective and on the objective planes, situates this life at an early stage of the dialectical journey that begins with the simplest, most abstract, and least differentiated notions (being and nothingness in *Logic*; the will lacking a fixed object in *Philosophy of Right*, and so forth). Individuation, concretization, and organismic complexity are, on the contrary, signs of an advanced dialectical development; what they convey is that enough negations and self-negations have taken place to determine the inner content of the entity in question, be it a will, being, or a form of life.

The lifeblood of dialectical determination is negation, which mediates the world in understanding, renders it concrete, makes it our "own." External reality must be negated as something independently confronting us if it is to be understood in the elementary school of wisdom, by digesting externally posited foodstuffs, or, in a higher school, where to grasp a book you have no other choice but to break its spine. "Free will" must be negated in an object to which it binds itself if it is to become concrete, just as the simple standoff of being and nothingness must be overcome in the dialectic of becoming if it is to move on to something other than an empty philosophical abstraction. (To make sense of Hegel's conception, picture being as a blank sheet of paper—hence, virtually indistinguishable from nothingness—breathing with the possibility of anything whatsoever scribbled on it. When you write on this sheet, you negate its blinding emptiness, all the while concretizing some of its abstractly and vaguely anticipated possibilities.) Since the plant has no clearly demarcated "self," however, it cannot say "no" to itself either, which is why the relatively indeterminate proto-form of the leaf keeps coming back in every metamorphosis it undergoes. For comparison's sake, we should note that to be human is, in Hegel's system, to be purely self-negating. Our determinative capacity to speak—and, especially, to say "I"—negates the singularity of *this* tree, *this* table, *this* cup, and even *this* living-breathing creature that I am in the universality of the word. (The example of the word "I" is particularly delicious: a marker of human individuality, it is so generic that anyone can apply this word to her- or himself, negating the very singularity it is meant to express.) The plant's silence, in turn, is a symptom of its powerlessness, its essential incapacity to negate itself.

One implication of the power of self-negation—to wit, the most potent power—is that the more dialectically advanced subjectivity gains the right to negate both itself and one that is less advanced. Whereas a tree cannot set itself against itself nor against the milieu of its growth, humans do so every time they open their mouths, whether to eat or to speak. Locomotion can also do the trick, for, as soon as we turn around, *this* tree right here vanishes and something else assumes its place in the indeterminacy of what is *here*.[21] Along with the animals, we negate plants that are incapable of negating themselves every time we take a bite into them or move away from them. But it is exclusively as humans that we negate plants (and animals) by giving them names, attaching a universal linguistic label to *this* oak and *this* dog. Or, as a bitter joke goes, first the European inhabitants of North America cleared huge extensions of forests on the continent and then they named streets in the suburbs after the very trees they felled.

The Sex Life of Plants, or Beyond Oppositionality

In Hegelian dialectics, a sexualized creature is one that is necessarily highly individualized. Why? Because, in keeping with the unquestioned heteronormative background of dialectics, sexuality hinges on a principle of opposition between the sexes that pits the self against another of a different sex. In the oppositional relation to the other, we finally discover ourselves. To be a little more nuanced, Hegel, in line with Aristophanes before him and Sigmund Freud after him, thinks that the masculine and the feminine principles coexist in every sexed being "on account of the original identity of formation," but only one of these becomes predominant: "in the female, it is necessarily the passive moment [*das Indifferente*], in the male, the moment of duality [*das Entzweite*], of opposition."[22] Sexuality is a convoluted opposition between masculine oppositionality and feminine nonoppositionality, and, therefore, it stands, on the whole, under the sign of masculinity.

As Elaine Miller has incisively noticed in her book *The Vegetative Soul*, Hegel's construction of feminine identity parallels his conception of the plant's "selfless" self.[23] The passivity, indifference, and nonoppositionality of plants and women are so many side effects of a profound ontological weakness that centers on the incompleteness of their individuation.

Following a deplorable dialectical train of thought, in contrast to men and animals, women and plants do not derive their sense of self from an opposition to the other or to their environment. Further, Hegel does not hesitate to add to the list of those who are ontologically weak men who live in "Southern latitudes": "The externality of the subjective, selflike unity of the plant is objective in its relation to light.... Man fashions himself in more interior fashion, although in Southern latitudes he, too, does not reach the stage where his self, his freedom, is objectively guaranteed."[24] As I explain elsewhere,[25] Hegel believes that, in the South, human subjectivity, like that of plants, is largely determined by light, causing the inhabitants of these parts of the world to be neglectful of their subjective interiority. Externally determined by abundant sunshine, living beings are not free; neither Southern men nor any women nor plants contain the principle of their activity within themselves and thus fail to set themselves up in opposition to their environments as purposeful subjects. The cunning of dialectical reason is such that the human and the plant cease to be monolithic concepts: Hegel elevates the North European ideal of the industrious and free man at the expense of the shared mode of being of plants, women, and those humans of both sexes who live in the global South.

Stressing the affinities between plants and women was not a one-time shameful slip on Hegel's part. It traverses his entire body of writing. In *Philosophy of Right*, he juxtaposes the difference between men and women onto the difference between animals and plants. "Men," he writes, "correspond to animals, while women correspond to plants because their development is more placid and the principle that underlies it is rather the vague unity of feeling."[26] The implication is that, if plants were to articulate their experience in words, they would probably describe it in terms of the feeling of the feminine "vague unity," of oneness with their "other." The stakes of this laughable argument are nonetheless exceptionally serious, seeing that it is immediately put in the service of legitimating the exclusion of women from the political sphere—the realm of frictions and oppositions *par excellence*. "When," Hegel continues, "women hold the helm of government, the state is at once in jeopardy."[27]

We can spend plenty of time criticizing, for all the right reasons, Hegel's views on women, people living in the global South, and plants. But there is a deeper, methodological problem with his overall method, which we risk leaving unnoticed in our indignation. Succinctly put, the issue is that dialectics automatically organizes differences into oppositional formations and, in the case of those that escape its sweeping theoretical move, devalorizes them as scattered, indifferent, and, hence, inessential. In an overarching oppositional framework, the dice are invariably loaded in favor of the purely oppositional pole—men, Northerners, animals. But what if vegetal and human sexualities are much freer than the logic of oppositionality makes them out to be? What about the so-called nonproductive or nonreproductive sexuality, Freudian polymorphous perversity, gender identities that do not fit into the Hegelian dualism, and, finally, the sexual reproduction of plants? Don't all of these "immature" manifestations, as Hegel would be wont to classify them, encapsulate the very kernel of sexuality?

Plants, in particular, lead a playful, promiscuous, hybridizing version of a sex life. With their plastic sexual morphologies, they invite pollinating insects to join a long-distance, cross-kingdom ménage à trois. They incestually pollinate themselves with the help of "bisexual" or "perfect" flowers. They switch sexes at different stages of their growth, as in the cases of *Cannabis sativa* (wild marijuana) or *Humulus japonicus*.[28] And they synthesize many of the same sex hormones as the ones found in mammals (e.g., estrogen).[29] The discovery of these hormones in plants puts in doubt Hegel's theoretical assertion that, as less developed than its animal analogue, plant sexuality is restricted to a single organ, namely their flowers:

> The different individuals [plants] cannot therefore be regarded as of different sexes because they have not been completely imbued with the *principle* of their opposition—because this does not completely pervade them, is not a universal moment of the entire individual, but is a separate part of it.... The sexual relation proper must have for its opposed moments entire individuals whose determinateness, completely reflected into itself, spreads through the whole individual.[30]

To sum up, given that plant sexuality is indeterminate, does not suffuse the whole plant, and pertains to a subject incapable of "self-reflection" or self-relatedness, it is utterly *im*proper and refers to a feature borrowed from the dialectically higher life of animals.

Sexuality, then, is a luxurious appendage of plant life. The entire vegetal "genus-process" becomes redundant and "on the whole, superfluous since the process of formation and assimilation is already reproduction as production of fresh individuals."[31] Plants can reproduce asexually, but when they resort to sexual reproduction, they push the limit of their mode of existence, treading upon the territory of animal life. Hegel, indeed, locates vegetation on the verge of selfhood, at the unstable border between nonindividuation and individuation: "The plant ... does not attain to a *being-for-self* but merely touches the boundary-line of individuality. It is at this boundary, therefore, where there is a show of *division* into sexes."[32] That is why so much rides on the argument that the sexual function is circumscribed to a part of a plant instead of suffusing all of its tissues: by conceding to plants a rudimentary, inessential, partial sexuality, Hegel ensures their stagnation on the threshold of "being-for-self," which is inappropriate to them qua plants. Vegetal difference is not easily translatable into a "*division* into sexes" or into the ideal of self-relational subjectivity. Yet what appears to be a failure or a deficiency in the dialectical scheme is the practical success of plant sexuality and subjectivity that are not paralyzed in oppositional molds.

The freest finite existence is, precisely, the one that hovers around the "boundary-line of individuality," without either crossing it once and for all or falling back into the nocturnal anonymity of the elemental. The reproduction of plants is the omen of their freedom, a laboratory of unpredictable clonal multiplications, cross-pollinations, self-fertilizations, and grafting. Do the seemingly inexhaustible possibilities explored in this laboratory substantiate Hegel's plea to view sexuality as a luxurious and ultimately dispensable excess over the vegetal "genus-process"? And what does the humanly enforced asexual reproduction hold in store for plants and, above all, for Hegel's favorite grapes? Predictably enough, a future in which we continue to impose abstinence on plants is grim; it is a future of greatly diminished diversity and a nearly identical genetic makeup in three-quarters of the world's grape varieties.[33] After eight thousand years of viniculture, with the abstinence it imposed on wine grapes, there is very little vininature left. The gases of fermentation that, on the olfactory and symbolic levels, used to be redolent of culture now reek of irreversible decay.

The Vegetable Kernel of the Dialectical Shell

Dialectical philosophy is brimming with plant metaphors, allegories, and synecdoches illustrating its theoretical points. We have seen, in the *Encyclopedia*, different philosophies likened to fruits, none of which represents the "fruitness" or the universal essence of fruit (read: of philosophy) better than all the others. Most emblematically, though, in *Phenomenology of Spirit*, Hegel maps the entire historical development of philosophy onto the reproductive stages of a fruit-bearing tree. No longer offered on an equal footing, philosophies are the snapshots of a gradual maturation of Spirit and its truth, now presenting itself in a bud, now blossoming forth, and now bearing fruit.

Conventional opinion, Hegel writes, "does not comprehend the diversity of philosophical systems as the progressive unfolding of truth, but rather sees in it simple disagreements." Philosophy is more like a plant that metamorphoses as it grows: "The bud disappears in the bursting-forth of the blossom, and one might say that the former is refuted by the latter; similarly, when the fruit appears, the blossom is shown up in its turn as a false manifestation of the plant, and the fruit now emerges as the truth instead."[34] Now, if philosophy is akin to a blossoming and fructiferous tree, then the plant is similar to philosophy. Each of its reproductive stages is a "refutation" of the earlier ones, as though the plant were caught up in a protracted argument with itself, an argument as lasting as its entire lifetime. This embodied argument is coextensive with life because the bud, the blossom, and the flower are not the objective truths of the plant, whose vitality—like that of any other creature—is inseparable from the possibility of becoming something other than what it is at any given point in time. But what exactly is the common denominator of philosophy and the tree onto which its history is transposed?

Philosophy and the tree are two distinct shells that cover over the same kernel of Spirit. The one is Spirit in the form of thinking, including the self-reflection of Spirit thinking about Spirit itself. The other is Spirit in its earliest organic form, striving toward the light of the sun as a growing shoot and passing through successive reproductive metamorphoses. Thinking and material reality are not, as in Cartesian philosophy, independent substances but variations on Spirit in its journey toward absolute self-knowing that arrives at its destination when it fully knows, suffuses, and elevates into itself the entire world. To play devil's advocate, Hegel would concede that Descartes, too, was not entirely wrong: the tree and a philosophical meditation *are* two radically different things before the latter manages to recognize itself in the former. Dualism (the belief in two incompatible substances) and monism (the conviction that a single substance constitutes the whole) are both true in one sense and false in another sense, which is another way of saying that their truth and falsehood should be indexed to the degree of Spirit's maturation as it marches through the world.

Why, nonetheless, does Hegel choose a plant to lay out the dialectics of truth and not, say, an animal? Why does he compare the most imperfect, extroverted, unreflective form of life to philosophy?

A scandalous hypothesis now suggesting itself to us is that dialectics as a whole is vegetal. Both before the plant appears on the scene of Hegel's philosophy of nature and after it is negated and surpassed by animal life, the principle of vegetal existence instigates dialectical unrest. This principle is metamorphosis. While animals sometimes experience metamorphosis, such as when a caterpillar is transformed into a butterfly, these experiences are rare, one-time occurrences limited to the early phases of organismic development in a small number of species. An animal's final shape is normally defined as early as the embryonic stage; the plant's, on the other hand, is not. This simple example of the end's presence as a potentiality in the beginning should have cemented the bond of dialectics and animal nature. It did not. To the extent that he relies on Goethe's botany, Hegel pays close attention to the diversity of vegetal forms, overlaying a simple essential unity of the leaf. The metamorphosis of this plant organ will shed light on the vegetal penchant of dialectics.

Whether intentionally or not, when Goethe and Hegel speak of the plant and its life, they have philosophy in mind. For Goethe, it was the flower, with its objective capturing of light in a bedazzling spectrum of colors, that symbolized the culmination of Spirit's heroic ascent from the darkness of the soil (the unconscious) to the bright day of knowledge. In Hegel's case, what the philosopher writes about the growth of plants applies to the metamorphoses of philosophical systems. Recall the lines I have cited above: "the whole growth (*Production*) of the plant shows the same uniformity and simple development; and this unity of form is the leaf." Does the same insight not hold for philosophy? Rewriting this sentence, we obtain the following: Despite the diversity of systems of thought, the whole growth of philosophy shows the same uniformity and simple development, and this unity of form is Spirit. Like the generic leaf, whose expansion and contraction underlies the emergence of the seed and the petal, the stalk and the fruit, the unity of the spiritual form is not at all obvious. Not directly given, it is a *metaphysical* unity, which dwarfs all the refutations of one individual moment by another—for example, of the blossom by the fruit or of medieval by modern philosophy. Wasting no time on a comparison of apples and oranges or, more pertinently, cherries and grapes on the marketplace of ideas, we can study the transformed forms of the same plant that is Spirit.

More unequivocally still, Hegel likens Spirit to a plant in his *Lectures on the Philosophy of History*. There, he quietly recycles Kant's notion of the plant as a product of its own activity in the idea of Spirit's self-production:

> Spirit is essentially the result of its own activity; its activity is the transcending of immediate, simple, unreflected existence,—the negation of that existence, and the returning into itself. We may compare it with the seed; for with this the plant begins, yet it is also the result of the plant's entire life. But the weak side of life is exhibited in the fact that the commencement and the result are disjoined from each other. Thus also is it in the life of individuals and peoples.[35]

Hegel draws the dialectical circle in all its magnificence: Spirit and the plant begin with the end results of their immediate life, condensed in the seed. The plant's outward growth without return to itself—the very movement the dialectician has previously denounced—closes onto itself in a circle, in the process of reproduction dialectically negating growth. To be sure, vegetable self-reflection takes its toll. It is declared weak because of the separation of the commencement from the outcome, of the mother plant from the fruit that falls from it, both in time and in space. But no less weak are the achievements of cultural activity whereby Spirit produces itself, presumably, on a more elevated dialectical plane. "Thus also is it in the life of individuals and peoples" means that, by the time the seed of a given culture has yielded its fruit, it has become obsolete and lost the living impulse that had animated it. In the end, the new seed still enveloped in the fruit and the tree that nourished it fall apart and fall out with each other.

At this late hour, at the close of the chapter, we cannot avoid mentioning that dialectics steps up to the plate of philosophical analysis quite late, when the living impulse is waning or, as Hegel poetically expresses this, when the owl of Minerva spreads its wings at dusk and things are already grey.[36] Dialectics is unable to accompany the living unfolding of thought, let alone the organic growth of a plant, "as they happen" but retraces these itineraries of Spirit in retrospect, once they are (almost) completed. Looking back, it recaptures the products of Spirit that are at hand, drained of life. All it finds are ways of thinking petrified in systems, grapes already fermented, and flowers preserved as mementos of a dead friend.

The reference to dry flowers brings us to one of the epigraphs to our intellectual herbarium, borrowed from Hegel's epistolary reflection, that the "flowers are of course dry and life has vanished from them. But what on earth is a living thing if the spirit of man does not breathe life into it? What is speechless but that to which man does not lend his speech?"[37] The posthumous existence of dry flowers imbued with human meaning is an example of nature's afterlife, when the previously mute plant commences to speak, albeit in the voice of Spirit. The Hegelian redemption of nature is thinkable on the condition that the immediate biological life of natural beings dries up and is ready to receive the breath of a higher, spiritual vitality. All the same, Spirit is not satisfied with the sacrifice of plant and animal existences; it also feeds on itself, productively negating the previous moments of its own life. The flowers receive their sense after they are filed in a herbarium, grapes acquire secret meaning after they have fermented into wine, ancient Greek philosophy comes into its own when its heyday is long past and it is digested in German thought . . .

So, where does this leave us? Aren't we underwriting dialectical violence in compiling an intellectual herbarium? It would seem so, save for a small but nonetheless important disclaimer. *The Philosopher's Plant* has plotted a decidedly un-Hegelian redemption of vegetal life, in that it has referred philosophy back to the plants themselves, showing how they bestow sense upon and enliven abstract conceptualities. Instead of enunciating *the philosophy of botany*, it has reveled in *the botany of philosophy* and, in doing so, has given the final word to plants.

PART IV

POSTMODERN PLANT-SUBJECTS

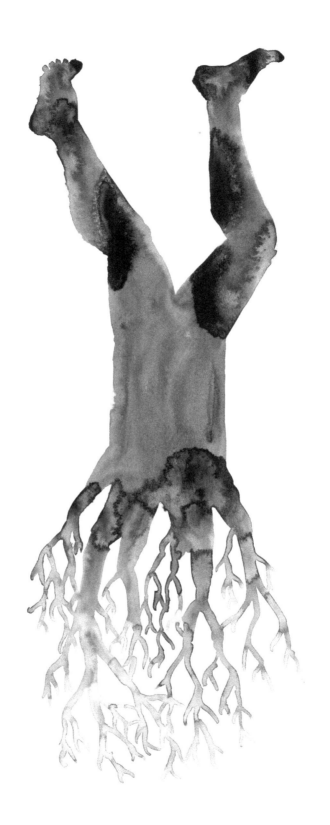

10

HEIDEGGER'S APPLE TREE

Face to Face with a Blossoming Tree

So much has been said and written about the piquant details of Heidegger's life that any future mentions of his shameful "Nazi period" or the affair with his gifted student Hannah Arendt are only likely to distract from the content of his philosophy. The best strategy to adopt is to accept the advice Heidegger himself gave in a lecture on Aristotle. A perfect factual summary of a thinker's biography, he opined, would be: "He was born, he worked, and he died."[1] In this bare-bones statement, the first and the third verbs do not in the least distinguish a philosopher from other humans, animals, and even plants, though the question of death in nonhuman organisms merits a separate debate.[2] The middle verb, "worked," flanked by the beginning and the end of life, is the one that makes all the difference, so much so that it comes to represent everything that occurs between these two extremes, absorbing into itself all meaningful biographical content. But what, you will ask, is entailed in philosophical "work" for Heidegger? Neither the long hours spent in archives nor contributions to the advancement of technical and ultimately irrelevant debates. Genuine work is accomplished in one's dedication to the task and the call of thinking that aims to think "what is," orienting oneself to being as a whole.

If Plato's philosophizing took place in the shade of a plane tree whose physical height was outdone by the immeasurably distant world of Ideas, then Heidegger lets us in on another primal scene of philosophy: a thinker standing face to face with a tree. Here,

> We stand outside of science. Instead, we stand before a tree in bloom, for example—and the tree stands before us. The tree faces us. The tree and we meet one another, as the tree stands there and we stand face to face with it. As we are in this relation of one to the other and before the other, the tree and we *are*. This face-to-face meeting is not, then, one of these "ideas" buzzing about in our heads.[3]

There is a sense of radical transhuman egalitarianism in the narration of a common experience of facing a tree in bloom, which, we are told later on in the book, is a "well-shaped" apple tree.[4] It is an encounter in the most robust sense of the word, a meeting that is mutual, one where we stand before a plant and the plant stands before us, we face it and it faces us, we *are* and it *is*. What makes a full-fledged relation to the apple tree possible is that we share being (and, to some extent, the state of being alive) with it, even though a human and a tree have quite different styles of existence at their disposal. The simultaneous commonality and singularity of being, uniting us with and separating us from a tree, will be a nagging concern of Heidegger's philosophy.

To take part in the "primal scene" of facing a tree, we are enjoined to abandon many of our preconceptions about the chemical composition, biological makeup, cultural symbolism, or commonsense inconspicuousness of greenery. But how deceptive is the ease of standing in front of a growing being without any sort of projections and representations that make of it what it is not! Such a stance must be earned by those patient enough to accomplish a tremendous work of phenomenological reduction, putting aside their expectations about the tree. (Hence, the specification that the meeting is not "one of these 'ideas' buzzing in our heads.") From the dusty sarcophagus of a library, Heidegger's thought comes out into the field, or at least peers into the backyard, so as to encounter the tree in its own being. As Heidegger construes it, this move is not at all linear: it is not a progression patiently building on the labor of thinkers before him. On the contrary, it is a leap "out of the familiar realm of science and, as we shall see, out of the realm of philosophy"—a leap that lands "on that soil upon which we live and die, if we are honest with ourselves."[5] This soil is the material support we share with the tree.

Ironically, for all his snubbing of philosophical precedents, Heidegger is not the first philosopher who recommends that we *leap*. Before him, Kierkegaard famously wrote about his own "leap of faith," and Nietzsche endorsed a thinking that leapt and danced. It is true that the Heideggerian leap does not land in the abyss of faith, much less in a Dionysian orgy of "joyful wisdom." Sober through and through, it remains under the influence of a third philosopher, Edmund Husserl, who called for a return "to the things themselves." Is the apple tree one of those things? Lest we rush to unwarranted conclusions, to label the tree *real* and Heidegger's approach *realism* is to fall prey to a grave misunderstanding. "Reality," derived from the Latin word for the thing (*res*), is a coy construct that obfuscates realism's allegiance to and origination from metaphysical thought. But what exactly is the problem with the metaphysical tradition? Why does it not warrant our standing on the soil, whereon we live and die and wherein the apple tree is rooted?

Heidegger's version of the history of metaphysics is a story of failed attempts to name (interpret, understand) being. We can see this quite plainly if only we leaf through our intellectual herbarium, registering how each thinker disappointed this humblest of expectations and, consequently, was prevented from facing the tree as tree.

After Plato called being *eidos* (Idea), he located truth in the Idea of the tree, rather than in the trees themselves, and prioritized other Ideas, such as that of beauty, over that of the tree. Aristotle conceived of being as the "unmoved mover" and, focusing on the problems of animation and entelechy, reduced plants to the poor bearers of vegetal souls. Plotinus converted the plant into the vegetable dimension of the One, his Parmenidian misnomer for being.

Augustine was still less interested in actual vegetation, preferring to treat it as the symbol of spiritual reality. For him, as for all medieval philosophers, perfect and self-sufficient being is none other than God, while plants are the least autonomous of all creatures. Avicenna slotted plants into an intricate hierarchy of souls and reduced them to their instrumental value (e.g., for a human diet or medicine) even as Maimonides turned them into hapless quasi-things bearing the full brunt of the Law.

Leibniz's word for being was "substance," the same as in the thought of Spinoza and Descartes; for him, plants were the most unabashedly material expressions of the one substance. Kant thought of being as the "thing-in-itself," beyond the limits of our practical and conceptual grasp. Within these limits, plants were reduced to scientifically knowable matter prepared for reproduction, to useful resources, and, at best, to the placeholders of universal beauty. Hegel called being "Spirit" and implied that actual plants had to lose their immediate biological life—to be preserved as dry mementos or fermented into bread or wine, for instance— to be reborn into the glorious world of Spirit.

On each page of this intellectual herbarium the plants themselves are forlorn: they are supposed to point to a reality beyond themselves, a reality ranging from Ideas to Spirit. The forgetting of the growing trees, herbs, or flowers corresponds to and stems from the forgetting of being in the midst of attempts to name it. Our ethical failures—be they in relation to other human beings, animals, or plants—are the direct consequences of this forgetting that consistently drives us out of this world and away from the material ground of our lives, that commits us to a "higher" reality, and that devalues whatever or whoever surrounds us. Heidegger's ontology, locating being in the beings themselves, is therefore fundamental also in this important sense: it is the ground for the ethics of respecting beings *in their own being*.

The ethics of ontological respect lies outside the purview of the "familiar realm of science," which is blind to an apple *as* apple, a being in its being. The negative reference to science holds a clue as to why Heidegger elected this particular tree and its fruit as an example. Newton's apple might have hit the scientist on the head, but, instead of relating to it in its singularity, Sir Isaac dissolved the fruit in a mathematically configured law of physics. In *Zollikon*, his last seminar, Heidegger himself speaks of Galileo, who conducted experiments with the simultaneous falls of an apple and a melon from the same height. Galileo, he says, "disregarded the tree, the apple, and the ground in observing the fall of the apple. He saw only a point of mass falling." Indeed, "this forced him to abstract from everything else, that is, from qualities—for instance, from the fact that an apple is an apple, this is a tree, and this is a meadow." The object of his interest "was neither in the apple, nor in the tree from which it fell, but only in the measurable distance of the fall."[6]

The tendency of modern science to see in objects and processes, in space and time, concrete expressions of mathematical or mathematizable principles is nothing new. As I have just mentioned, the metaphysical history of philosophy viewed both beings and events as the dispensable and usually distorted reflections, expressions, or signs pointing toward a higher, ideal, and true reality. Already for the Pythagoreans that reality was numerical, as all material entities were the materializations of numbers. Although modern science is (typically) not in the business of speculating about the question of origins, it also translates beings into quantities, neglecting, as Heidegger complains, their qualities, such as the sweetness of an apple, which we can only experience by biting into it. It has no notion of a unique place, whose atmosphere is ineluctably colored by the moods, memories, and associations of those who inhabit or pass through it. Denied the heterogeneity of places, science leaves us with physical space, which is an empty grid indifferently occupied by a human, a tree, or a house, as so many points that can be mapped onto it. Modern scientific rationality is but an extreme version of the logic subtending Western metaphysics.

Savvy readers will object that Heidegger's critique of science is in dire need of correction, insofar as the theory of relativity and the non-Euclidean conceptions of geometry and of space are concerned. Granted: in contemporary physics, it is not a matter of indifference which body occupies a portion of space, since its force field warps what we used to think of as an empty undifferentiated grid. And this is not to mention the issue of black holes that infinitely slow down the passage of time for an object approaching their rim, subatomic physics with laws of its own, or the threshold beyond which space and time virtually merge, forming a space-time continuum. These corrections notwithstanding, Heidegger's basic point is still valid: science, much of philosophy, and our common sense are rarely (if ever) satisfied with the given as given or with beings as beings. We seem compelled to add something else to the given—its Idea, substance, thingness—or to subtract something from it—its perishable body, materiality, finitude—or, more often than not, to perform both operations at the same time. An apple is never just an apple: it is a fruit handed by Eve to Adam in the Garden of Eden; a conjunction of vitamins, carbohydrates, and acids holding a determinate number of calories; a mass falling from the height of the branch, on which it has ripened, and interacting with the mass of the earth through the planet's gravitational field . . .

All this needs to be dropped overboard like unnecessarily heavy luggage, excoriated from the realm of thinking *after* metaphysical philosophy, which, according to Heidegger, exhausted and completed itself in the Nietzschean inversion of Platonism. But what Heidegger prescribes is easier said than done since even our perceptions (say, of an apple) are tainted with the scientific, imaginary, or conceptual interpretations that have been accruing in human cultures for millennia. If Plato beseeched us to awaken to the radiance of Ideas from the apparent certainties of physical reality as though from a nightmare, Heidegger asks us to awaken from this very awakening, so that we could meet beings—whether human or not—for the first time on their own and our turf, in the sphere of finite existence. The apple that fell on Newton's head did not interrupt his slumber but only deepened it. Awakening would be accepting the apple and the apple tree just as they are. For all the buzz around the Enlightenment, we are still sound asleep: we do not yet know—or perhaps we had once known and have now forgotten—the meaning of the assertion "being is" or "an apple tree is."[7] That is why Heidegger takes the task of ontological *anamnesis* (literally, un-forgetting) upon himself. It remains to be seen how his interpretation of the meaning of being bodes for plants.

The Blossoming of Being

The apple tree, in front of which we are still standing, is at the most beautiful juncture of its reproductive cycle; it is blossoming. Why does Heidegger point this out? Did he pen these lines at the height of spring, envisioning a renewal of philosophy that would parallel that of organic nature after a long period of wintery torpor? Did he want to highlight the still unaccomplished promise of the apple tree, its blossoms still not metamorphosed into fruits? This promise would bring the tree even closer to us, who are facing it, since we, humans, are made of the nonactualized possibilities that grant us our future. (In the order of existence, "higher than actuality stands possibility," Heidegger writes in his magnum opus, *Being and Time*.)[8] Or, is something else afoot here?

The answer is buried in the second part of *What Is Called Thinking?*, many pages after the initial encounter with the blossoming apple tree. Using it as a heuristic device, Heidegger separates the meaning of "blossoming" as "the given something that is blossoming—the rosebush or apple tree," on the one hand, and "the act of blossoming," on the other.[9] "Blossoming," in line with other participles or English gerunds, boasts a substantive and a dynamic dimension. It signifies a blossoming something (a noun) and the blossoming *of* something (a verb). Heidegger's point is that the same ambiguity haunts the word "being," which "means something in being, and the act of being."[10] The tragedy is that, in regards to being, we have collectively repressed its active sense as a verb. Just as there are no blossoming things without the act of blossoming, so there are no beings without the exercise of being. And just as the process of blossoming is nothing separate from the blossoming trees and flowers, so the process of being cannot come detached from the beings themselves. To retrieve "being" as a verb, Heidegger implies, we must undertake yet another reduction—that of beings to their own being, countering centuries of forgetting this most basic of ontological categories. The thorny path toward such retrieval meanders through unmistakably vegetal imagery; blossoming, for example, gathers into itself the entire question of ontico-ontological difference (the difference between beings and their being).

An exceptionally perceptive and original reader of the Greeks, Heidegger could not have been unaware of the etymological and conceptual linkages of *phuton* and *phusis*, the plant and nature. *Phusis* refers to "that which arises,"[11] reminiscent of vegetal germination; it is the name for "the event of standing forth, arising from the concealed,"[12] alluding to a plant growing from its roots hidden in the earth; and it encompasses all of being as "what flourishes on its own, in no way compelled."[13] Given this rich sense of nature, the plant should have been interpreted not as a part of its total growth but as a being that concentrates in itself (if only potentially) all natural existence. What is more, in light of Heidegger's ontological conception of *phusis* as one of the ancient words for "being," the plant would stand for a being that comes closest to the activity of being as such: flourishing, arising from the concealed, and so on. So conceived, nature is the common "ground of beings,"[14] which is also the case of the plant, whose principle of vitality potentiates the existence of all other living creatures.

The vegetative basis of human existence is apparent in the architectonics of *Being and Time*. Richard McDonough, to name but one commentator, attributes this connection to Heidegger's organicism, with its "ideology of plantlike rootedness in the cultural soil," "plantlike submission to its [Dasein's: human being's] world," and "plantlike lack of substantial center."[15] For a large part of our existence, we vegetate, "go with the flow," sleepwalk through life without as much as questioning the everyday concerns we pursue or thinking about the inevitability of our deaths. Heidegger sees the hustle and bustle of activity, into which we plunge and which we call "life," as an imperfect escape from the thought of mortality. We are dispersed in the world through everything we pursue in it, precisely because we (unconsciously) desire to flee from the terrifying and unrepresentable center of our existence—the future event of our death. But this is where the analogy with plant life crumbles. While dispersion in the world is one of the possibilities proper to humans, who occasionally glimpse and recoil from the terrifying center of finite existence, it is the destiny of plants that are necessarily decentered and that are exposed to the elements in a manner that animals and humans are not. The equation of cultural "soil" to the earth, wherein plants are rooted, is fallacious. And human and vegetal acts of "blossoming" are not of the same order.

In his 1955 memorial address celebrating the 175th birthday of the composer Conradin Krauzer, Heidegger confirms the assumption that the works of human genius would have not come to fruition were it not for the artist's and thinker's rootedness in the cultural soil that feeds their creativity. He cites with approval Johann Peter Hebel's aphorism, "We are plants which—whether we like to admit it to ourselves or not—must with our roots rise out of the earth in order to bloom in the ether and to bear fruit,"[16] and offers his own interpretation: "The poet means to say: For a truly joyous and salutary human work to flourish, man must be able to mount from the depth of his home ground up into the ether. Ether here means the free air of the high heavens, the open realm of the spirit."[17] A blooming talent is rooted in the home culture, much like the blossoming of actual flowers is dependent on the plant's rootedness in the earth. Conversely, estrangement, diaspora, exile, being-out-of-place—conditions that in Hebel's and Heidegger's Germany would have been associated with the Jews—correspond to vegetal uprooting and hamper the flourishing of human works.

The organicist metaphor apparently gives license to a nationalist and possibly racist cultural politics. The "home ground" evokes the total belonging of individuals to their milieu, their immersion in the dark and moist materiality of the cultural soil, full of biodegraded, decomposed, and recycled ideas, images, and symbols. We might say that plants can also feel at home *or not*, depending on the soil into which they are transplanted, the climate in which they are cultivated, and neighboring species that facilitate or impede their flourishing. For Heidegger, of course, the notion that plants are "at home" or "not at home" would sound ludicrous. To be at home or to be exiled from a familiar dwelling—those are the positive and negative modes of being appropriate to humans alone. These states presuppose both active and passive transactions with the world, to which we not only submit, as McDonough has it, but which we also construct. If, according to Heidegger's oft-cited classification, "the stone (material object) is *worldless*; the animal is *poor in world*; [and] man is *world-forming*,"[18] then the absence of plants from this hierarchy is symptomatic of their absolute abjection, an extreme "poverty-in-the-world" bordering on the worldnessness of a stone.

In a much later essay, "The Origin of the Work of Art," Heidegger retracts his prior statements on the poverty of plant and animal world. A harsher verdict is passed: they have none. "A stone is worldless. Plant and animal likewise have no world; but they belong to the covert throng of a surrounding into which they are linked."[19] Simply put, plants and animals are an integral part of the environment (*Umwelt:* literally, "the world around") teeming with living beings. Never mind the rich vitality of the "covert throng"; the biological life of plants and animals does not measure up to the subtlety of human existence, even as the intricacies of the environment pale against the background of the world. Why? Because, Heidegger avers, what is missing from this throng is language: "Where there is no language, as in the being of stone, plant, and animal, there is also no openness of what is, and consequently no openness either of that which is not and of the empty."[20] The world is forged out the environment through language, which plants and animals lack, despite the evidence for their capacity to communicate among themselves and with other living beings. The worldlessness of the stone is an upshot of its muteness; the abjection of plants a result of their seeming silence, shrouding the biochemical means of communication; the exclusion of animals an outcome of the nonsymbolic nature of their interactions.

A Plant's "Being-in-the-World"

How can we stand face to face with a blossoming apple tree and still accept the simple metaphysical trinity stone-animal-human (which, by the way, excludes plants) as valid? Convinced that the plant is closer to a worldless thing than to a being with a world of its own, we miss out on the challenge Heidegger sets in *The Fundamental Concepts of Metaphysics*, namely to make "the plant-character of the plant . . . originarily *accessible*."[21] The trick is that under no circumstances will we be at the point of retrieving the plant-character (i.e., the being) of plants *originarily* because only the plants themselves are privy to such access. All we can do is speculate on how plants subjectively form and are formed by their world, that is to say, what it is like to be a plant.

Heidegger himself gives us precious few guidelines for this exercise in philosophical imagination. Take wakefulness and sleep. "We do not say that the stone is asleep or awake," he notes. "Yet what about the plant? Here already we are uncertain. It is highly questionable whether the plant sleeps, precisely because it is questionable whether it is awake."[22] This uncertainty itself is significant. To say that a plant is awake would be to claim that it is, somehow, conscious. What largely determines vegetal activity above ground level is the plants' tending toward and photosynthetic processing of sunlight. We would expect that in the absence of light, plants would be asleep. And they are! Anyone who has seen the time-lapse footage contrasting plant movements in the light and in the dark is struck by the difference between their purpose-oriented waking movements and the dreamy and somewhat chaotic vacillations at night. Although the metabolism of plants does not slow down in darkness, their movements change in keeping with the Aristotelian understanding of sleep—which Heidegger, incidentally, admires—as *akinesia*, the languor of motion and of *aesthesis* (sensation).[23]

The second guideline for what it is like to be a plant has to do with its language. In a word, we might sum up Heidegger's take on nonhuman language as a "relation without articulation," that is, without the identification and naming of beings as beings: "It is a basic determination of Da-sein to be open for being claimed by the presence [being] of something. A plant is related to light as well, but it is not open to light *as* light. For it, the sun or the light is not present as sun or light."[24] The plant's ontological heedlessness to the very thing it depends upon does not invalidate its ontic, physical openness to light, toward which it turns with every inch of its green body. It is claimed by the presence of light without, in turn, grasping that which claims it *as light*. The plant's relation to luminosity is itself dark, unarticulated, and inarticulate. The vegetable autotroph harnesses solar radiation for its life process, converting it into chemical energy. The abject poverty of its world, if it has one, is attributable to a combination of its ontological indifference to being as being (light as light) and ontic openness to beings and their effects.

But what do creatures like ourselves, who cannot perform the simplest act of photosynthesis, know about openness to "light as light"? For us, light is always refracted through symbolic language, even when it blinds us, as a consequence of having raised our gaze toward the sun. For the plant, the memory of light, stored at the cellular level, is the trace of light itself, ready to be retrieved and interpreted at any given moment, for instance, as a cue to the best blossoming time. The language of plants is by the same token the language of the things themselves, interpreted not in symbolic sequences but in spatial configurations. Plants actively establish relations of contiguity with other plants and with minerals, with sunlight, and with animals, participating in the chains of material interpretation that add up to life itself. They are both the living architects and the architectural marvels of the ecosystems they inhabit. That is their styling of the world. The medieval and early modern *natura naturans* ("nature naturing") and *labora laborans* ("the work working") are the two mutually complementary dimensions of the Heideggerian "the *world worlds*"[25] and "being is."

A work of art such as a Greek temple, Heidegger argues, affords us access to a world: "The temple-work, standing there, opens up a world and at the same time sets this world back again on earth, which itself only thus emerges as native ground.... The temple, in its standing there, first gives to things their look and to men their outlook on themselves."[26] Couldn't we say exactly the same about a tree that, like the Greek temple, gives the earth itself its look (this is what we call "landscape") or manifests the ferocity of a storm raging above it and causing its branches to creak and bend? The "look" the temple and the tree bestow upon other beings is nothing other than Plato's Idea, *eidos*, brought down to earth, phenomenalized, made visible, and converted into a nontranscendental condition for visibility. The worlds of nature and art, *phusis* and *technē*, become available to a discerning gaze starting from the magnificent tree or the building that integrates parts of the environment into a coherent whole ready for interpretation. The tree and the temple gather the elements that surround them into the unity and unicity of place. Not related *to themselves*, they make all other relations possible. They do not open the world by speaking in the sense we usually attribute to the word—naming, referring to this as that, considering light as light—but by spurring a network of material, spatial references underlying the formality of symbolic language.

The deficiency Heidegger diagnoses in a plant's comportment toward light migrates into his account of an animal's engagements with a plant. Or, better, with parts of a plant, seeing that no animal is in a position to form the idea of it as a whole with its above- *and* below-ground portions included. We will not be shocked to learn that the part of a plant Heidegger himself favors is the blossom:

> In sucking at the blossom the bee does *not comport itself* toward the blossom *as something present or not present*.... This is not to say that something like a directedness toward scent and honey, *a relation toward*..., does not belong to behavior, but there is no recognitive self-directing toward these things. More precisely, there is *no apprehending* of honey *as* something present, but rather a peculiar captivation, which is indeed related to the honey. The drive is captivated.[27]

In their turning toward the sun, the leaf and the flower do not objectify the light they receive in abundance; the bee that instinctually flies toward a blossom does not perceive it as an object ("something present or not present"). It is not that phenomenological intentionality is entirely irrelevant to animal drivenness: "directedness toward" and "relation toward" name an intentional comportment, at least in the case of a bee attracted to a blossom. The missing piece that renders animal (and, even more so, vegetable) intentionality defective is "recognitive self-directing" or directedness toward oneself in the course of striving toward an external target. The captivation of the drive is peculiar because the behavior it either stimulates or inhibits is oriented wholly outward. A bee returns to its hive from the field, but it can't return to itself, remaining imprisoned, as it were, in exteriority.

For the sake of contextualization, I should mention that Heidegger, among many other twentieth-century philosophers, relied heavily on the writings of an Estonian biologist, Jacob von Uexküll, who enunciated his theory of *Umwelt* (the surrounding world or environment) in *A Foray Into the Worlds of Animals and Humans*. The pivotal idea of this monograph, later on elaborated by the contemporary German philosopher Peter Sloterdijk in his series of books *Spheres*,[28] is that every animal finds itself in the middle of a distinct world of things and processes holding some degree of significance for it. In fact, a world is this very circle of practical significations, or, as Heidegger puts it, an "encircling ring."[29] Some of the rings partially overlap, when the same things prove to be equally vital for different kinds of animals; others barely touch. But the crux of the matter is that von Uexküll's plants are never the centers of their own circles of significance, or *Umwelten*, but represent green backgrounds for the habitats of animals and humans. The same holds for Heidegger's work. In the interactions of biological agents, the "woodworm, for example, which bores into the bark of the oak tree is encircled by *its own* specific ring. But the woodworm itself . . . finds itself in turn within the ring encircling the woodpecker as it looks for the worm. And this woodpecker finds itself in all this within a ring encircling the squirrel, which startles it as it works."[30] Not meriting circles of their own, the oak tree and the blossom that attracts a honeybee are the material supports for the various overlapping rings of life. At best, they are the scattered points within, outside, or on the circumference of animal and human spheres of activity.

The human ring, in accordance with this logic, is the widest because of its ontological slant, that is, because it swallows up "what is" in its totality. It is open to the greatest number of beings and to being as a whole. In illustrating this thesis, Heidegger chooses to contrast the human not to its animal other but to a plant "which has in common with man the fact that it is alive. But the plant, in its living being, is completely confined within itself, dull, without relation to anything else that we call 'revealed.' "[31] Everything pivots, then, on (1) the denegation of a vegetal world qua world and (2) on creating the gradations of dis-closure within the region of life. Gone are the days when, in the course *Phe-nomenological Interpretations of Aristotle*, Heidegger drafted the equation "*Leben = Dasein*," "Life = Existence."[32] The German thinker's subsequent philosophical itinerary will evince a steady narrowing down of existence to a peculiar mode of life temporally related to itself and living in antici-pation (whether avowed or not) of its death. Only a finite living creature advanced enough to look its death in the face will earn the appellation "Dasein." But, if the fundamental concepts of metaphysics are "world, finitude, and solitude," as the title of Heidegger's 1929–1930 lecture course specifies, then plants, excluded from all three notions at once, are thereby expelled from the purview of metaphysics for good.

Do Plants Die?

With several critical interjections in the mix, we have accompanied the case Heidegger had made against the thinking of plants as beings inhab-iting a world of their own. The argument that plants are never alone is, perhaps, more forthright: both their openness to the inorganic world and their largely nonindividualized growths, often making it difficult to dis-tinguish singular plants from plant communities, point in the direction of their nonsolitary existence. But isn't it quite absurd to say that plants do not belong under the rubric of finitude? In short, don't they, like all other creatures, die?

First, sifting through biological data, we are struck by the fact that the lifespan of plants is far from uniform. From seasonal pea vines to centuries-old oaks and olive trees, it varies so tremendously that the distinction between the annual and the perennial plants overflows the quantitative difference between months, years, and centuries and plugs directly into the ontological register of the plants' being. Second, as the author of *In Praise of Plants* recaps,[33] when plants do die, they often don't "pass away" in their entirety, the way an animal organism does. Branches of the same tree may continue to thrive while others have dried up and rotted away, a new offshoot may germinate from the roots of an already hollowed trunk, and so forth.

Keeping in mind the pitfalls of such generalizations, the conclusion is that death, for plants, does not carry with it the same finality as it does for animals and humans. For the latter, the moment of death is negatively integrating, as it befalls and nullifies our entire being, negates our "temporal stretching" between the past and the future, and is experienced as a possibility that is our ownmost, nonrelational, and not to be outstripped.[34] In the plant kingdom, however, death is an event that neither integrates vegetable being (which is decentralized and nonorganismic) nor necessarily spells out the end of its life. Difficult as it might be for us to comprehend this, it is an event that can, in some cases, be overcome, survived, and perhaps even made useful for further proliferation and growth. And things get still more complicated in light of the blurry boundaries between "individual" growth and asexual reproduction (e.g., apple trees propagated by grafting), thanks to which plant communities can live virtually indefinitely.

Among the three metaphysical concepts Heidegger has singled out, finitude stands out as the one that gives meaning to the other two. Radical individuation is accomplished in the face of death, which cannot be shared with anyone else and before which Dasein is solitary. Our being-in-the-world is, simultaneously, disturbed by the thought of mortality and functions as a diversion from the intolerable anticipation of death. All that we deemed significant fades in comparison to this singular event, producing such an intense state of anomie that we flee back to the world, with its mundane concerns, from the traumatic face-to-face with our death. And so, if finitude is subtracted from the list of metaphysical keywords, then the rest of these are immediately invalidated. That is why the question of animal and plant mortality is so pressing.

The issue at hand is not finitude as an objective fact but the relation of finite creatures to the future of their death. Heidegger's unstated assumption in this respect is that plants and animals are finite beings, though they do not know it. As in the philosophy of Hegel, self-relation implies the negation of oneself (i.e., one's immediate, "natural" existence) and therefore an exercise in dying, imagining oneself already dead. Life is split into, on the one hand, mere life, as lived by plants, animals, and by humans for a large portion of our existence, and, on the other hand, a living oriented toward death, which we experience in but a few exceptional moments that strike us like lightning. As Heidegger puts it in his lectures on Nietzsche, "We . . . use 'life' only to designate beings that are vegetable or animal; we thereby differentiate human being from these other kinds, human being meaning something more and something other than mere 'life.' "[35] The razor-thin difference between mere life and authentic existence is death.

But there is yet another rift within life, separating its "mereness" from living with *logos* (reason, speech, voice). Transfixed by a text of Aristotle, Heidegger repeats after the great philosopher: "The distinguishing feature of man is the *logos*," which isolates the human from the broad field of life shared with plants and animals.[36] What compensates for the seeming banality of this claim is that, in Heidegger's thought, *logos* comes to occupy the structural place of death. Humans, unlike plants, have to decide on their own being-human by exercising *logos* and by facing up to their mortality; if they do not make this decision, Heidegger echoes Aristotle as much as the political thought of Carl Schmitt, they "would sink down to the level of a plant."[37] "Yet this decision," Heidegger continues, "also brings with it the step over into the realm of non-being, of the null, the contrary and the erroneous. Only where there is all this, and where it is conceived as necessary, only there is there also greatness, what is to be affirmed, the noble and the true. The animal and plant know neither the one nor the other—nor their opposition."[38] The fundamental decision on our own being anchors the parallel between mortality and *logos*, both of them elevating human beings above the fray of "mere life." The noble and the ignoble, the true and the false, matters of life and death are thus the exceptionally human preoccupations. When plants wither away, they do not die nobly (heroically) or ignobly, in error or in truth, while humans do, depending on whether their sovereign decision was to assume their humanness or not. But if, having renounced *logos*, human beings become ontologically indistinguishable from plants, then do they also become plantlike and wilt passively when they are too frightened to face up to their mortality?

Heidegger furnishes the answer in *Being and Time*. There, he lumps together plant and animal deaths in the phenomenon of "perishing," *Ableben*:

> The ending of that which lives we have called "perishing." Dasein too "has" its death, of the kind appropriate to anything that lives.... Dasein too can end without authentically dying, though on the other hand, *qua* Dasein, it does not simply perish. We designate this intermediate phenomenon as its "demise." Let the term "dying" stand for that way of being in which Dasein is towards its death.[39]

Plants and animals do not die; they perish. True dying is a being-to-ward-death, that is to say, a directedness toward, an intending of something paradoxically unintended and nonobjectifiable (death is never something present as an object for the one who dies). We will come back to this point in a moment. For now, suffice it to mention that inauthentic dying does not merge, conceptually or semantically, with perishing. In their demise, humans seem to pass away like plants or animals ("to die like a dog," as the saying goes), but they will never die the purely natural death of other living creatures. Even the most inauthentic death of Dasein is a negative modification of the possibility of dying authentically. When push comes to shove, Heidegger does not go as far as Aristotle, who thinks that humans can sink to the level of plants. Heidegger's inauthentic existence meets plants and animals halfway, in the "intermediate phenomenon" of demise that mimics their perishing despite the possibility of dying that remains ever present for it.

"Being-toward-death" is a term that obstinately clings to the phenomenological concept of intentionality as "directedness-toward." Nonetheless, that toward which one is when one is directed toward death is not a conventional *noema* (the intended target of the intending). Death is not an object; it is nothing present, and it is not given to comprehension as such. Haven't we already heard the same descriptions applied to the plant's nonarticulated relation to light? What if the human approach to death were virtually indistinguishable from the vegetal comportment toward light, with the proviso that plants do not have the option of avoiding that toward which they grow? Don't we, oddly enough, draw our individuality from the most personal, unshareable future of our death, much like a plant is individuated in its very being by sunlight?

Although the equation Life = Dasein has been discarded ("the ontology of Dasein ... is superordinate to the ontology of life": the former is "higher" precisely because it incorporates a relation to death),[40] its simple logic continues to disturb Heidegger's thought. Since Dasein shares mere life with other creatures, it also dies in a way "appropriate to anything that lives." Among the vast array of "anything that lives," in *Being and Time* Heidegger chooses to concentrate on plants. The point of comparison for the coming-to-an-end of a human is the ripening of the fruits, perhaps even the very apples that developed from the blossoms of the tree that grows in the philosopher's backyard. From the generality of an end appropriate to all finite beings, we are invited to descend to the particularity of human and vegetable endings that retrospectively illuminate the being of the two kinds of beings. Here is what Heidegger has to say on the subject:

> Ripening is the specific being of the fruit. It is also a kind of being of the "not-yet" (of unripeness); and, as such a kind of being it is formally analogous to Dasein, in that the latter, like the former, *is* in every case already its not-yet.... But even then, this does not signify that ripeness as an "end" and death as an "end" coincide with regard to their ontological structure as ends. With ripeness, the fruit *fulfills* itself. But is the death at which Dasein arrives, a fulfillment in this sense?... For the most part, Dasein ends in unfulfillment.[41]

Whereas, having delivered ripe fruits, a plant lives up to its promise, the human coming-to-an-end is always a disappointment and a nonfulfillment, because at the hour of death countless existential possibilities are still unrealized. Heidegger keeps the Aristotelian teleology of nature, progressing from latent potentialities to their actualization, intact for all merely living beings, save for Dasein. As a consequence of his selective appropriation of Aristotle, the vis-à-vis with a blossoming apple tree comes to an impasse not because the plant and we are separated in space but because the two temporalities, the vegetal and the human, do not intersect. The future of possibilities is distinct from that of actualized potentialities: the "not-yet" of a plant is foreign to that of a human.

If we neither live nor die as plants do, what permits us to stand face to face with them? An anthropocentric projection of human individuality (a face) onto a faceless living being? Or, conversely, a transposition of plantness onto certain aspects of human existence?

Returning to *What Is Called Thinking?* will allow us to find out what being face to face with a blossoming apple tree conceals. Right before the episode with which this chapter commenced, Heidegger offered his take on the Greek *eidos*. Earlier in the chapter, we took *eidos* to mean "the look of things." As Heidegger elaborates, "The word 'idea' comes from the Greek *eido* which means to see, face, meet, be face-to-face."[42] Clearly, the tree in the backyard is not one of those ideas swarming in our minds. But standing face to face with a tree is an idea in the more original sense of the word! Faithful to his critique of Nietzsche, Heidegger does not wish to "overturn" Platonism, only to locate the earthly in *eidos* itself. All along, he says between the lines, the world of Ideas has been not above us but right in front of our eyes; it is made apparent every time we find ourselves face to face with beings, because *eidos* is their look or face. A blossoming tree, devoid of anything resembling a human face, has an eidetic one, the outlines of which come through when we stand next to it, taking care not to project any other representations onto its luxuriant blossoms. A philosophical encounter with the tree, on the ground wherein it is rooted, demands phenomenological attention to the way it looks. But, above all, this rendezvous symbolizes the end of an era known as "metaphysical."

11

DERRIDA'S SUNFLOWERS

Three Scenes of Reading Plants

Scene 1. Seventeen-year-old Jackie is seated on a bench in Algiers's La-ferrière Square immersed in the "ecstatic bedazzlement" of reading Jean-Paul Sartre's *Nausea*. At times, he would tear his gaze from the book, raising his "eyes toward the roots, the bushes of flowers or the luxuriant plants, as if to verify the too-much of existence, but also with intense movements of 'literary' identification: how to write like that and, above all, not write like that?"[1] [Press the *pause* button . . .]

This scene is full of mirrors. On the one hand, the excess of human existence is reflected in the luxuriance of vegetable growth, as ecstatically bedazzling as the book and its subject matter. On the other hand, the young Jackie literally identifies with and instantly rebels against the style of the French *maître*. The teenager reads two things at once: the text composed by Sartre and the world of plants, which supplements the existential insights of *Nausea*. The Book of Nature and a book of philosophical literature absorb him, vying for his attention, which is, as always, torn between two objects and thus, at the height of its concentration, slips into distraction. Despite Jackie's impression that he has found a confirmation of existential excess in the exuberance of plants, to read one of these is to neglect, if only for a split second, the other. It is impossible to establish an absolute correspondence between the terms in a comparison, brought together, here and elsewhere, by a fictional "as if" ("as if to verify"). The process of verification, aiming at verity, is fraught. The mirror is broken, even when it seems to be reflecting most faithfully.

Come think of it, the mirroring effect is more than double. Besides Sartre's text, the existence of plants, and the reader on the bench, there is also Jacques Derrida who retrospectively reflects on the episode and we, the readers of another book, namely *Negotiations*, with its flashbacks to the time in Algiers. Reflection—spatial and temporal, physical and intellectual—both separates and interrelates the reflecting and the reflected. The marginal, auxiliary, contextual ramifications of the reading scene parachute us right into the thickets of deconstruction.

Not all the mirrors are set up on the same level, though. The quasi-cinematic sequence, commencing with the traveling shot of the gaze, reveals that the reader of *Nausea*, who looks up to and at the same time distances himself from Sartre, also looks up to plants. Counterintuitively, he raises his eyes to the *roots* of the square's lush vegetation. A position at once humble and subversive, this is the deconstructive stance par excellence. To assume it is to underlie and undercut what is deconstructed, not by taking the place of the foundation, of the ground or of the soil that sustains concepts and systems of thought, but by pointing out how the foundation destabilizes itself all by itself and thus becomes unfounded, abyssal. Such is, no doubt, also the preferred standpoint of the poet Francis Ponge, who was the subject of a little-known book by Derrida:[2] to place oneself in one's writing practice a little below the surface and, from there, to stretch up and down simultaneously.[3] In a word, to be transmuted into a germinating seed of sense.

Derrida would agree to turn himself—his work, his words, or his neither-words-nor-concepts (e.g., *différance*)—into seeds solely on the condition that the passage from sowing to germination is not assured. Declining a dutiful insemination of meaning, deconstruction disseminates it, "spills" it "in advance,"[4] mischievously spreads it for nothing, without the expectation of any yields or returns. In most cases, Derrida will encrypt at least as much as he makes appear in his writing, and, sometimes, he will conceal bits of meaning in the very moment of disclosing it. This strategy, which we might mistake for capricious extravagance, elucidates the routine operation of any text, where countless semantic morsels are hidden, including from the author herself. Deconstruction draws on the unconscious stratum of textuality, where words, phonemes, and expressions unexpectedly and surreptitiously work as shibboleths, restricted passwords, or codes. Their sense is not merely buried in the semantic ground like a seed or a root, whose hiddenness facilitates the rest of plant growth. It is (or it could be) lost on us, irretrievably. To the excess of existence and of vegetal growth in the Algiers episode we must add the excess of meaning that borders on meaninglessness. [Hit the *fast forward* button, and on to the 1970s!]

Scene 2. J. D. is composing missives to an anonymous lover. These half-ironic, half-autobiographical letters will be compiled in the "Envois" section of *The Postcard*. For now, he is impatient, not even seated as he was [*rewind!*] on a bench in Laferrière Square. Instead, he writes, "here I am again standing up to write to you . . . , so often standing, incapable of waiting—and I do it like an animal, and even standing against a tree sometimes."[5] He is no longer identifying with another author but compares himself to an animal that leaves its marks in the vicinity of a tree. Plant matter furnishes ready support for the writing procedure: still living, it props up the writer's bodily frame; already dead and recycled into a postcard, it receives the blows of his pen. The animal is impatient, while the plant—the tree and the paper—endures everything with forbearance. Edgy, J. D. will exploit this patience of the plant.

In one of the missives, he mocks the hypersymbolic "language of plants," charging the word "the sunflower," *le tournesol*, with a surplus of meaning: "When are you coming back? I will call Sunday at the latest. If you are not there, leave them a message. Leave, for example, so that they won't understand a thing, as in the Resistance, a sentence with 'sunflower' to signify that you prefer that I come, without sunflower for the opposite."[6] A tiny image or a mirror of the sun, the sunflower is not itself, or, at least, it does not signify itself. As a cipher for something else altogether, it is overcoded, hypersymbolized, overwritten with an alien meaning. Too-much of existence = too-much of sense. Derrida does not object to this potentially damaging excess. There is no proper meaning that would belong to the sunflower alone, all by itself, just as there is no completely idiosyncratic meaning of the human. [We are replaying the previous scene backward, now lowering our gazes from the plant to the human, still in an attempt to capture the exuberance of existence.]

Why the sunflower? We will never know for sure, but conceivably the choice of the plant has to do with its movement of turning, or returning, toward the sun, as indicated in the French word *tournesol*. If so, then who is the sun and who the sunflower? Assuming that the beloved is meant to return, is she the *tournesol* vis-à-vis the solar author of these lines? Or is he the one searching for her, as the flower scans the sky for sunlight? The "sentence with 'sunflower'" is, after all, used "to signify that you prefer that I come." Who mirrors or follows whom? The text itself prohibits a precise determination of the place of the sun and of the flower, the origin of life and the plant that tracks the movement of the celestial body across the horizon. We cannot dispel this indeterminacy with the help of better, more accurate explanations. It is here to stay, interfering with the fixed positions allotted to the organic and the inorganic, the earthly and the heavenly, the lover and the beloved, "you" and "I" in the scheme of Western metaphysics.

J. D.'s sunflower is more than a symbol; it is, like Augustine's pear, the symbol of a symbol. "Without sunflower for the opposite" means "without a codeword for the opposite," that is, for the message that would convey the beloved's preference that the lover not arrive. Undecidability coincides with a resolute and unconditional "yes" to the other, an affirmation uncoupled from the possibility of negation. What better figure for a "yes" that knows no "no" than a sunflower, a plant, which, in contrast to an animal, does not oppose its inorganic other (sunlight) but loyally follows it? If unconditional and unconditionally affirmative hospitality is what we are after, then our identification with an animal standing against a tree will not do. We would need to entrust our subjectivity to that very tree or to the sunflower. Especially because the sunflower has already appropriated our humanness for itself, well in advance of our interference with it. How so? [Skip to the next scene.]

Scene 3. Jacques Derrida in a vast field of sunflowers. He is (standing or sitting?) in the middle of a virtual field, where the flowers of rhetoric are growing. And, to shake off the age-old temptation of gazing directly at the sun, he is staring at its reflection in the sunflowers: "Unceasingly, unwillingly, we have been carried along by the movement which brings the sun to turn in metaphor; or have been attracted by what turned the philosophical metaphor toward the sun. Is not this flower of rhetoric (like) a sunflower? That is—but this is not exactly a synonym—analogous to a heliotrope?"[7] Since Plato's Sun/Good analogy, philosophy has felt the seduction of the light (though not of the warmth) emitted by the celestial body, to which it turned like a heliotrope—a sunflower, for instance. The philosophical emphasis on the clarity and distinctness of ideas recycled the most obvious effects of sunlight, causing "the sun to turn in metaphor," even as "the philosophical metaphor [turned] toward the sun." At its transcendentally purest, philosophy could not avoid metaphoricity, just as the metaphor did not chart an escape route from philosophy but was the very thing that threw us into the midst of philosophical discourse.

Given the precedents, we are already used to the fact that the sunflower is a codeword for something else [*rewind*, once more]. In the first place, it is associated with heliotropism, with which it does not entirely coincide, as Jacques Derrida admits. If sunflower "is not exactly a synonym" of heliotrope, this is because it is but one among many kinds of flowers and leaves that track the movements of the sun. Its semantic relation to other heliotropes is a synecdoche, a rhetorical device whereby a part stands in for the whole. Add into the mix the insight that our thinking and language are also heliotropic, and you will see how the sunflower represents us, before we represent it. Its turning toward the sun anticipates our turning: we are the mimes of flowers!

In the second place, "sunflower," as the synecdoche of heliotropism, is a watchword for metaphoricity, or, as I have written above, the symbol of a symbol. As such, it imbibes that which is properly human: "Thus, metaphor means heliotrope, both a movement turned toward the sun and the turning movement of the sun."[8] On the margins of philosophy, in the virtual field of meaning, Jacques Derrida *reads through* the sunflowers, rather than *reading them*. Standing in for heliotropism or for metaphor, they stand out from the field of beings at the price of their singularity, stripped of the self-generated and lived sense of their vegetable existence. The virtualization of the world in chains of meaning and representation seems to dispense with the actual growing flowers. And, indeed, the most common misinterpretation of the deconstructive *il n'y a pas de hors-texte*, "there is no outside-text"[9]—often erroneously translated as "there is nothing outside the text"—levels this very accusation.

Before drawing the curtain on the three scenes of reading, let us rid ourselves of the assumption that the virtual is the antithesis of the real, especially in deconstructive discourse. The "real" seventeen-year-old Jackie on a bench in Algiers is on the same footing with the "virtual" Jacques Derrida roaming semantic fields and with the author of *The Postcard*, J. D., who purposefully interlaces what we would call "fact" and "fiction." I can access the experiences of my teenage self only through memory and language—the same mediations that will bring my fictional personae to life. Kant, as we remember, found it pointless to talk about the tulip itself, outside our theoretical, practical, or aesthetic approaches to it. Derrida carries this Kantian impulse further, showing the impossibility of referring to a flower (or to oneself) outside of language. Even mutely pointing to a referent is a kind of signification, according to one of his predecessors, Edmund Husserl.

Our virtual intellectual herbarium is itself a supplement to the real gardens, fields, and forests where plants grow. But the supplement in deconstruction always comes first, before what it supplements. It is on the basis of the prevailing idea of the plant and its significance (or insignificance) on the scale of beings that the so-called natural resources are managed and agriculture is organized on the industrial model. To change these practices we would first need to alter the supplementary notion of the plant.

Virtualized, a heliotrope "can always become a dried flower in a book"—in preparation for its filing in a herbarium. "There is," Derrida continues, "absent from every garden, a dried flower in a book."[10] This very absence, which makes every garden what it is, is what we have been cataloging, from Plato onward.

Plastic Plants, Wasted Seeds, and Other Useless Artifacts

In addition to the virtual flowers of rhetoric and the actual sunflowers, artificial garlands are sometimes indistinguishable from the floral arrangements they imitate. The topic of artificial flowers pops up in Derrida's strangest, most uncanny book, *Glas*, where, mixed with long quotes from letters, dictionary definitions, and other marginalia, we encounter commentaries on the philosophy of Hegel in the left-hand column of the text and meditations on the literary output of Jean Genet in the right-hand column. If we glean some of the references to natural and artificial flowers from the "Genet" side of the book, we will obtain the following:

[The flowers of rhetoric] quickly begin to resemble those mortuary wreaths [*couronnes*] that are thrown over the walls of the cemetery. These flowers are neither artificial nor entirely natural. Why say "flowers of rhetoric"? And what would the flower be when it becomes merely one of the "flowers of rhetoric"?[11]

The most natural flowers are the most artificial, like the virginity of the Holy Virgin.[12]

The effort to *render* the flower can only fail.... The flower is nothing, never takes place because it is never natural or artificial. It has no assignable border, no fixed perianth, no being-wreathed.[13]

The cult function of natural flowers lends them an air of artifice. Funerary wreaths, flowers used for the worship of Virgin Mary, and, in a not-so-different sense, the flowers of rhetoric are withdrawn from their immediately pragmatic use within the chains of signification or food supply. Suspended between nature and culture, they exemplify the workings of *différance*—a neologism that combines the effects of differing and deferring as well as the different and the deferred. In this vein, culture "is" nature, deferred and different from itself. And vice versa. The flowers of *Glas* "are neither artificial nor entirely natural" because they are the flowers of *différance*, void of a fixed identity. That is why "the flower is nothing, never takes place": it takes place in what does not have a fixed place in the order of being, that is, in *différance*.

Unless they fulfill a cult function, flowers are either useless adornments (aesthetic objects) or the promises of fruit (the objects of future utility). For its part, deconstruction sides with aesthetic uselessness, on the condition that this playful inutility extends beyond the confines of the "critique of judgment" to the sphere of being (and nothingness) as a whole. As we have seen, reminiscing about Kant's tulip, Derrida has termed the critical untethering of uselessness and of the flower that symbolizes it "the *sans* of the pure cut," where the word *sans*, "without," is homophonous with *sang*, "blood," and shares affinities with *sens* (sense, meaning, direction).[14] Deconstruction goes further in that it untethers this untethering from aesthetics, disrupting the sense, meaning, and directionality assumed by Kantian philosophy. The flower is freed from its limited aesthetic freedom when it is extricated from the webs of identity. "It has no assignable border, no fixed perianth," declares the end of the critical project fixated on setting apart the different domains of human activity.

But the cult function of flowers never vanishes without a trace; it is, to use the language of high modernity, secularized. The key to Genet's flowers, adorning the beginning of *Glas*, is buried in the "Hegel" column at the end of the book. There, Derrida analyzes (though "analyzes" is not the right word; better, "writes around") Hegel's take on "flower religion," which "is innocent insofar as the war internal to animality is not yet unchained in it."[15] Why are flowers innocent, presumably like those who worship them?—Because

> the flower is neither an object nor a subject, neither a not-I nor an I.... Innocent to be sure, therefore not culpable, not guilty, but its innocence is declared only insofar as the flower is capable of culpability, culpable [*coupable*] of being able to become culpable, cuttable [*coupable*]. Among all these opposites, the essence of the flower appears in its disappearance, vacillates like all the representative mediations, but also excludes itself from the oppositional structure.... The flower at once cuts itself (off) by and from itself and abysses itself.[16]

The cult function of flowers is not restricted to the religious celebration of the Virgin Mary or to funerary arrangements. Flowers, and plants broadly speaking, are the instruments for the expiation of their nonexistent guilt (hence, of *our* guilt). Their culpability/cuttability, indicated in the same French word *coupable*, reinscribes them into the order of the Maimonidean *arbor sacra*, of the most naked life that can be terminated with impunity. The flower, like the plant it represents, is sacrificed to the continuation of human and animal lives; its essence "appears in its disappearance" as a mediation between the bud and the fruit, between the inorganic and the organic, between the innocent and the guilty, between the uselessly beautiful and the nourishing, between religious sacredness and mundane dietary concerns. But, more importantly, the flower and the plant are sacrificed for the purpose of expiating our guilt before the animals that humans have been exploiting and consuming for millennia now. Some of today's prohibitions of animal exploitation go hand in hand with the unrestricted instrumentalization of plants. No matter of how practical the context, an unethical engagement with vegetal life abides by the rules of sacrificial logic, itself predicated on the flower's culpability/cuttability.

At the crossroads of various oppositions, in which it does not participate ("excludes itself from the oppositional structure"), the flower is confirmed as the placeless place of *différance*. "Neither a not-I nor an I," it dislocates the conventional categories of ethics, for which a clear-cut distinction between subject and object is a must. The nonidentity of the flower is the first cut, thanks to which it differs from itself or defers its coincidence with itself, "cuts itself (off) by and from itself." The second cut, now initiated by a human hand, deepens the first, detaching the flower from its root, from the organic connection to the soil, from the world of nature, which has hitherto determined plant growth. In a brief period of time when a culled rose is still fresh and there are no signs of withering, one can easily conflate it with a plastic replica. The resemblance is more than merely formal or empirical. The "natural" flower is cut off from the process of reproduction, as well as from nutrition and growth. It is denaturalized, put in the service of culture as a symbol of love, grief, or gratitude. Or, perhaps, it is plucked gratuitously, for nothing, for no apparent reason, and thus transplanted into the "place of zero signification,"[17] i.e., *différance*, which makes signification possible.

So the flower is, at the same time, hypersymbolic and nonsignifying, overloaded with and empty of sense. As in the case of a metaphor, which is itself a heliotrope, its meaning should be prefaced by the French *plus de*: *plus de métaphore* conveys "more metaphor" and "no more metaphor." The affirmation of more X and no more X, disrespectful toward the most fundamental principles of formal logic, is consistent with the prelogical, if not the presemantic, nonprinciple of *différance*. Apropos of a plant, the indeterminacy haunting every sign and every thing is amplified, in that its status—subjective or objective?—remains enigmatic across the board of Western philosophy and, particularly, in the thinking of Hegel. As an object, it receives layers upon layers of significance, which we attribute to it; as a subject, it signifies itself and, therefore, keeps itself inaccessible and opaque in the face of our lived hermeneutic ventures. And the same goes for its classification as natural or artificial. If artificiality is taken literally, as the application of human skill or artistry, technique or technicity, then many plants we consider natural are also artificial. After countless generations of humanly controlled hybridization, grafting, and cultivation, plants that have all the appearance of naturalness are also, to a certain extent, artificial. They are at the epicenter of the unavoidable cross-contamination of nature and culture.

In the virtual field of textuality, which produces real effects, another sort of contamination occurs: the author's proper name mutates into a common noun normally attached to a flower. The author is Jean Genet, and the plant is a broom flower (in French, *genêt*). "Apparently, yielding to the Passion of Writing," writes Derrida, "Genet made himself into a flower. While tolling the *glas* (knell), he has put into the ground, with very great pomp, but also as a flower, his proper name."[18] Or, again: "Improper then is the flower name, the accent of the *genêt* that is hardly pronounced."[19] Derrida himself frequently plays with his name, inscribing it in words like "already," *déjà* (*Derrida J*acques) or in expressions such as "behind the curtain," *derrière le rideau* (homophonous with "Derrida") or *j'accepte* ("I accept," partly homophonous with "Jacques").[20] What is unique about the becoming-flower of a name is that the most human artifact is denaturalized, estranged from us, thanks to its renaturalization, its burial in the ground and flourishing in the shape of a flower. Although the funereal bell tolls for him, Genet does not die, or he dies and is resurrected in a broom flower. He spreads his name as one would spread seed, with the willingness to lose his human identity for the sake of a floral afterlife.

Needless to say, Derrida is extremely dissatisfied with this interpretation, which is why he begins it with the word "apparently." Literature, as much as communication, are not at the behest of information transmission, where the seeds of sense germinate in the exact way they were intended to. The message does not arrive, despite what appears to be its successful arrival—such is the message of *The Postcard*. To entrust a name (above all, one's proper name) to the unpredictable machinations of language, to bury it in the semantic soil, is to risk everything without any assurances of yields, let alone resurrection. Hence, Derrida's motto will be: "To plant seeds by 'dispersing' without the slightest hope left of arriving at one's ends."[21] At best, he will retain the melancholy hope that his name, his seed, or his writings would be "biodegradable,"[22] in other words, would dissolve into the cultural soil, shed their recognizable identity, and, staying buried in and as this soil, nourish the future of thinking and writing.

From the uselessness of a cut flower to the seed spilled or spread out-side the scheme of its calculated displacement in expectation of germi-nation, deconstruction coordinates a series of disruptions in the plant's reproductive cycle. It does this to mark a rift in the history of metaphys-ics between, on the one hand, a productivist approach to meaning and life and, on the other, a wasteful expenditure of both that no longer fits within this history.

Armed with transcendental guarantees, Plato and Hegel, each in his own way, engage in a calculated displacement of the seed. "*Plato* wants to emit. Seed, artificially, technically. . . . To sow the entire earth, to send the same fertile card to *everyone*."[23] Whether emitted or sown, released in an animal or a plant mode, Plato's seed is destined to everyone—a message of truth's universality, residing in the immortal realm of Ideas. Plato hides himself (and his seed) behind Socrates, who will carry out this act of a universal sowing of the universal. He dissimulates himself so as to find himself everywhere, in *everyone*: "Himself, he wants to issue seed . . . , he wants to sow [*semer*] the entire world, and the best lever at hand, look, is S., the sterile midwife."[24] In other words, Plato conceals his seed in the other (Socrates) in order to recover it in all the other others.

Hegel, too, disperses the seed only to gather whatever will issue from it: "The Life of the Concept is a necessity that, in *including* the disper-sion of the seed, in making that dispersion work to the profit of the Idea, *excludes* by the same token all loss and all haphazard productivity. . . . Seminal difference [is] thus repressed."[25] In the dialectical back-and-forth the identity of a being (say, a plant) is temporarily lost, so as, after its initial negation, to be recovered at a higher level (say, in human and animal nutrition). Difference is invariably included under the overar-ching umbrella of sameness; the seed is recuperated in a mature plant. Meaning is inseminated in Spirit that unfolds itself in history, not dis-seminated in the absolute loss of sense or in its haphazard, unpredictable semantic effects.

In *Margins of Philosophy* Derrida opposes the Platonic-Hegelian insem-ination of meaning to its dissemination in the dyad Nietzsche-Bataille.[26] At stake is a distinction between two kinds of heliotropes: the metaphys-ical sunflower and the postmetaphysical waste of solar, biotic, human, or other kinds of energy. For Friedrich Nietzsche, the massive appendage of purposiveness is the irrecoverable squandering of the will, in "that every purposive action is like the supposed purposiveness of the heat the sun gives off: the enormously greater part is squandered."[27] The sunflower tracking the sun and the thinking turned toward solar tropes register this unfathomable loss. Georges Bataille dubs such excessive expenditure without any returns "general economy," which he contrasts to the restricted economy of transactions based on the rules of reciprocity (give and take).[28] The energy a sunflower invests in the production of seeds is indeed exorbitant when measured against the new plants that will issue from it. Life—whether vegetable or human—is this immoderate waste. In the process of living we throw ourselves away, along with the products of our life-activity. Like plants that spread their pollen or seed, entrusting their future to blind chance. Thus, we have, "on the one hand, cultivation, agri-culture, knowledge, economy; on the other, art, enjoyment, and unreserved spending."[29] But the one hand acts with as well as against the other. The effectiveness of cultivation presupposes unreserved spending, random plant varieties, and seeds that will never germinate. Total control over the outcome is a hollow illusion.

Phytophallogocentrism

With a wink to the German philosopher Ludwig Klages, who came up with the term *logocentrism*, Derrida coined the word *phallogocentrism* to mark the confluence of two privileges: that accorded, in the Western tradition, to speech, logic, coming to light, or rationality (*logos*) and that bestowed upon the patriarchal or masculine manifestations of *logos*. Why, then, did we add the prefix *phyto-*, plant-, to this antilogic neologism?

One of the ideas behind phallogocentrism is that, worshipping the light of reason, thinkers salute its phallic erection. Already in the writings of Sigmund Freud, the sun's rising and setting symbolized male sexual excitation and the ejaculatory release of tension. The metaphorical sun of philosophy, similar to the one that shone over the British Empire, neither rises nor sets: it is the burning center of what Derrida calls "the metaphysics of presence"—"the exigent, powerful, systematic and irrepressible desire" for a "transcendental signified,"[30] that is, for what lies outside the chains of signification and embodies an atemporal truth (the Ideas, God, Reason itself, and so forth). The metaphysics of presence purged of shadows, lacunae, obscurities, or absences is the impossible erection of *logos* that maintains itself forever and that, on Derrida's reading, is the perverse fantasy of all Western philosophers.

The association of plants with solar phallocentrism harkens to the thought of Bataille. As he notes in "The Solar Anus," "Beings only die to be born, in the manner of phalluses that leave bodies in order to enter them. Plants rise in the direction of the sun and then collapse in the direction of the ground. Trees bristle the ground with a vast quantity of flower shafts raised up to the sun."[31] Heliotropism is an extreme form of phallocentrism, a plant's banding erect in the direction of the solar erection. And the sunflower is the most phytophallogocentric plant of all, in that it shamelessly mimics the phallic movements of the sun.

In Derrida's singular vocabulary, the essence of masculine sexuality subsumes, besides the sun and plants, the becoming-present in general, growing and appearing: "To come, glisten, glow, shine, appear, be present, grow (*phuein*): to band erect."[32] When, in coming to light, phenomena and vegetal growth display themselves, the exhibition of their presence carries unambiguous sexual overtones, albeit not those of feminine sexuality. The germination of a seed, coming to light from the dense opacity of the soil, is the synecdoche of all phenomenal appearances, driven by and imitating the phallic rays of light. Nature demonstrates itself as a gigantic phallus.

Regardless of all the suggestive phallic imagery, the banding-erect of phenomena and of plants is not altogether metaphysical. The shining of phenomena—their appearing before us—is finite, as it depends on the attention we dedicate to them. Presence is mixed with absence and death in phenomenology as much as in vegetal growth, which does not preclude decay. The moment *phyto-*, combining plants and growth, comes to supplement phallogocentrism, which in Derrida's texts forges an alliance with the vegetal, the whole erected structure of metaphysics collapses. Stated otherwise, plant life deconstructs the metaphysics of presence, forcing its eternally upright phallus to fall.

As always, deconstructive thought does not resort to an external critique of metaphysics but, rather, pulls on a thread that internally unravels the fabric of the deconstructed object. Although it represses death, absence, and nonappearance, the metaphysics of presence still (unconsciously) contains them in its deepest, darkest recesses. That is how two contradictory effects emanate from the same thing: erection is, in itself, a premonition of castration. "The phallic flower is cuttable-culpable. It is cut [*se coupe*: also "it cuts itself"], castrated, guillotined, decollated, unglued. . . . Flower, trance: the *simul* of erection and castration."[33] Whatever is present presents itself to the chance of passing away. The strength of presence is one and the same as its utter vulnerability. The culling of flowers, that is, of the sexual organs of plants, is made possible by their very erection. In eschewing the finality of death and in insisting on the purity of its timeless display, metaphysics castrates itself.

What about the Kantian cut tulip? Does it not illustrate the activity of critique, with its penchant for drawing up limits and hence cutting out what does not belong within the critically delimited sphere? If so, then critique is, in a certain sense, castration, de-banding the erection of an all-powerful reason. By the same clean stroke, the aesthetic cutting of the tulip off from the nutritive and reproductive processes inaugurates its freedom. We may surmise, then, that castration, anticipated in the fall of every erection, and, more generally, the deflation of metaphysics are liberating, insofar as they lighten the burden of safeguarding presence uncontaminated by absence. Along similar lines, the philosophical acceptance of finitude liberates the subject from the chimera of eternal life that happens elsewhere, beyond the world here-below. From the culled flower we learn that there is no life that does not contain the seeds of death.

While the deconstruction of *logos* in phallogocentrism is concerned with the cracks of absence in the façade of "pure presence," the deconstruction of patriarchy and masculine sexuality is focused on the fluidity of sexual identities. Signifying too much, the flower evokes phallogocentrism as well as its obverse: "Thus the flower (which equals castration, phallus, and so on) 'signifies'—again!—at least overlaps [with] virginity in general, the vagina, the clitoris, 'feminine sexuality,' matrilineal genealogy."[34] It is not that deconstruction, in consenting to the castration of the flower/*logos*, arrives at feminine sexuality by way of disavowal, equating it with the lack of phallus. Pure absence is as metaphysically inflected as the dream of pure presence. Steering clear of these extremes, Derrida suggests that the sexual significance of the flower is unspecifiable. It hinges on the "overlaps" of the phallus (and its castration) with the vagina and the clitoris, or, to put this differently, on the sexual version of *différance*. The more botanically inclined among us will immediately think of hermaphroditic plants, which incidentally include most flowering varieties, and certain species, such as *Arisaema japonica* and *Spinacea oleracea*, that can change their gender over time in what is known as "sequential hermaphroditism."[35] Is *logos* also—sequentially or simultaneously—hermaphroditic, its phallogocentrism notwithstanding?

To simplify a little, Derrida's response to this question is a resounding *yes!* Were deconstruction to substitute feminine sexuality for the default masculinity that has dominated Western thought, it would have reproduced the very same either-or structure that metaphysics prides itself on. Incomparably more persuasive is the argument that repressed femininity has always been at the bosom of phallogocentrism. In what guise or guises?

The autism of Occidental reason that listens and talks to itself alone is what Derrida calls "autoaffection," a quasi-masturbatory self-touching, endeavoring to exclude the other at any price.[36] "Hearing-one-self-speak," responsible for the formation of the soul in Aristotle and in Husserl, is the prototype of such autoaffection. But even the narcissistic self-touching of the psyche and of reasonable discourse is not isolated from their other. The instant the one (the One) gloriously tautological *logos* separates from itself, if only for the purpose of relating back to itself, otherness breaks through in the space of this separation. Its division, however temporary, signals its heteroaffection,[37] which, in the case of phallogocentrism, implies the irruption of feminine sexuality. A beautiful illustration of this inversion is the French *s'aimer*, which can mean in different contexts, "to love oneself," "to be loved," or "to love each other" and which, as the English translator of *The Postcard* Alan Bass emphasizes, sounds like *semer*—"to scatter," "to plant seeds."[38]

In the course of jealously guarding its immutability, ensconced in the transhistorical certainties of metaphysics, phallogocentrism has no other choice but to open unto its other. Much in the same fashion, if you try to hold air in your lungs and avoid breathing in or out, you will eventually exhale all the more forcefully, your respiratory tract exposed to the exteriority of the atmosphere. The flower touches itself—its petals touch each other—when it is closed in a bud. But, lo and behold, its time to blossom comes and it " 'blows [*éclôt*],' the petals part [*s'écartent*]."[39] It parts against itself, heteroaffects itself, delivers itself and its pollen to the outside. In botanical jargon, the parting of the petals is known as dehiscence, a *terminus technicus*, the meaning of which Derrida locates also outside the world of plants, invoking, for example, "the interminable *dehiscence* of the supplement (if we may be permitted to continue to garden this botanical metaphor)."[40] The flower deflowers itself at the peak of blossoming, and *logos* interrupts its own monologue in the middle of addressing itself to itself. Internally decentered, phytophallogocentrism falls apart into multiple outgrowths.

The Trouble with the Supplement and the Place of Plants

The marginalization of plants in Western philosophy makes them the perfect candidates for deconstruction, which is fond of pointing out the tacit centrality of the margins. Derrida uses the words *parergon* (what is beside the work, *ergon*) and *supplement* to describe the counterintuitive relation of the core to the periphery, reversing the order of priority so that what is outside, secondary, and inessential turns out to be the condition of possibility for the centerpiece it supplements.

Take, for example, the wooden frame in which Van Gogh's *Sunflowers* is encrusted. That is the classic *parergon*, superadded to a work of art. The frame has inner and outer edges—a thickness that leaves us uncertain as to where the work ends and the nonwork begins. Its borders are made of boards, of wood, which "better than stone ... names matter (*hylē* means wood). These questions of wood, of matter, of the frame, of the limit between inside and outside, must, somewhere in the margins, be constituted together."[41] "Somewhere in the margins," that is to say, in the world of plants. It is this world that is situated at "the limit between inside and outside" of life, that supplies the materials for the frame, and that influences the first philosophical enunciation of matter. The Aristotelian conception of matter and form, to which Derrida alludes, relies on the metaphor of a carpenter working on a piece of wood, giving it the intended shape, transforming it into a usable thing. The form works, whereas matter passively endures the saw, the rasp, and the chisel. The plants, in turn, are the matter of matter; they are what the wooden boards of the frame are made of. They are, therefore, doubly passive.

Derrida deconstructs this passivity of the frame, of matter, and of wood. In intimating that the frame works, he hints that matter and wood do so as well: "The frame labors [*travaille*] indeed. Place of labor, structurally bordered origin of surplus value, i.e., overflowed [*débordée*] on these two borders by what it overflows, it gives [*travaille*] indeed. Like wood. It creaks and cracks, breaks down and dislocates even as it cooperates in the production of the product."[42] The work of matter, wood, and the frame is, at the same time, support and resistance. In fact, matter is nothing but the difference between the resistance and the support that it gives. Through this circuitous path, we are led back to the Latin coinage, which we have already come across on several occasions: *natura naturans*, "nature naturing," as a corollary to *labora laborans*, "labor laboring." Plant life, likewise, is *natura naturans* not only in a passive relation to the outside elements but also as a continual shaping of its own world.

Be forewarned: the deconstructive paths will be as meandering as ever, and it is doubtful that they are worth pursuing with reference to the priority of plants and matter. The risk is high that, when the trappings of *parergon* and supplementarity are removed, only the foregone conclusions of common sense will remain. We have no need of high theory to realize that plants support life on earth or that, without matter, the formative drive would have been unable to put itself to work. Most likely, such is the fate of all deconstructive insights when they are *directly applied* to any given problem, losing, in the process, their playful and somewhat opaque style. But the style, too, is a supplement: though apparently insignificant, it shapes the content it stylizes. After all, in deconstruction, the supplementarity and parergonality of matter, wood, and the plants does not simply prioritize them over form or over animals but renders them more indeterminate than ever. The criterion of usefulness (including Nietzsche's potent "usefulness for life," which he deployed against philosophical nihilism) is useless there where the distinctions between natural and artificial flowers no longer apply. The trademark of deconstruction's resistance to idealism is that it does not rally under the banner of materialism but foregrounds the inner contradictions troubling every *-ism*.

The logic of the supplement further complicates the place of plants in Derrida's thought. Habitually, the French thinker ties the idea of supplementarity to the relation of speech and writing. Writing is the "dangerous supplement" of speech that, according to philosophers ranging from Socrates to Rousseau, gives authors the license to dodge direct responsibility for what they convey. According to this metaphysical bias, writing is the dead letter of the text as opposed to the living spirit of speech.

It is, therefore, further removed from the presence of the things themselves than actual speech. Derrida explains why the supplement is so feared: the supplementing adds something to the supplemented and at the same time supplants it, replaces it, occupies its proper place.[43] Writing usurps the priority of speech. Supplementarity, combining the addition and replacement of meaning, is the very principle of signification.

How does all this affect plants? For Derrida's Rousseau, the real catastrophe, in the literal sense of a sudden reversal or downturn, ensues when "Nature becomes the supplement of art and society."[44] But

> that botany becomes the supplement of society is more than a catastrophe. It is the catastrophe of the catastrophe. For in Nature the plant is the most *natural* thing. It is natural *life*. The mineral is distinguished from the vegetable in that it is a dead and useful Nature, servile to man's industry. When man has lost the sense and the taste of true natural riches—plants—he rummages in the entrails of his mother [mining the earth] and risks his health.[45]

Derrida paints with broad brushstrokes when he attributes to plants the quality of "natural *life*." Across our intellectual herbarium, we have espied how uncertain the philosophical distinction between the vegetable and the mineral has always been, with the plants consigned to a grey area between dead stones and living animals. In effect, Derrida might be ventriloquizing Rousseau, for whom "conversing with plants" is a supplement to a failed attempt to converse with, love, and form attachments to humans.[46] Nothing, however, assures the naturalness of plant life that, precisely qua life, is an exception from the evident vivacity of animals. The placement of plants in the category "natural *life*" is, in and of itself, a supplementation of these two oft-incompatible things, namely nature and life.

In contrast to Rousseau, Derrida would not be averse to viewing nature and "the most *natural* thing" as the supplements of art and society. The supplementarity of nature and of plants is a win-win solution that respects deconstruction's aversion to the discourse of origins (natural or otherwise) while implying that the marginality of plants dissimulates their indispensability to "art and society." Plants and nature, in the capacity of supplements, are slotted into the same structural position as writing: apparently accessory yet crucial to what they supplement.

The elegant solution nevertheless fails to address the ethical dilemmas inherent in the human treatment of vegetation. Rousseau's willingness to converse with plants imparted to them the sort of dignity that goes along with ethical subjectivity. Derrida's playful conflation of natural and artificial flowers, along with his adherence to the supplementarity of plants, intensifies their objectification and marginalization. The subtle twists and turns of deconstruction betray its predilection for the flowers of rhetoric over the sunflowers growing in a field, no matter how porous the conceptual borders separating them. So does Derrida deserve the same response as Novalis received from the German student protesters in the 1960s? Then, the German Left reacted against Novalis's imaginary *blaue Blume*—the blue flower at the center of the novel *Heinrich von Ofterdingen*—which had become a symbol of Romanticism and bourgeois high culture. The students' chant was: *Schlagt die Germanistik tot, färbt die blaue Blume rot!*—Strike Germanistics dead, paint the blue flower red! What color should we paint Derrida's sunflower for it to acquire ethical relevance and dignity?

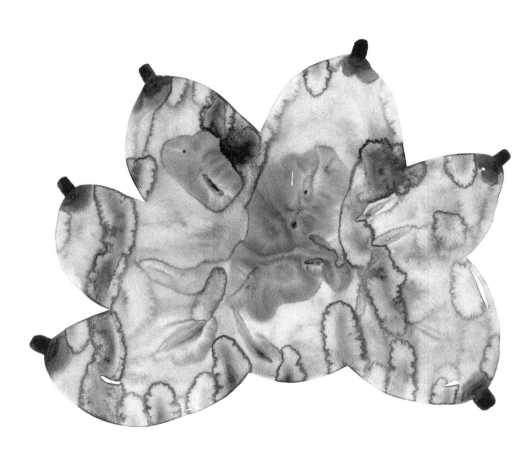

12 IRIGARAY'S WATER LILY

Contemplating a Flower with Buddha

Despite the opinion, prevalent today both in academic and nonacademic quarters, that philosophy is a thing of the past, a thing to be found exclusively in the textbooks of intellectual history, the love of wisdom is flourishing like never before. Having thrown off the straightjackets of metaphysical reasoning, living thought turns toward corporeity stamped by finitude and sexuate difference, to the world around us, to the rhythms of the earth, and to a wealth of non-Western philosophical traditions.

The work of Luce Irigaray is open to and rooted in all these dimensions of experience, which it has been able to regain at the dusk of metaphysics. Hers is a growing body of thought, not in the banal though still true sense that we can expect many more books to come from this incredibly prolific philosopher but in the sense that her thinking is attuned to and nourished by natural, and especially vegetal, growth. Books are the late fruit of her daily practice that involves walks in nature, yoga, breathing (not only with the lungs but with the whole body, through the skin), contemplation, and thinking. In the prologue to *I Love to You*, Irigaray puts this in terms of her "vital rhythm," reminiscent of the rhythms of growth: "My vital rhythm does not always enable me to cope with so much procrastination, misunderstanding, and tardiness. Fortunately, I walk, I contemplate, I think, I write."[1] If "life is what grows,"[2] then she dispenses thought back to life—her own and that of others, including its nonhuman varieties.

Among other-than-human forms of life, the vegetal stands out in Irigaray's oeuvre, so much so that it comes to stimulate the unfolding of her thought. "All my work develops as a plant grows,"[3] she admits. This will not have been the first time when plants have provided Irigaray with a model for thinking, living, and cultivating subjectivity. A recurrent image, which crops up time and again in her writings, is that of Buddha contemplating a flower. The image of "thought . . . ready to listen to nature, to the sensible,"[4]

> Buddha's gazing at the flower is not an inattentive or predatory gaze, nor the decline of the speculative into flesh. It is both material and spiritual contemplation, furnishing thought with an already sublimated energy.... Indeed, Buddha contemplates the flower without picking it. He gazes at what is other to him without uprooting it.... Buddha's gazing at the flower might provide us with a model. So might the flower.[5]

Buddha's gaze, respecting the flower's integrity, could be symbolic of Irigaray's philosophy that proposes to bridge matter and spirit, nature and culture, without betraying either the one or the other. Material-spiritual contemplation is a part of cultivation: of the flower as much as of the one who gazes at it. In the word "cultivation," favored by Irigaray, we ought to hear the meaning, which the philosopher invests in it, namely, care for what grows. The image of contemplation we are now contemplating is certainly not frozen; the flower does not appear as a still life. At the height of nondomineering attention, Buddha's gaze accompanies the growth of the flower without indifference, grows *with* it, and welcomes it in all its otherness (unless the flower is not altogether foreign to him, considering his history of incarnations). Although he does not directly meddle with it, Buddha cares for the flower's growth. Cultivation, then, is not the molding of *phusis*—that is to say, of everything and everyone that or who grows—in accordance with the predetermined parameters of reason or, worse yet, the violent uprooting of what grows by itself.[6] Quite the opposite, it is the culturing of nature, for instance, by putting ourselves in its service, protecting, sharing and promoting the myriad of growths that comprise it.

There is much to be said about Irigaray's reluctance to identify the species of the flower Buddha is contemplating. For one, were she to single it out, she would run the risk of consecrating that variety at the expense of all others. Additionally, to attach a scientific, or even a colloquial, name to the flower is immediately to cut short our infinite and infinitely attentive *rapprochement* to it by converting it into a representative of its species. Once identified as X, the flower will be known, instead of perceived. As an alternative, "Buddha's contemplation of the flower," revisited in *To Be Two*, "suggests that we learn to perceive the world around us, that we learn to perceive each other between us: as life, as freedom, as difference."[7] While knowledge focuses on an entity as a totality, perception accentuates the fine grains of difference, particularly the spaces in between, which we usually overlook as we hurriedly pass by a flowerbed or the elderly person sitting on a bench next to it. It is in this in-between of a genuine encounter (e.g., between Buddha's gaze and the flower) that life, freedom, and difference blossom and that we, too, gain the space necessary for living and flourishing.

Provided that we are attentive to the text itself, through which we get in touch with a part of Luce Irigaray's vital pace, we will get a clue to the kind of flower Buddha is contemplating there. By naming the flower, I am not capitulating before the speculative impulse and the desire to know and to identify. I merely want the reader to imagine more vividly the model it might provide us with, while taking care not to capture the flower without remainder in its image or an idea.

Before hinting at the species of the flower, Irigaray relates Buddha's teaching that encouraged each one "to awaken his own skin," just as Buddha "breathes and even laughs, with all his skin."[8] She has not mentioned plants yet, but the unstated premise is evident: to be initiated into this essentially superficial way of breathing, supplementing the activity of the lungs, we must seek guidance from vegetal respiration. Totally exposed to the atmosphere, which they replenish with oxygen, plants breathe throughout their entire extension and, most of all, through the leaf. Inhaling with the skin, perceiving the world with our whole bodies, we grow a little plantlike. "If we were more attentive," Irigaray adds, "we would be flowers capable of opening ourselves to the light of the sun, and also of love, and of reclosing ourselves in the interiority or the intimacy of the heart, as can be observed in tantric iconography, where the *nymphaea* opens or closes in accord with places of the body and the movement of energy, of breath."[9] *Nymphaea*, or the water lily, thus makes its fleeting appearance, bordering on a spectral apparition.

The most iconic portrayals of Buddha depict him as sitting on the corolla of a lotus flower, which resembles a water lily despite certain undeniable dissimilarities between the two, notably in the carpels, the flowers' female reproductive organs. (One of the outmoded botanical designations for lotus is *Nymphaea nelumbo*.) But *nymphaea* is precisely not a lotus. Its name alludes to the nymphs, Greek nature goddesses dwelling in and caring for a particular locale. The etymology of *nymphaea* points back to the Greek *nymphē* ("a bride" or, literally, "a veiled one") and contributes to the formation of the Latin *nūbere*, "to take in marriage," the source of the English *nuptials*.[10] In violation of metaphysical categorization, it is a flower that fuses the vegetal, the human, and the divine.

We have already spotted the nymphs Pharmaceia and Oreithyia in the first chapter of our intellectual herbarium, where we concluded that, for the Socrates of *Phaedrus*, a charming corner of the countryside populated by nymphs, river gods, and the god of the northern wind was the *ur*-place of myth. The Athenian gadfly saw it as his life's task to fight against the alluring power of such fables, intimately linked to nature as much as to the feminine, with the help of speeches governed by reason — in a word, *logos*. It is only fitting that a flower named after the nymphs would marshal the energy, attention, or rhythm of life and of breath, incommensurable with those of *logos*, which has "become authoritarian through the immobilization of breathing."[11] And that it would do so by alluding to the marginalized and fetishized others of Western rationality — to her, the goddess of a place, and to him, an Eastern practitioner of spiritual and bodily enlightenment.

The water lily instructs us on how to breathe, how to be attentive and exposed to the world while keeping close to "the interiority or the intimacy of the heart," where we can regather ourselves. The skin and the lungs, the flower open and closed, are the mutually complementary organs and figures of breath. The tantric iconography of *nymphaea*, emphasizing both the inhalation and the exhalation of air, prompts Irigaray to question the deconstructive privileging of absolute exposure, dispersion, dissemination, and perhaps evasion. At the antipodes of Spirit, which only knows how to breathe in without breathing out, deconstruction exhales without inhaling; it skips a beat and falls out of rhythm when it lumps subjective self-gathering with other excesses of metaphysics. Between East and West, woman and man, the one and the other, the rhythmic vacillations of opening and reclosing are indispensible for the cultivation of subjectivity, where to be is to be two.

Does the flower's (or the subject's) composure in itself, the petals (or thoughts) cradling the intimacy of its interiority, retrieve the dream of metaphysical essence? With reference to another flower, Irigaray's essay "Belief Itself," composed in 1980 for a conference on the work of Jacques Derrida, responds in the negative. After the rose has blossomed, "the place in which the rose once touched herself, lip to lip, has disappeared. You will never see it." Nor does the place that has been revealed harbor a previously hidden essence: "In the heart of the flower there is nothing— but the heart."[12] Autoaffection, the being-in-touch-with-itself of a living being, is neither the primary nor the most significant element of our (and the flower's) constitution. Similar to the diastolic and the systolic movements of heartbeat, both autoaffection and heteroaffection, which refers to being-in-relation-with-the-other, are the cardinal moments in subject formation.

The rose, to be sure, does not follow the same cadence of opening and closing its blossom as a water lily or a lotus, and Irigaray is well aware of this. An aphorism in *Elemental Passions* reads: "The oriental lotus and the mystic rose: different flowerings."[13] Unlike the lotus, the rose, after it has bloomed, remains open until it fades away. Yet this fading holds a promise of regeneration: "Even as the rose opens up, it already knows about shedding petals, dying down, lying dormant, not as an end but as a recovery."[14] Its cycle of energy, which entails both growth and decay, is not diurnal but seasonal. It still exists in and by virtue of a rhythmic alternation, if not of day and night then of summer and winter, in tune with the positions of the sun and the earth. Humans, however, have re- belled against the time of *phusis*. In contrast to the rose and the lotus, we have cut ourselves off from the ambient and cosmic cycles, such that the opening of *our* world has meant the closure of the environment. Tread- ing dangerously, we have come to believe that for the human to blossom, the rest of *phusis* must fade away. Irigaray's work, in turn, urges us to lis- ten to the muted vegetal rhythms in our life and thought, where growth has been stunted by the prejudices of metaphysics and the arrhythmia of modern existence.

Lest we forget, the other point of comparison for the water lily, the lotus, and the rose is the physical context of their growth. The aquatic environment of the water lily (and of the lotus) is distinct from the purported stability of the soil wherein the rose is rooted. The classical elements of water and earth are replete with strong connotations of sexual or sexuate differences, while the interplay between the feminine and a fluid milieu is a source of dread and uncertainty for philosophers, be they as daring as Friedrich Nietzsche.[15] Like air, liquid cannot be arrested in the molds of identity, and it cannot be divided against itself in the manner of a furrowed earth. A metaphysical search for secure grounds, hard foundations, and the bedrocks of knowledge has never been far from the terrestrial solidity, itself associated with the rigidity of phallic erection and artificially projected onto the otherworldly reality of "true being." The distinct flowerings of the rose and the lotus (or the water lily) imply differences between the places and paces of their growth as well as between the elements in which they bathe or into which they burrow. Although it would be erroneous to graft such differences directly onto the modes of subject formation in the feminine and masculine, or in "the East" and "the West," there is an undeniable correlation between the *nymphaea* and *nymphē*, the lotus and Buddha, "the pick driven into the earth-mother's womb in order to build the sacred enclosure of the tribe" and the rose that blooms there, "recall[ing] something of blood"[16] and of the rape of nature.

Flowering-With

So, what is the model of plant subjectivity that emerges from Irigaray's texts? Returning to the episode of Buddha and Luce Irigaray gazing at the flower, we discover the following semilyrical description:

> [The flower] sways with the wind, without rigidity. It also evolves within itself; it grows, blossoms, grows back. Some of them, those I find most engaging, open with the rising sun and close up with the evening. There are flowers for every season. The most hardy among them, those least cultivated by man, come forth while preserving their roots; they are constantly moving between the appearance of their forms and the earth's resources.[17]

The flowers Irigaray finds most engaging are redolent of the one Buddha is engaged with: water lilies that "open with the rising sun and close up with the evening." A flower grows *with* the elements and the seasons, not against them. Swaying with the wind, it does not oppose the movements of the air and, therefore, is no longer the forerunner of phallic erection (and castration) that it was for Bataille and for Derrida. In itself, a flower is open to the other, which is why its evolution "within itself" is indistinguishable from its outward growth and blossoming. A flower flowers with the wind and the sun while showing obeisance to the nightfall and keeping in touch with the earth's equally nocturnal resources. In a sense, a flower is the act of flowering-with, a vegetal variation on Heidegger's *Mitsein*, being-with. That is why "plants live together without difficulty."[18] Being-with or flowering-with is the meaning of their being, which is ultimately accessible to them alone.

Everything Western philosophers from Aristotle to Hegel have discarded and devalued about plants is lovingly retrieved, reassessed, and cultivated at the tail end of the metaphysical tradition. For instance, the nonoppositional nature of plants, compared to animals, was for Hegel a sign of their ontological weakness, which on Irigaray's reading bespeaks perseverance and tenacity shorn of confrontation. The indeterminacy of vegetal growth, which used to instill terror into Aristotle, is the *apeiron*—the infinite—in the finitude of plant life, well in excess of the limits set by *logos*. "The plant appears with borders, with a form, but to express it as such amounts to having already deprived this plant of its vegetal life. Indeed its form is never definite: it evolves according to the hour, the day, the season, the year."[19] The becoming of plants, their plasticity, is the offshoot of their nonoppositionality, which is why their flourishing is, in itself, a growing with and a flowering with the other.

We have been acquainted with the recent philosophical revaluation of plant qualities in Derrida's deconstruction of Western metaphysics. In Irigaray's philosophy, however, the accentuation of vegetation is markedly different. To discern this shift in emphasis, I recommend that we read the above quotation from *In the Beginning, She Was* side by side with the characterization of "her," referring at once to nature, woman, or Goddess, ten pages further into the text: "She is, but not solid, nor uniform, nor finite. She is, but also void, multiple, indefinite. Infinite? She resists the limits he intends to impose on her."[20] Obviously, she (nature, woman, or Goddess) shares the indeterminacy, fluidity, and multiplicity with plants. A miniature mirror of *phusis*, the plant gives off a double reflection, also including feminine subjectivity. The flower model does not lay claim to universality but affirms the bond—much sullied by the archetypal metaphysician, by him who "intends to impose limits"—between "her" and the vegetal world.

In the conclusion to *The Vegetative Soul*, Miller notes that Irigaray strives to restructure "the feminine imaginary (thereby effecting the possibility of a feminine subjectivity) by way of reworking the symbols of nature."[21] The co-belonging and the solidarity of the plant, the woman, and nature have nothing to do with a trivially negative (and utterly wrong) explanation highlighting their common exclusion from the realm of culture. Like nature itself in the ancient Greek sense of *phusis*, the plant and the woman are the least static of living subjects. Metamorphosis, if not transmorphosis, is at the heart of their respective existences. Still, plants and their growth are not merely "the symbols of nature," into which Miller transcribes them. In the preceding chapter, I have argued that hypersymbolism is the Achilles' heel of deconstruction, as far as its treatment of plants is concerned. To reduce them to mere symbols or even metaphors, no matter how thoroughly reimagined, is by the same stroke to reappropriate them for *logos*, which has been for millennia sanctioning their exploitation—and that of women, as well. In all of her written work, be it philosophical or poetic, Irigaray vigilantly guards against the reduction of plants (or of any other living beings for that matter) to symbols by moderating the theoretical impulse with practical contemplation and by letting them grow, leaving them be, freeing them from the noise of *logos*. She foments that silence which "safeguards things . . . , lets them be before any monstration, any appearing; left to their will, their growth."[22] Buddha, after all, gazes at the flower in unperturbed silence.

There is, in fact, no flowering-with, no being-with, outside of this silence, "leading back to a deeper or more blossomed level of Being."[23] At a more blossomed level, being is revealed as growing, as becoming, as not-One. The abiding insight of Irigaray's thought is that the human is (at least) two—man and woman—and that these two correspond to different ways of growing, cultivating subjectivity, and relating to the world. The biological fact or facticity of internal sexual organs in women and external ones in men is not devoid of significance for their culturally mediated approaches to the world. Nor should we ignore the fact or facticity of women welcoming their lovers within their bodies and, potentially, engendering a child within themselves, as opposed to the males begetting outside themselves. Manners of relating to the other and creations of the worlds of immanence or transcendence are the lived interpretations of these embodied, sexuate differences.[24] The flourishing of plants that live together with other plants and with the elements is akin to the blossoming of her who lives together with the other in herself. Compared to the masculine subjects who, conveying "a meaning in some way closed," "converse above all with their own self and with speech," "the feminine subject ... takes an interest in the relation between two, in communication between people."[25] The *with* of vegetal nonoppositionality and the feminine welcome of the other draw their inspiration from the same source of a "more blossomed level of Being."

To reject the oneness of being is, at the same time, to repudiate a certain narcissism. Narcissus—a mythological hero and a plant (daffodil)—is the counterflower of Irigaray's water lily. Rather than letting himself be surrounded by a watery milieu, he separates from its immanence, turning it into a liquid mirror, in which to contemplate his own image. Narcissus loves himself to the point of interposing himself in the place of the other. His silent stare at his own reflection has nothing in common with Buddha's equally wordless gaze at the flower. The former is the origin of narcissistic discourse, whereby *logos* converses with itself alone; the latter is the cultivation of silence that permits the other surrounded by loving care to grow in its otherness. Amid a summary of what the traditions of India have taught her, Irigaray highlights the "renunciation of narcissistic self-importance, the first condition of listening and of speaking."[26] But even then this renunciation is not bitterly oppositional; it is not a question of the water lily versus the daffodil. To be two is to give place to transcendence as much as to immanence, to dispersing as well as to gathering oneself, to self-relation as much as to the relation to the other, to letting be and to fabrication ... It is, in any case, to resist the "nostalgia of the one," corresponding at times to "the self-love of Narcissus" and at other times to "the desire to be or to possess the whole."[27]

The vegetal and feminine openness toward the other within themselves involves a unique paradigm of giving and sharing. Plant world puts itself in the service of life, "regenerating the air by metabolizing what has destroyed its properties."[28] In what it is and in what it does, it is *for* the other while remaining itself. That is what flowering-with at last conveys: finding one's conditions for flourishing in the other and dedicating oneself to the other's flourishing are not synonymous with losing oneself. Irigaray's example of such giving, in oneself and of oneself, is "the mother's silent teaching," her sharing of breath with the fetus.[29] The mother's unseen sharing of oxygen is probably the sole human instance of giving pure air to the other, reenacting the plants' gift to the world of the living. Only in a pathologically narcissistic culture will living for the sake of the other be conflated with self-sacrifice. Giving (of) oneself is not self-abnegation but sharing; if the mother gave her breath or life "without keeping some of it, without remaining alive, the other would lose existence."[30] The plants, also, share themselves, though they do so perhaps not freely, not having made the choice to do so. Yet theirs is an enviable fidelity to the other, a faithfulness we can only dream of.

Vegetal Fidelities

A plant's growth is the first indication of faithfulness to its milieu. Rooted in a place, which it does not oppose, it adheres to the ground and strains toward the sky, which it enriches with oxygen. In a recent interview, Irigaray has extended the scope of the tree's fidelity from the inorganic other to itself: "What I said concerning a tree is that it is more faithful to itself than we can be, first, because it cannot separate off from its roots as we do as humans. It also remains more purely natural, whereas we become a blend of nature and cultural constructions that are not in continuation with respect to our nature."[31] In its faithfulness to itself, a plant is attentive to its other, that is, to the elements and the inorganic world. A cork tree growing on one of the rolling hills in the Alentejo region of Portugal registers the shifts in temperature, the amounts of sunlight, the force of the wind rustling in its branches, the richness of the soil that nourishes it. Inseparable from the place of its growth, it keeps faithful to itself all the while monitoring the world's fluctuations, seasonal rotations, comings and goings.

When she embraces that love which does not annihilate the otherness of the other, Irigaray yearns to learn fidelity from the plants themselves. "I love you upon the threshold of this permanent alterity," she writes, "offered to my attentive senses and spirit. I wish that the flowers themselves could help me in such fidelity."[32] Fidelity to the other as other requires that alterity be permanent, inassimilable to the lover's self.[33] It also spells out a precarious (and, for humans, elusive) balance between opening up to the world and gathering in oneself, between following the other with the senses and with spirit, for no attentive comportment is possible except in the difference between these two. The flowers, such as those tracking the movements of the sun and the changes of day or night, are exceptionally faithful to the "objects" of their attention, to the point of changing *with* them. The diurnal rhythm of the water lily is the best proof of its vicarious transformation.

Imperceptibly, we have circled back to the origin of the word *nymphaea* I documented in the first section of this chapter. *Nymphē* is a bride, a betrothed. In other words, she is the one who has pledged fidelity to the other. Not to the masculine appropriative subject of metaphysics but to the entire world, toward which her diffuse and receptive attention is turned. The love of wisdom that is philosophy will henceforth overlap with this attentive fidelity. Indeed, who can teach us how to be faithful better than *nymphaea*? While abiding in her watery milieu, she has embarked on the path of truth, the semantics of which lie dormant in "betrothed."[34] The veil of *nymphē* is the floral, material instantiation of this very truth as dis-closure, simultaneously revealing and concealing both the subject of loving attention and the world she tracks without ever having enough of it. Life itself, above all in its vegetal configuration, takes the place of Heideggerian being that, in its very appearance, encrypts itself: "Life never speaks simply. It shows itself in its flower, hides itself in its roots."[35]

How to be faithful to life that both shows and hides itself? Fidelity is a barely visible thematic thread that weaves its way through Irigaray's corpus. More often than not, this theme is entwined with attention, on the one hand, and with the vegetal world, on the other. In *I Love to You*, Irigaray rereads the ignorant and injurious attribution of passivity to women and to plants in the context of their attentive fidelity to the world:

> And so one might well wonder if women are closer to the vegetable world than to the animal world.... Could it be that in this proximity there lies an accurate explanation of her relation to passivity?... Her so-called passivity

would not be part of an active/passive pair of opposites but would signify a
different economy, a different relation to nature and to the self that would
amount to attentiveness and to *fidelity* rather than *passivity*.[36]

On Irigaray's terms, we are not dealing with the restricted economy of
cognitive attention or mental concentration on a given object but with
the attentiveness of the whole body, which coincides with our breathing through the skin and with the plant's openness to its environment.
Thinking is reunited with growth, both material *and* spiritual, whence it
has first arisen. Faithfully following whatever we pay attention to, we let
our gaze and our entire rapt flesh wander after the "target" that ends up
targeting *us*.

In this wandering, typically conflated with passivity, we stay true to
the world around us and to ourselves as creatures whose growth and
flourishing depend on this world, not the least in its floral dimension.
Through attentive fidelity, we become the betrothed of what or whom we
follow. Momentarily, we metamorphose into water lilies and ultimately
into the places of truth that exceeds the narrow scope of understanding,
the truth that emanates from the other, be it a flower or a star: "You my,
stars, masters of the universe, are my guardians and my peace, the font
of my duties and my fortunes. Bound to you in some mysterious way, I
try to be faithful without understanding. . . . Attentive, I am sometimes
amazed, sometimes terrified, even though, in a certain sense, I put more
faith in you than in myself."[37] Attention undisturbed by understanding
clears the space for thinking *and* for life—for the wonder, with which
philosophy begins, and for existence, which is not forced into the ready-
made categories of cognition.

So durable is the thread of fidelity that it allows us to refashion the
fabric of Aristotelian teleology, particularly that of plant growth and reproduction. In a disagreement between Plato and his illustrious student,
Irigaray implicitly takes the side of Aristotle, as long as the appropriate-
ness of the seed to the plant germinating from it is understood in terms
of continued faithfulness. A flower, according to her, "exists and can
blossom not by conformity to an image or an idea but by faithfulness to
a seed, an earth, a nourishment that are proper to it."[38] Having cast aside
the regulative role of "an image or an idea" (hence, of *eidos*), she accepts
the felicitous fit of the blossoming plant, its seed, its soil, and nourish-

ment on the basis of a growing being's fidelity to the conditions that facilitate its growth. Again, the "proper" is not a matter of possession or appropriation; a flower is far from making its mineral nourishment, let alone the earth, its own. Aristotle's teleology manifests itself in a new light, when we distinguish in it the infrastructure for the plant's faithful correspondence to its past (the seed) and present (nourishment). The so-called correspondence theory of truth should have made this point perspicuous a long while ago: truth hinges on faithfulness and is therefore an issue of faith.

Besides the vegetal, every type of growth presupposes this abysmal foundation, since "growth cannot happen outside of a faithfulness to her—or Her—the one who gives life, who inspires or maintains love, she whom one knows without knowing her, through a knowledge irreducible to the logic of opposites."[39] Nonoppositional, nonbinary knowledge is the betrothed of growth, itself made possible by *her*: by nature, woman, or Goddess. For all its vociferousness, the *logos* that undergirds "the logic of opposites" drowns in the silence of growth, of her loving care, and of the Plotinian *nous*, which "by giving something of itself to matter, made all things in unperturbed quietness." Fidelity to the other beseeches us to be attentively silent.

Unfortunately, humans have not, for the most part, been faithful to themselves and to each other, to their own origin and destiny, or to the world around them. In what amounts to a betrayal of ourselves and of each other, we have historically opted for a cunning synecdoche, according to which one half of humanity—men—is interchangeable with the human as such. Oblivious to our principal task "to make the transition from nature to culture as sexed beings, to become women and men while remaining *faithful* to our gender,"[40] we have continued to associate our sexuate bodies with the reproductive function immersed in the frozen and consequently mutilated-beyond-recognition order of nature. Endeavoring to "master growth through playing with words" and further arresting the dynamic potentialities of *phusis*, we have invented speech that "wanders progressively away from the real in order to say the nonborn, the true from time immemorial, being—or Being."[41]

What conditions our triple going astray is the drift that has carried us away from any attachment to the place, from the need to spiritualize our bodies without rejecting their corporeality, and from a language that, in the beginning, still grew "starting from the same depths as vegetal growth."[42] Nonetheless, Irigaray is unwilling to ascribe human infidelities to our wholesale detachment from the plant world. Her preferred allegory in this respect is a tree whose sap has been thwarted, obstructed, or depleted, the plant gradually draining its own life entrusted to the spiritual "vitality" of *logos*.

In the aftermath of Plato's cave experiment, *logos* has been busily constructing an artificial analogue of life, one presumably better and more durable than worldly existence. *Logos* has been an *analogon*.[43] But "if breath emanates from life, it is not evident that this is always the case for *logos*. . . . Why abandon the sap of life for a diet that just as easily brings death to pass? . . . What kind of reason has in this way divided the world into two, cutting it from its living roots?"[44] A world divided into two is composed of the segregated realms of becoming and being, of what keeps growing and what knows no alteration, of natural life and purely spiritual life-death. To wit, this division is not absolute, seeing that *logos*, for all its limitations, still mimes life; being parodies a congealed flow of becoming; and an increasingly lifeless, sapless trunk sticks out of a living root.

Plato's divided line has organized, on an uninterrupted continuum, the intellect and the senses, ideas and appearances, the heavenly and the earthly plants. Plotinus' world tree has included maggot-infested material roots and the purified parts of the Soul of All in the vegetal image of the One. And Irigaray's critique of the human plant where "the sap for becoming is lost"[45] has acknowledged, perhaps despite itself, the continuity of a deadening *logos* and life. In a Nietzschean vein, we might say that *logos* is a perversion of life that has turned against itself and has crippled itself and everything around it without as much as detaching from its roots. A question from our first chapter thus resurfaces: Does the breakout from Plato's cave announce an absolute separation from earthly existence evocative of animal birth, or is it the soul's gradual, though no less traumatic, transition to another element, akin to that of a seedling germinating from the soil into the air and the light of the sun?

Even assuming that the thesis of radical continuity is upheld, it does not remedy our infidelity to ourselves, to the other, and to the world. Admittedly, we ought to qualify this infidelity as the poisonous fruit of *phallogocentric* reason, growing from men's dreams of pure transcendence that stunt growth: "Can we imagine the sap remaining eternally fecund at the top of the tree? This is not sure. Nature tells us the opposite. But, apparently, men have forgotten this lesson."[46] Their breathless aspiration to the top (of the tree, of the world or of worlds, of Ideas, of the Chain of Being, of Spirit) ignores the changes of season and the unwilled passage of time, the circulation of energy between the "below" and the "above," the in-between of growth, cultivation, and becoming-human. In their quest for immutable truths, spawning fixed correspondences between dead words and a lifeless reality, they lose sight of truth as betrothal. At best, they confine truth to mediation—think of Hegel's *Vermittlung*—which dissolves the two in a higher one. What they have forgotten is still more basic than nature's lesson about the seasonal changes that renew a plant's sap. It has slipped from their minds that meaningful fidelity is pledged only to what is inconstant, to what grows, in or from the middle, to what "knows completeness in the uncompleted."[47]

"We Still Fall Short of the Human"

Our unfaithfulness to ourselves has resulted in a preternatural situation where "between plant, animal, angel or god, we still lack the human. We still fall short of the human."[48] We should hear this likely baffling statement in several registers.

First, Irigaray conveys that the human has been traditionally defined with an eye to something or someone else—the ontological regions bordering on the upper and lower limits of the concept. Aristotelian metaphysics circumscribes humans along with the polity they create to the narrow stretch of theoretical terrain between the beastly and the divine. As sublime animals possessing *logos* and godlike figures who attain self-sufficiency in "thought thinking itself," Aristotle's men (and they are most certainly *men*) forego the elaboration of what it means to be human starting from everyday relations: between lovers, a mother and a daughter or a son, a brother and a sister, a father and a daughter or a son. And this is not to mention that, when it comes to the subhuman categories of metaphysics, they tend to ignore the plant.

Second, it follows that after millennia of Western philosophy and on the heels of this failure, "the human" has not yet been thought of, represented, or experienced as (at least) two, in the difference between men and women. The usurpation of the indeterminate concept of humanity by one half of the species, in what I've called a cunning synecdoche, implies incalculably more than a mere exclusion of women from its purview. It indicates that the human has been, thus far, erroneously conceived as an entity, rather than a relation of the one to the other. Defined by virtue of its hierarchically inferior or superior position vis-à-vis animality and divinity, the deficient, because one-sided, notion of the human boasts a nonrelational core. The exclusion of the feminine does not merely impoverish humanity but utterly annihilates it as a meaningful construct.

The third sense of Irigaray's insight is that the human is not a cultural, much less biological, given but a still unaccomplished task. We have glimpsed this singular mission in the quasi-Rousseauian desideratum to cultivate desire, to make a transition from nature to culture without leaving the materiality of growth, embodiment, and sexuate difference behind. To the extent that this mission has not yet been accomplished—and it is debatable whether it can be ever brought to completion—the human is lacking. In the words of Irigaray: "There remains work to complete: a house to build, a love to invent, a spirit to cultivate."[49] More precisely, she calls for a house, *oikos*, that would not seal us off from the rest of the environment and its ecology, a love that would be irreducible to hormonal fluctuations or to the surge of the drives, and a spirit that would not require the sacrifice of nature as a whole for its blossoming.

In response to the current fad of posthumanism, with its central claim that the human has been surpassed thanks to last century's technological advances, Irigaray rightly claims that we have not yet become human. In doing so, she finds herself in an unspoken agreement with Karl Marx, who in his early writings considered the course of events prior to the workers' universal emancipation to be the "prehistory of human society."[50] Sharing humanity between two is far from splitting a preexisting category of the human in half. It is, instead, inventing the human within a relation bereft of a simple unity, letting each grow toward the other as much as toward herself or himself and fostering a culture, a civil society, and a polity, based on such growth.

What is the role of plants in this transformation? It is not by chance that the words "growth" and "cultivation" pepper Irigaray's texts. The incompletion of the human may be seen as an intensification of vegetal indeterminacy, of the terrifying *apeiron* of growth, introducing, better than Descartes' God, infinity into the finite. It could well be that we would never become fully human, that the work cut out for us would not yield something like a final product, and that the task of cultivating spirit with and as nature would be ongoing. If so, then, in our kinship with plants, we would experience a constant metamorphosis of our forms, taking care not to assume one that would have been definite or definitive. In our lived passage through various modes of existence, we would not exclude the vegetal. Jointly with Irigaray, we would follow the lead of Brahma who, escaping from the god of winds, "takes refuge in a blade of grass; he takes root."[51] After all, even a blade of grass is inimitable and unique, as Leibniz has shown in his monadology. Being human is not incompatible with entrusting oneself to the most insignificant of plants.

The choice we are facing invites us to take our pick between two modes of incompletion. We are to decide whether we would fall short of the human by betraying our unique task *or* whether we would embark on the path toward humanity without realizing it fully thanks to the recognition of our (unavoidable though still enabling) limitation—the impossibility to become human in isolation from the other. Will we persist in the shape of a tree of death, or will we metamorphose into another kind of plant, faithfully stretching its branches in the direction of something or someone it will never reach? It is in this appreciation of our self-insufficiency that freedom, resembling "the sap that comes out of a delicate plant," will regenerate as the "blossoming of the possible"[52] outside the finality of its actualization.

NOTES

Prologue: Herbarium Philosophicum

1. Cook, *Jean-Jacques Rousseau and Botany*, 15, 17.
2. For a more detailed study of Rousseau's phytophilia, see Marder and Vieira, "Writing Phytophilia."
3. In the same letter, Rousseau writes, "It is necessary to follow the flowers from before their opening until the full maturity of the fruit, and it is in this succession that one sees the metamorphoses and a chain of marvels which hold every healthy mind who observes them in a continual admiration." Rousseau, "Elementary Letters on Botany," 155.
4. I am, of course, referring to Russell's *History of Western Philosophy*.
5. Miller, *Black Holes*, 151.
6. Hegel, *The Letters*, 60.
7. See Rousseau's *Reveries*.

1. Plato's Plane Tree

1. See Kennedy, *The Musical Structure of Platonic Dialogues*.
2. http://www.nycgovparks.org/trees/tree-census/2005-2006/summary.
3. See Sayre, *Plato's Literary Garden*.
4. Claudel, *La Connaissance de l'est*, 148.
5. See Carpenter, "Embodied Intelligent (?) Souls," 281–303.
6. Chamovitz, *What a Plant Knows*, 74.
7. I learned this last factoid from a conversation with Dr. Monica Gagliano.
8. See Irigaray, *The Speculum of the Other Woman*.

2. Aristotle's Wheat

1. The origin of the English "matter" is the Latin *materia*, which is derived from the same root as "mother," *mater*. It is tempting to conclude that, while the Greek *hylē* emphasizes the exterior aspect of matter, the Latin *materia* points toward the interiority of the origin or the source. We should not rush to this conclusion, however. The Portuguese *madeira*, etymologically proximate to *mater*, recovers the Greek signification, as it refers to the hard *inner* wood of a tree.

2. To be sure, there was also a separate word for wheat in Greek—*pyros*. Yet this does not eliminate the irreducible confusion inherent in the polyvalent *sitos*.

3. Ward, *Aristotle on Homonymy*, 7, 21–2, 58, 168.

4. Baracchi, *Aristotle's Ethics as First Philosophy*, 38.

5. Kant, *Critique of Judgment*, part 2, 66.

6. Gomez-Lobo, *Morality and the Human Goods*, 88.

7. On Baracchi's heterodox reading of Aristotle, the unmoved mover, characterized "in the language of desire and eros" as "that which is desired" and "the beloved," is "illuminated in terms of beauty, that is, of phenomenality." Baracchi, *Aristotle's Ethics as First Philosophy*, 50. If this is so, then it has more than one thing in common with the world of plants, the erotic vegetal soul, and the embodiment of phenomenal appearance as such in the seedling's partial emergence from the darkness of the soil.

8. See Cvrčková et al., "Plant Intelligence."

9. See Pollan, *The Botany of Desire*.

10. See Palmer et al., "Phenotypic and Developmental Plasticity in Plants."

11. The same parable is repeated in *The Politics* 1311a.

3. Plotinus' Anonymous "Great Plant"

1. Marder and Francione, "Michael Marder and Gary Francione Debate Plant Ethics."

2. See Wildon et al., "Electrical Signaling."

3. On the criteria of nondiscursive thought in Plotinus, see Emilsson, *Plotinus on Intellect*, chap. 4.

4. See Chamowitz, *What a Plant Knows*; Cashmore, "Crytpochromes"; and Garzón, "The Quest for Cognition in Plant Neurobiology."

5. Preus, "Plotinus and Biology," 53.

6. Hegel, *Early Theological Writings*, 261.

7. Novalis, *Philosophical Writings*, 80.
8. For the original formulation, see Porphyry, *On the Life of Plotinus*, 2, 20–30.

4. Augustine's Pears

1. Derrida, "Composing 'Circumfession,' " 31.
2. Burrus, Jordan, and MacKendrick, *Seducing Augustine*, 17.
3. Derrida, "Composing 'Circumfession,' " 31.
4. Arendt, *Love and Saint Augustine*, 40, 38.
5. Augustine, *Essential Sermons*, 78–79.
6. Augustine, *Essential Sermons*, 76.
7. Haraway, *When Species Meet*, 296.
8. Augustine, *Essential Sermons*, 34.
9. Augustine, *Essential Sermons*, 120.
10. Augustine, *Essential Sermons*, 62.
11. Augustine, *Essential Sermons*, 73.
12. Augustine, *On Order*, Book 1, Debate 1, 5.13.
13. Augustine, *On Order*, Book 1, Debate 1, 5.14.

5. Avicenna's Celery

1. Avicenna, *The Canon of Medicine*, iii.
2. Avicenna, *The Canon of Medicine*, 404.
3. Avicenna, *The Canon of Medicine*, 433, 435.
4. Afnan, *Avicenna*, 74.
5. Gohlman, *The Life of Ibn Sina*, 85.
6. Afnan, *Avicenna*, 74.
7. On the subject, he is reported to have said: "I prefer a short life with width to a narrow one with length." Quoted in Khan, *Avicenna*, 85.
8. See Lameer, "Avicenna's Concupiscence."
9. Gohlman, *The Life of Ibn Sina*, 83.
10. Avicenna, *Avicenna's Psychology*, 24.
11. Avicenna, *Livre de la Genese*, 64.
12. Avicenna, *Avicenna's Psychology*, 25.
13. Avicenna, *The Canon of Medicine*, 107.
14. Avicenna, *The Canon of Medicine*, 302.
15. Avicenna, *The Canon of Medicine*, 113.
16. Avicenna, *The Metaphysics of* The Healing, 341.
17. Avicenna, *A Compendium*, 38, 39.

18. Avicenna, *A Compendium*, 41.

19. Avicenna, *The Canon of Medicine*, 114.

20. Avicenna, *The Canon of Medicine*, 113.

21. Avicenna, *Livre de la Genese*, 64.

22. Avicenna, *The Canon of Medicine*, 113.

23. Avicenna, *A Compendium*, 23.

24. Avicenna, *Livre de la Genese*, 65; Avicenna, *The Canon of Medicine*, 113.

25. Avicenna, *A Compendium*, 38.

26. Avicenna, *Avicenna's Psychology*, 24.

27. Avicenna, *Avicenna's Psychology*, 25.

28. Avicenna, *A Compendium*, 37–8.

29. Avicenna, *Avicenna's Psychology*, 37.

30. See Pollan, *The Botany of Desire*.

31. Avicenna, *A Compendium*, 26.

32. Avicenna, *A Compendium*, 46.

33. Avicenna, *A Compendium*, 48.

34. McGinnis, *Avicenna*, 262.

35. Avicenna, *The Canon of Medicine*, 112.

36. For more on this reading of Aristotle, see my *Plant-Thinking*: "Although vegetal life lacks an objective end, Aristotle, like many philosophers in his footsteps, chases after its elusive first principle, a basic capacity and the unitary origin of the soul from which all others may be deduced. According to *De Anima*, the generic *dunamis* of this life is the nutritive faculty, *tō threptikon*, analogous to the fundamental haptic sense in animals (in a word, touch), which is only subsequently differentiated into other specific senses (413b, 1–10). *Tō threptikon*, Aristotle contends, is the precise place where the soul begins in a simple unity that will bestow vitality not only upon plants but also upon all living beings without exception. It is the minimal level of vitality that distinguishes living entities from mere things, and the plant stands right at the threshold of this distinction, given that no other capacities supplement *tō threptikon* in its sphere of existence" (38).

37. Avicenna, *A Compendium*, 31ff.

38. Bloch, *Avicenna y la izquierda aristotélica*, 19, et passim.

39. Avicenna, *A Treatise on Love*, 214.

40. Avicenna, *A Treatise on Love*, 216.

41. Avicenna, *A Treatise on Love*, 212.

42. Avicenna, *A Treatise on Love*, 216.

43. Avicenna, *A Treatise on Love*, 216.

44. Avicenna, *A Treatise on Love*, 215.

45. Avicenna, *A Treatise on Love*, 227.

46. Avicenna, *A Treatise on Love*, 227.

47. Avicenna, *A Treatise on Love*, 227.

48. Avicenna, *The Metaphysics of* The Healing, 312.

49. Avicenna, *A Treatise on Love*, 222

50. Avicenna, *A Compendium*, 15.

51. Avicenna, *A Compendium*, 16.

6. Maimonides' Palm Tree

1. Maimonides, *Acquisitions*, 86.

2. Agamben, *Homo Sacer*, 10.

3. Agamben, *Homo Sacer*, 21.

4. Maimonides, *Acquisitions*, 88.

5. Maimonides, *Acquisitions*, 7.

6. Maimonides, *Acquisitions*, 87.

7. Maimonides, *Acquisitions*, 88.

8. Compare with: "Whoever takes possession of ownerless property acquires title to it. Thus also in the case of deserts, rivers, and streams the law is that whatever is in them, as for example, plants, trees, and the fruits of the trees of the woods, has the status of ownerless property, and whoever is first to take possession of them acquires title to them." Maimonides, *Acquisitions*, 110.

9. Maimonides, *Seasons*, 7.

10. Maimonides, *Seasons*, 41.

11. Maimonides, *Guide*, 180, translation modified.

12. Maimonides, *Guide*, 274.

13. See Silverman, "Anthropocentrism," especially the section "Maimonides' *Via Negativa*," 121–126.

14. Maimonides, *Guide*, 309.

15. Maimonides, *Guide*, 275.

16. Maimonides, *Guide*, 81.

17. Maimonides, *Guide*, 56.

18. Maimonides, *Guide*, 35.

19. On the irreducibility of ambivalence in Maimonides, see Dobbs-Weinstein, "The Ambiguity of the Imagination," 95–112.

20. Maimonides, *Guide*, 60.

21. Maimonides, *Guide*, 80.

22. Maimonides, *Guide*, 35.

23. Maimonides, *Guide*, 35.

24. Maimonides, *The Ethical Writings*, 61. See also Melber, *The Universality of Maimonides*, 76ff.

25. Maimonides, *Ethical Writings*, 61–62.

26. Maimonides, *Guide*, 124.

27. Maimonides, *Guide*, 115.

28. Maimonides, *Guide*, 115.

29. Maimonides, *Guide*, 40.

30. Maimonides, *Guide*, 215.

31. Maimonides, *Cleanness*, 339.

32. Maimonides, *Cleanness*, 352.

33. Maimonides, *Cleanness*, 336.

34. Maimonides, *Seasons*, 43.

35. Maimonides, *Acquisitions*, 15.

36. Maimonides, *Cleanness*, 338.

37. Maimonides, *Acquisitions*, 193.

38. Maimonides, *Ethical Writings*, 64.

39. Maimonides, *Guide*, 337.

40. Maimonides, *Guide*, 337.

41. See Maimonides, *Agriculture*, esp. *Kilayim* 5:13.

42. Maimonides, *Acquisitions*, 191.

43. Maimonides, *Guide*, 318.

44. See Gagliano, Mancuso, and Robert, "Towards Understanding Plant Bioacoustics."

45. Nuland, *Maimonides*, 94.

46. Maimonides, *Guide*, 248.

47. Maimonides, *Guide*, 238–239.

48. Maimonides, *Guide*, 286.

49. Even then the "prophets . . . express their surprise that God should take notice of man, who is too little and too unimportant to be worthy of the attention of the Creator; how, then, should other living creatures be considered as proper objects of Divine Providence!" Maimonides, *Guide*, 287.

7. Leibniz's Blades of Grass

1. Leibniz and Clarke, *Leibniz and Clarke: Correspondence*, 22.

2. Hegel, *Logic*, 170.

3. Leibniz, *Philosophical Essays*, 32.

4. "Things which are uniform, containing no variety, are always mere abstractions: for instance, time, space, and the other entities of pure mathematics. There is no body whose parts are at rest, and no substance which does not have something which distinguishes it from every other." Leibniz, *New Essays*, 110.

5. Leibniz, *New Essays*, 57.

6. McCarthy, "The Philosopher as Essayist," 64.

7. Leibniz, *New Essays*, 58.

8. See Marder, "Plant Intentionality."

9. Leibniz, *Discourse on Metaphysics*, 15.

10. Leibniz, *Philosophical Essays*, 277.

11. Mates, *The Philosophy of Leibniz*, 17n6.

12. Spinoza, *Ethics*, 180.

13. Leibniz, *Monadology*, 228.

14. Leibniz, *Monadology*, 226, 227.

15. Swift, *The Works*, 217.

16. Leibniz, *Monadology*, 221.

17. Leibniz, *New Essays*, 317.

18. Leibniz, *Monadology*, 230.

19. Leibniz, *New Essays*, 254.

20. Leibniz, *New Essays*, 254–255.

21. Leibniz, *New Essays*, 255.

22. Leibniz, *New Essays*, 293, emphasis added.

23. Leibniz, *New Essays*, 307.

24. Leibniz, *New Essays*, 309–310.

25. Leibniz, *Monadology*, 221.

26. Leibniz, *Philosophical Essays*, 154.

27. Leibniz, *Philosophical Essays*, 155.

28. Leibniz, *Discourse on Metaphysics*, 38.

29. Leibniz, *Discourse on Metaphysics*, 39.

30. Leibniz, *Discourse on Metaphysics*, 37.

31. Leibniz, *New Essays*, 73.

32. Deleuze, *The Fold*, 35ff.

33. Leibniz, *Discourse on Metaphysics*, 14.

34. Leibniz, *Philosophical Essays*, 150.

35. See Holt, *Why Does the World Exist?*

36. Leibniz, *New Essays*, 56.

37. Leibniz, *New Essays*, 50–51.

38. Leibniz, *New Essays*, 114.

39. "Nature had need of animals, plants, inanimate bodies; there are in these creatures, devoid of reason, marvels which serve for exercise of the reason. What would an intelligent creature do if there were no unintelligent things?" Leibniz, *Theodicy*, 198.

40. Leibniz, *New Essays*, 139.

41. Leibniz, *New Essays*, 139.

42. Leibniz, *New Essays*, 139.

43. Leibniz, *New Essays*, 145.

44. Leibniz, *New Essays*, 232–233.

45. Leibniz, *Philosophical Essays*, 147.

46. Leibniz, *New Essays*, 232.

47. Leibniz, *Monadology*, 232.

48. Leibniz, *Philosophical Essays*, 104.

49. Leibniz, *New Essays*, 58.

8. Kant's Tulip

1. Kant, *Critique of Judgment*, 80.

2. Kant, *Critique of Judgment*, 140–141.

3. Quoted in Derrida, *The Truth in Painting*, 85.

4. Gasché's (*The Idea of a Form*, 67) explanation that "what is true of wildflowers is true, too, of the tulip: this flower, which had just been imported to Europe from Turkey, was, in Kant's time, a wildflower in all senses of the word" is clearly erroneous. Tulips were introduced in Europe from the Ottoman Empire around 1554, some two hundred years prior to Kant's time. After the tulipomania of the seventeenth century, they could not have been considered "wildflowers" in any sense of the word.

5. Kuehn, *Kant*, 115.

6. Kant, *Notes and Fragments*, 510.

7. Goody, *The Culture of Flowers*, 11ff.

8. Kant, *Notes and Fragments*, 498.

9. Derrida, *The Truth in Painting*, 85ff.

10. Derrida, *The Truth in Painting*, 117.

11. Bernstein, *The Fate of Art*, 161.

12. Bernstein, *The Fate of Art*, 161.

13. Kant, *Critique of Judgment*, 4.

14. Kant, *Critique of Judgment*, 8.

15. Kant, *Opus Postumum*, 182–183.

16. Kant, *Opus Postumum*, 247.

17. Immanuel Kant, *Critique of Judgment*, second part, 19.

18. Kant, *Critique of Judgment*, second part, 19.

19. Caygill, *Kant Dictionary*, 238.

20. Kant, *Critique of Judgment*, second part, 18.

21. Kant, *Critique of Judgment*, second part, 18.

22. Kant, *Critique of Pure Reason*, 397.

23. Kant, *Critique of Pure Reason*, 397.

24. Kant, *Critique of Judgment*, 76.
25. Akpinar et al., "Plant Abiotic Stress Signaling."
26. Kant, *Observations*, 329.
27. Kant, *The Metaphysics of Morals*, 198.
28. Kant, *Critique of Practical Reason*, 28, 63.
29. Kant, *The Metaphysics of Morals*, 162.
30. Kant, *Critique of Practical Reason*, 66.
31. See Marder, *Plant-Thinking*.
32. Butler, *Precarious Life*, 130.
33. Kant, *The Metaphysics of Morals*, 193.
34. Kant, *Critique of Practical Reason*, 70.
35. Kant, *The Metaphysics of Morals*, 192.
36. Kant, *The Metaphysics of Morals*, 192.
37. Kant, *The Metaphysics of Morals*, 192.
38. Kant, *Notes and Fragments*, 9.
39. Kant, *Critique of Judgment*, 136–137.
40. Kant, *Critique of Judgment*, 136.
41. Kant, *Critique of Judgement*, 142.
42. Kant, *Critique of Judgment*, 72.
43. Kant, *Critique of Judgment*, 72.
44. Kant, *Critique of Judgment*, 87.
45. Kant, *Critique of Judgment*, 89.
46. Kant, *Critique of Judgment*, 88.
47. Kant, *Critique of Judgment*, 76.

9. Hegel's Grapes

1. Hegel, *Correspondance*, 301, my translation.
2. Hegel, *Correspondance*, 303. For more on Hegel's relation to his travels, see Pinkard, *Hegel: A Biography*.
3. Hegel, *Phenomenology of Spirit*, 65.
4. Hegel, *Phenomenology of Spirit*, 65.
5. Hegel, *Phenomenology of Spirit*, 438.
6. Hegel, *Phenomenology of Spirit*, 451.
7. Hegel, *Aesthetics*, 42.
8. Hegel, *Logic*, 23. For a further analysis of this passage, see Benjamin, *The Plural Event*, 85ff.
9. Hegel, *Phenomenology of Spirit*, 58ff.
10. Hegel, *Philosophy of Nature*, 303.
11. Hegel, *Phenomenology of Spirit*, 146.

12. Hegel, *Phenomenology of Spirit*, 146.

13. Hegel, *Philosophy of Nature*, 301.

14. Hegel, *Philosophy of Nature*, 309.

15. Hegel, *Philosophy of Nature*, 336.

16. Hegel, *Phenomenology of Spirit*, 420.

17. Hegel, *Philosophy of Nature*, 314–5.

18. See the Society of Plant Signaling and Behavior: http://www.plantbehavior.org.

19. Genoud and Métraux, "Crosstalk in Plant Cell Signaling."

20. Hegel, *Philosophy of Nature*, 316.

21. Hegel, *Phenomenology of Spirit*, 60–61.

22. Hegel, *Philosophy of Nature*, 412–413.

23. See Miller, *The Vegetative Soul*.

24. Hegel, *Philosophy of Nature*, 306.

25. Marder, "The Life of Plants and the Limits of Empathy," 270.

26. Hegel, *Hegel's Philosophy of Right*, 263.

27. Hegel, *Hegel's Philosophy of Right*, 263.

28. See Freeman et al., "Sex Change in Plants."

29. See Janeczko and Skoczowski, "Mammalian Sex Hormones in Plants."

30. Hegel, *Philosophy of Nature*, 344.

31. Hegel, *Philosophy of Nature*, 343.

32. Hegel, *Phenomenology of Spirit*, 149.

33. See Wade, "Lack of Sex Among Grapes Tangles a Family Vine."

34. Hegel, *Phenomenology of Spirit*, 2.

35. Hegel, *Lectures on the Philosophy of World History*, 50, translation modified.

36. Hegel, *Hegel's Philosophy of Right*, 13.

37. Hegel, *The Letters*, 60.

10. Heidegger's Apple Tree

1. Safranski, *Martin Heidegger*, 1.

2. See the fourth section of the present chapter.

3. Heidegger, *What Is Called Thinking?*, 41.

4. Heidegger, *What Is Called Thinking?*, 173.

5. Heidegger, *What Is Called Thinking?*, 41.

6. Heidegger, *Zollikon Seminars*, 30, 154, 28.

7. Heidegger, *What Is Called Thinking?*, 172–173.

8. Heidegger, *Being and Time*, 63.

9. Heidegger, *What Is Called Thinking?*, 220.

10. Heidegger, *What Is Called Thinking?*, 220.

11. Heidegger, *Poetry, Language, Thought*, 98–99.

12. Heidegger, *Introduction to Metaphysics*, 16.

13. Heidegger, *Nietzsche*, 1:81.

14. Heidegger, *Poetry, Language, Thought*, 98

15. McDonough, *Martin Heidegger's* Being and Time, 169, 170.

16. Quoted in Heidegger, *Discourse on Thinking*, 47.

17. Heidegger, *Discourse on Thinking*, 47–48.

18. Heidegger, *The Fundamental Concepts of Metaphysics*, 177.

19. Heidegger, *Poetry, Language, Thought*, 43.

20. Heidegger, *Poetry, Language, Thought*, 71.

21. Heidegger, *The Fundamental Concepts of Metaphysics*, 179.

22. Heidegger, *The Fundamental Concepts of Metaphysics*, 62.

23. Heidegger, *The Fundamental Concepts of Metaphysics*, 62.

24. Heidegger, *Zollikon Seminars*, 217.

25. Heidegger, *Poetry, Language, Thought*, 43.

26. Heidegger, *Poetry, Language, Thought*, 41–42.

27. Heidegger, *The Fundamental Concepts of Metaphysics*, 243.

28. See, for instance, Sloterdijk, *Bubbles*.

29. Heidegger, *The Fundamental Concepts of Metaphysics*, 277.

30. Heidegger, *The Fundamental Concepts of Metaphysics*, 277.

31. Heidegger, *Being and Truth*, 137.

32. Heidegger, *Phenomenological Interpretations of Aristotle*, 64.

33. Hallé, *In Praise of Plants*, 117ff.

34. Heidegger, *Being and Time*, 308.

35. Heidegger, *Nietzsche*, 2:26.

36. Heidegger, *The Fundamental Concepts of Metaphysics*, 313.

37. Heidegger, *Being and Truth*, 46.

38. Heidegger, *Being and Truth*, 47.

39. Heidegger, *Being and Time*, 291.

40. Heidegger, *Being and Time*, 291.

41. Heidegger, *Being and Time*, 288.

42. Heidegger, *What Is Called Thinking?*, 41.

11. Derrida's Sunflowers

1. Derrida, *Negotiations*, 264.

2. Derrida, *Signsponge*.

3. Ponge, *Nouveau Nouveau Recueil*, 109.

4. Derrida, *Dissemination*, 268.

5. Derrida, *The Postcard*, 26.

6. Derrida, *The Postcard*, 42.
7. Derrida, *Margins of Philosophy*, 250.
8. Derrida, *Margins of Philosophy*, 251.
9. Derrida, *Of Grammatology*, 158, 227–228.
10. Derrida, *Margins of Philosophy*, 271.
11. Derrida, *Glas*, 13R.
12. Derrida, *Glas*, 54R.
13. Derrida, *Glas*, 86R.
14. Derrida, *The Truth in Painting*, 83ff.
15. Derrida, *Glas*, 246L.
16. Derrida, *Glas*, 246L.
17. Derrida, *Glas*, 31R.
18. Derrida, *Glas*, 12R.
19. Derrida, *Glas*, 188R.
20. Derrida has also written a book, *Signsponge*, on the poet Francis Ponge, whose name becomes a thing (a sponge), exemplifying the event of literature.
21. Derrida, *The Postcard*, 239.
22. See Derrida, "Biodegradables."
23. Derrida, *The Postcard*, 28.
24. Derrida, *The Postcard*, 101.
25. Derrida, *Dissemination*, 48.
26. Derrida, *Margins of Philosophy*, 271.
27. Nietzsche, *The Will to Power*, 351.
28. Bataille, *The Bataille Reader*. See especially the section titled "General Economy," 165–220.
29. Derrida, *Dissemination*, 150.
30. Derrida, *Of Grammatology*, 49.
31. Bataille, *Visions of Excess*, 7.
32. Derrida, *Glas*, 148R.
33. Derrida, *Glas*, 21R, 22R.
34. Derrida, *Glas*, 47R.
35. Schlessman, "Gender Diphasy," 140–141.
36. See, for instance, Derrida, *On Touching*, 274.
37. Derrida, *On Touching*, 270.
38. Bass, "Glossary," xv.
39. Derrida, *Glas*, 21R.
40. Derrida, *Margins of Philosophy*, 220.
41. Derrida, *The Truth in Painting*, 54–55.
42. Derrida, *The Truth in Painting*, 75.
43. Derrida, *Of Grammatology*, 145.

44. Derrida, *Of Grammatology*, 147.
45. Derrida, *Of Grammatology*, 148.
46. Derrida, *Of Grammatology*, 148.

12. Irigaray's Water Lily

1. Irigaray, *I Love to You*, 11.
2. Luce Irigaray, *In the Beginning, She Was*, 23.
3. Luce Irigaray, letter to Michael Marder, July 3, 2013, private correspondence.
4. Irigaray, *I Love to You*, 139.
5. Irigaray, *I Love to You*, 24–25.
6. "Do we have to fell a tree before cultivating it? If that were the case, what would we cultivate? An idea of the tree, but not the tree itself." Irigaray, *I Love to You*, 40.
7. Irigaray, *To Be Two*, 23.
8. Irigaray, *To Be Two*, 59.
9. Irigaray, *To Be Two*, 59.
10. Onions, *Oxford Dictionary of English Etymology*, 618; Skeat, *Concise Dictionary of English Etymology*, 310.
11. Irigaray, *Between East and West*, 51.
12. Irigaray, *Sexes and Genealogies*, 48.
13. Irigaray, *Elemental Passions*, 79.
14. Irigaray, *Sexes and Genealogies*, 48.
15. See Irigaray, *Marine Lover of Friedrich Nietzsche*.
16. Irigaray, *Sexes and Genealogies*, 47.
17. Irigaray, *I Love to You*, 25.
18. Irigaray, *To Be Two*, 3.
19. Irigaray, *In the Beginning*, 57.
20. Irigaray, *In the Beginning*, 66–67.
21. Miller, *The Vegetative Soul*, 190.
22. Irigaray, *The Way of Love*, 32.
23. Irigaray, *The Way of Love*, 17.
24. See, for instance, Irigaray, *Sharing the World*, 33ff.
25. Irigaray, *The Way of Love*, 24.
26. Irigaray, *Between East and West*, 21.
27. Irigaray, *To Be Two*, 57.
28. Irigaray, *Sharing the World*, 66.
29. Irigaray, *Between East and West*, 79–80.
30. Irigaray, *Between East and West*, 80.
31. Luce Irigaray, "Interview with Emily Parker".

32. Irigaray, *To Be Two*, 13.

33. Hence, "some seeds die when one wants to assimilate them, to make them one's own, instead of offering them a hospitable place to take root, to develop, to blossom." Irigaray, *In the Beginning*, 67.

34. On the connection of truth to betrothal, see Critchley, *Things Merely Are*, 12.

35. Irigaray, *In the Beginning*, 33.

36. Irigaray, *I Love to You*, 38.

37. Irigaray, *To Be Two*, 7.

38. Irigaray, *In the Beginning*, 33.

39. Irigaray, *In the Beginning*, 87.

40. Irigaray, *I Love to You*, 30, emphasis added.

41. Irigaray, *In the Beginning*, 54–55.

42. Irigaray, *In the Beginning*, 27.

43. Irigaray, *In the Beginning*, 15.

44. Irigaray, *In the Beginning*, 34–35.

45. Irigaray, *Sharing the World*, 26.

46. Irigaray, *Sexes and Genealogies*, 108.

47. Irigaray, *In the Beginning*, 31.

48. Irigaray, *To Be Two*, 10.

49. Irigaray, *To Be Two*, 4.

50. Marx, *Early Writings*, 426.

51. Irigaray, *Between East and West*, 41.

52. Irigaray, *Sharing the World*, xix.

BIBLIOGRAPHY

Afnan, Soheil. *Avicenna: His Life and Works*. London: George Allen & Unwin, 1958.

Agamben, Giorgio. *Homo Sacer*. Translated by Daniel Heller-Roazen. Stanford, Calif.: Stanford University Press, 1998.

Akpinar, B.A., et al. "Plant Abiotic Stress Signaling." *Plant Signaling and Behavior* 7 (2012): 1450–1455.

Arendt, Hannah. *Love and Saint Augustine*. Chicago: University of Chicago Press, 1996.

Aristotle. *Metaphysics*. Loeb Classical Library, vols. 271 and 287. Cambridge, Mass.: Harvard University Press, 1933–1935.

——. "De Plantis." In *Minor Works*. Loeb Classical Library, vol. 307, 141–236. Cambridge, Mass.: Harvard University Press, 1963.

——. *Generation of Animals*. Loeb Classical Library, vol. 366. Cambridge, Mass.: Harvard University Press, 1942.

——. *Nicomachean Ethics*. 2nd ed. Loeb Classical Library, vol. 19. Cambridge, Mass.: Harvard University Press, 1934.

——. "On Generation and Corruption." Translated by Harold Joachim. In *The Basic Works of Aristotle*, edited by Richard McKeon. New York: Random House, 1941.

——. *On the Soul. Parva Naturalia. On Breath*. Rev. ed. Loeb Classical Library, vol. 288. Cambridge, Mass.: Harvard University Press, 1975.

——. *Parts of Animals, Movements of Animals, Progression of Animals*. Loeb Classical Library, vol. 323. Cambridge, Mass.: Harvard University Press, 1937.

——. *The Physics*. rev. ed. Loeb Classical Library, vols. 228 and 255. Cambridge, Mass.: Harvard University Press, 1934–1957.

——. *Politics*. Loeb Classical Library, vol. 264. Cambridge, Mass.: Harvard University Press, 1932.

Augustine, Saint. *Confessions*. Translated by Henry Chadwick. Oxford: Oxford University Press, 2009.

——. *Essential Sermons*. Edited by Boniface Ramsey. Hyde Park, N.Y.: New City Press, 2007.

——. *On Order = De Ordine*. Translated by Silvano Borruso. South Bend, Ind.: St. Augustine's Press, 2007.

——. *The City of God, Against the Pagans*. Translated by R. W. Dyson. Cambridge: Cambridge University Press, 1998.

Avicenna. *A Compendium on the Soul*. Translated by Edward Abbott van Dyck. Verona: Stamperia di Nicola Paderno, 1906.

——. *A Treatise on Love by ibn Sīnā*. Translated by Emil Fackenheim, *Medieval Studies* 7 (1945): 208–228.

——. *Avicenna's Psychology*. Oxford: Oxford University Press, 1952.

——. *Livre de la Genese et du Retour*. Translated into French by Yahya J. Michot. Oxford: Oxford Centre for Islamic Studies, 2002.

——. *The Metaphysics of* The Healing. Translated and annotated by Michael E. Marmura. Provo, Utah: Brigham Young University Press, 2005.

——. *The Canon of Medicine*. Translated by Oskar Cameron Gruner. New York: AMS, 1973.

Baracchi, Claudia. *Aristotle's Ethics as First Philosophy* (Cambridge: Cambridge University Press, 2008).

Bass, Alan. "Glossary." In *The Postcard: From Socrates to Freud and Beyond*, by Jacques Derrida. Chicago: University of Chicago Press, 1987.

Bataille, Georges. *The Bataille Reader*. Edited by Fred Botting and Scott Wilson. London: Wiley-Blackwell, 1997.

——. *Visions of Excess: Selected Writings, 1927–1939*. Edited by Allan Stoekl. Minneapolis: University of Minnesota Press, 1985.

Benjamin, Andrew. *The Plural Event: Descartes, Hegel, Heidegger*. London: Routledge, 1993.

Bernstein, Jay. *The Fate of Art: Aesthetic Alienation from Kant to Derrida*. Philadelphia: Pennsylvania State University Press, 1992.

Bloch, Ernst. *Avicenna y la izquierda aristotélica*. Madrid: Editorial Ciencia Nueva, 1952.

Burrus, Virginia, Mark D. Jordan, and Karmen MacKendrick. *Seducing Augustine: Bodies, Desires, Confessions*. New York: Fordham University Press, 2010.

Butler, Judith. *Precarious Life: The Powers of Mourning and Violence*. London: Verso, 2006.

Carpenter, Amber. "Embodied Intelligent (?) Souls: Plants in Plato's *Timaeus*." *Phronesis: A Journal of Ancient Philosophy* 55, no. 4 (2010): 281–303.

Cashmore, A. R. "Cryptochromes: Enabling Plants and Animals to Determine Circadian Time." *Cell* 114 (2003): 537–543.

Caygill, Howard. *Kant Dictionary*. London: Wiley-Blackwell, 1995.

Chamovitz, Daniel. *What a Plant Knows: A Field Guide to the Senses*. New York: Scientific American / Farrar, Straus & Giroux, 2012.

Claudel, Paul. *La connaissance de l'est*. Paris: Gallimard, 2000.

Cook, Alexandra. *Jean-Jacques Rousseau and Botany: The Salutary Science*. Oxford: Voltaire Foundation, University of Oxford, 2012.

Critchley, Simon. *Things Merely Are: Philosophy in the Poetry of Wallace Stevens*. London: Routledge, 2005.

Cvrčková, Fatima, Helena Lipavská, and Viktor Žárský. "Plant Intelligence: Why, Why Not, and Where?" *Plant Signaling and Behavior* 4 (2009): 394–399.

Deleuze, Gilles. *The Fold: Leibniz and the Baroque*. London: Continuum, 2006.

Derrida, Jacques. "Biodegradables: Seven Diary Fragments." Translated by Peggy Kamuf. *Critical Inquiry* 15 (Summer 1989): 812–873.

——. "Composing 'Circumfession.'" In *Augustine and Postmodernism: Confessions and Circumfession*, edited by John Caputo and Michael Scanlon. Bloomington: Indiana University Press, 2005.

——. *Dissemination*. Translated by Barbara Johnson. Chicago: University of Chicago Press, 1983.

——. *Glas*. Translated by John P. Leavey and Richard Rand. Lincoln: University of Nebraska Press, 1986.

——. *Margins of Philosophy*. Translated by Alan Bass. Chicago: University of Chicago Press, 1985.

——. *Negotiations: Interventions and Interviews, 1971–2001*. Translated by Elizabeth Rottenberg. Stanford, Calif.: Stanford University Press, 2002.

——. *Of Grammatology*. Translated by Gayatri C. Spivak. Baltimore, Md.: Johns Hopkins University Press, 1997.

——. *On Touching—Jean-Luc Nancy*. Translated by Christine Irizarry. Stanford, Calif.: Stanford University Press, 2005.

——. *Signésponge / Signsponge*. Translated by Richard Rand. New York: Columbia University Press, 1984.

——. *The Postcard: From Socrates to Freud and Beyond*. Translated by Alan Bass. Chicago: University of Chicago Press, 1987.

——. *The Truth in Painting*. Translated by Geoffrey Bennington. Chicago: University of Chicago Press, 1987.

Dobbs-Weinstein, Idit. "The Ambiguity of the Imagination and the Ambivalence of Language in Maimonides and Spinoza." In *Maimonides and His Heritage*, edited by Idit Dobbs-Weinstein et al., 95–112. Albany: SUNY Press, 2009.

Emilsson, E. K. *Plotinus on Intellect*. Oxford: Clarendon, 2007.

Freeman, D. C., T. K. Harper, and E. L. Charnov. "Sex Change in Plants: Old and New Observations and New Hypotheses." *Oecologia* 47, no. 2 (1980): 222–232.

Gagliano, Monica, Stefano Mancuso, and Daniel Robert. "Towards Understanding Plant Bioacoustics." *Trends in Plant Science* 17, no. 6 (2012): 323–325.

Garzón, F. C. "The Quest for Cognition in Plant Neurobiology." *Plant Signaling and Behavior* 2 (2007): 208–211.

Gasché, Rodolphe. *The Idea of Form: Rethinking Kant's Aesthetics*. Stanford, Calif.: Stanford University Press, 2003.

Genoud, Thierry, and Jean-Pierre Métraux. "Crosstalk in Plant Cell Signaling: Structure and Function of the Genetic Network." *Trends in Plant Science* 4, no. 12 (1999): 503–507.

Goody, Jack. *The Culture of Flowers*. Cambridge: Cambridge University Press, 1993.

Gohlman, William. *The Life of Ibn Sina: A Critical Edition and Annotated Translation*. Albany: SUNY Press, 1984.

Gomez-Lobo, Alfonso. *Morality and the Human Goods: An Introduction to Natural Law Ethics*. Washington, D.C.: Georgetown University Press, 2001.

Hall, Matthew. *Plants as Persons: A Philosophical Botany*. Albany: SUNY Press, 2011.

Hallé, Francis. *In Praise of Plants*. Cambridge: Timber, 2002.

Haraway, Donna. *When Species Meet*. Minneapolis: University of Minneapolis Press, 2007.

Hegel, G. W. F. *Aesthetics: Lectures on Fine Art*. Translated by T. M. Knox. Oxford: Oxford University Press, 1998.

——. *Correspondance*. Vol. 2, *1813–22*. Paris: Gallimard, 1963.

——. *Early Theological Writings*. Translated by T. M. Knox. Chicago: University of Chicago Press, 1975.

——. *The Letters*. Translated by Clark Butler and Christiane Seiler. Bloomington: Indiana University Press, 1984.

——. *Hegel's Philosophy of Right*, translated by T. M. Knox. Oxford: Oxford University Press, 1967.

——. *Lectures on the Philosophy of World History*. Translated by H. B. Nisbet. Cambridge: Cambridge University Press, 1981.

——. *Logic: Encyclopedia of the Philosophical Sciences, Part II*. Translated by William Wallace. Oxford: Oxford University Press, 1975.

——. *Phenomenology of Spirit*. Translated by A. V. Miller. Oxford: Oxford University Press, 1979.

——. *Philosophy of Nature: Encyclopedia of the Philosophical Sciences, Part II*. Translated by A. V. Miller. Oxford: Oxford University Press, 2004.

Heidegger, Martin. *Being and Time*. Translated by John Macquarrie and Edward Robinson. New York: Harper & Row, 1962.

——. *Being and Truth*. Translated by Gregory Fried and Richard Polt. Bloomington: Indiana University Press, 2010.

——. *Discourse on Thinking*. Translated by John Anderson and Hans Freund. New York: Harper & Row, 1966.

——. *Introduction to Metaphysics*. Translated by Gregory Fried and Richard Polt. New Haven, Conn.: Yale University Press, 2000.

——. *Nietzsche*. 2 vols. Translated by David Farrell Krell. San Francisco: Harper San Francisco, 1979–1984.

——. *Phenomenological Interpretations of Aristotle*: *Initiation into Phenomenological Research*. Translated by Richard Rojcewicz. Bloomington: Indiana University Press, 2001.

——. *Poetry, Language, Thought*. Translated by Albert Hofstadter. New York: Harper Collins, 2001.

——. *The Fundamental Concepts of Metaphysics: World, Finitude, Solitude*. Translated by William McNeill and Nicholas Walker. Bloomington: Indiana University Press, 1995.

——. *What Is Called Thinking?* Translated by J. Glenn Gray. New York: Harper & Row, 1968.

——. *Zollikon Seminars: Protocols-Conversations-Letters*. Edited by Medard Boss. Evanston, Ill.: Northwestern University Press, 2001.

Hesiod. *Theogony, Works and Days, and Testimonia*. Loeb Classical Library, vol. 57N. Cambridge, Mass.: Harvard University Press, 2007.

Holt, Jim. *Why Does the World Exist? An Existential Detective Story*. London: Norton, 2012).

Homer, *Iliad, Books I–XII*. Loeb Classical Library, vol. 170. Cambridge, Mass.: Harvard University Press, 1924.

Irigaray, Luce. *Between East and West: From Singularity to Community*. Translated by Stephen Pluháček. New York: Columbia University Press, 2002.

——. *Elemental Passions*. Translated by Joanne Collie and Judith Still. London: Athlone, 1992.

——. *I Love to You: Sketch of a Possible Felicity in History*. Translated by Alison Martin. New York: Routledge, 1996.

——. *In the Beginning, She Was*. New York: Bloomsbury, 2013.

——. "Interview with Emily Parker," *Journal of the British Society for Phenomenology*, special issue "On Ecology," forthcoming in 2014.

——. *Marine Lover of Friedrich Nietzsche*. Translated by Gillian C. Gill. New York: Columbia University Press, 1991.

——. *Sexes and Genealogies*. Translated by Gillian C. Gill. New York: Columbia University Press, 1993.

——. *Sharing the World*. London: Continuum, 2008.

——. *The Speculum of the Other Woman*. Ithaca, N.Y.: Cornell University Press, 1985.

——. *The Way of Love*. London: Continuum, 2002.

——. *To Be Two*. Translated by Monique Rhodes and Marco Cocito-Monoc. London: Continuum, 2000.

Janeczko, Anna, and Andrzej Skoczowski. "Mammalian Sex Hormones in Plants." *Folia Histochemica et Cytobiologica* 43, no. 2 (2005): 71–79.

Kant, Immanuel. *Critique of Judgment*. Translated by James C. Meredith. Oxford: Clarendon, 1953.

——. *Critique of Practical Reason*. Edited by Mary Gregor. Cambridge: Cambridge University Press, 1997.

——. *Critique of Pure Reason*. Cambridge: Cambridge University Press, 1999.

——. *Notes and Fragments*. Cambridge: Cambridge University Press, 2010.

——. *Observations on the Feeling of the Beautiful and the Sublime and Other Writings*. Cambridge: Cambridge University Press, 2011.

——. *Opus Postumum*. Edited by Eckart Förster. Cambridge: Cambridge University Press, 1993.

——. *The Metaphysics of Morals*. Edited by Mary Gregor. Cambridge: Cambridge University Press, 1996.

Kennedy, J. B. *The Musical Structure of Platonic Dialogues*. Durham, N.C.: Acumen, 2011.

Khan, Aisha. *Avicenna (Ibn Sina): Muslim Physician And Philosopher of the Eleventh Century*. New York: Rosen, 2006.

Kuehn, Manfred. *Kant: A Biography*. Cambridge: Cambridge University Press, 2002.

Lameer, Joep. "Avicenna's Concupiscence." *Arabic Studies and Philosophy* 23 (2013): 277–289.

Leibniz, G. W. *Discourse on Metaphysics and Other Essays*. Edited and translated by Daniel Garber and Roger Ariew. Indianapolis, Ind.: Hackett, 1991.

——. *Monadology (An Edition for Students)*. Edited by Nicholas Rescher. Pittsburgh, Penn.: University of Pittsburgh Press, 1991.

——. *New Essays on Human Understanding*. Edited by Peter Remnant and Jonathan Bennett. Cambridge: Cambridge University Press, 1996.

——. *Philosophical Essays*. Edited by Roger Ariew and Daniel Garber. Indianapolis, Ind.: Hackett, 1989.

——. *Theodicy: Essays on the Goodness of God, the Freedom of Man, and the Origin of Evil*. Translated by E. M. Huggard. Peru, Ill.: Open Court, 1985.

Leibniz, G. W., and Samuel Clarke. *Leibniz and Clarke: Correspondence*. Edited by Roger Ariew. Indianapolis, Ind.: Hackett, 2000.

Maimonides, Moses. *The Code of Maimonides: Book Three: The Book of Seasons*. Translated by Solomon Gandz and Hyman Klein. New Haven, Conn.: Yale University Press, 1961.

——. *The Code of Maimonides: Book Seven: The Book of Agriculture*. Translated by Isaac Klein. New Haven, Conn.: Yale University Press, 1979.

——. *The Code of Maimonides: Book Ten: The Book of Cleanness*. Translated by Herbert Danby. New Haven, Conn.: Yale University Press, 1954.

——. *The Code of Maimonides: Book Twelve: The Book of Acquisitions*. Translated by Isaac Klein. New Haven, Conn.: Yale University Press, 1951.

——. *The Ethical Writings of Maimonides*. Edited by Raymond Weiss and Charles Butterworth. New York: New York University Press, 1975.

——. *The Guide for the Perplexed*. Translated by M. Friedländer. New York: Dover, 1956.

Marder, Michael. "Plant Intentionality and the Phenomenological Framework of Plant Intelligence." *Plant Signaling and Behavior* 7, no. 11 (November 2012): 1365–1372.

——. *Plant-Thinking: A Philosophy of Vegetal Life*. New York: Columbia University Press, 2013.

——. "The Life of Plants and the Limits of Empathy." *Dialogue* 51, no. 2 (2012): 259–273.

Marder, Michael, and Gary Francione. "Michael Marder and Gary Francione Debate Plant Ethics." http://www.cup.columbia.edu/static/marder -francione-debate.

Marder, Michael, and Patricia Vieira. "Writing Phytophilia: Philosophers and Poets as Lovers of Plants." *Frame: Journal of Literary Studies* 26, no. 2 (November 2013): 39–55.

Marx, Karl. *Early Writings*. New York: Penguin, 2005.

Mates, Benson. *The Philosophy of Leibniz: Metaphysics and Language*. Oxford: Oxford University Press, 1989.

McCarthy, John. "The Philosopher as Essayist: Leibniz and Kant." In *The Philosopher as Writer: The Eighteenth Century*, edited by Robert Ginsberg. Cranbury, N.J.: Associated University Presses, 1987.

McDonough, Richard. *Martin Heidegger's* Being and Time. New York: Peter Lang, 2006.

McGinnis, Jon. *Avicenna*. Oxford: Oxford University Press, 2010.

Melber, Jehuda. *The Universality of Maimonides*. New York: Jonathan David, 1968.

Miller, Elaine. *The Vegetative Soul: From Philosophy of Nature to Subjectivity in the Feminine*. Albany: SUNY Press, 2002.

Miller, J. Hillis. *Black Holes*. Stanford: Stanford University Press, 1999.

Nietzsche, Friedrich. *The Will to Power*. Translated by Walter Kaufman and R. J. Hollingdale. New York: Vintage, 1968.

Novalis, *Philosophical Writings*. Edited and translated by Margaret Mahoney Stoljar. Albany: SUNY Press, 1997.

Nuland, Sherwin. *Maimonides*. New York: Schocken, 2005.

Onions, C. T., ed. *Oxford Dictionary of English Etymology*. Oxford: Oxford University Press, 1966.

Palmer, C. M., S. M. Bush, and J. N. Maloof. "Phenotypic and Developmental Plasticity in Plants." *eLS* (June 2012).

Pinkard, Terry. *Hegel: A Biography*. Cambridge: Cambridge University Press, 2000.

Plato. *Euthyphro; Apology; Crito; Phaedo; Phaedrus*. Loeb Classical Library, vol. 36. Cambridge, Mass.: Harvard University Press, 1914.

——. *The Republic*. Loeb Classical Library, vols. 237 and 276. Cambridge, Mass.: Harvard University Press, 1930–1935.

——. *Timaeus; Critias; Cleitophon; Menexenus; Epistles*. Loeb Classical Library, vol. 234. Cambridge, Mass.: Harvard University Press, 1929.

Plotinus, *The Enneads*. Translated by A. Armstrong. Loeb Classical Library, 7 vols. Cambridge, Mass.: Harvard University Press, 1966–1988.

Pollan, Michael. *The Botany of Desire: A Plant's-Eye View of the World*. New York: Random House, 2001.

Ponge, Francis. *Nouveau Nouveau Recueil, 1967–1984*. Paris: Gallimard, 1992.

Porphyry. "On the Life of Plotinus and the Order of His Books." In *Ennead*, vol. 1: *Porphyry on the Life of Plotinus. Ennead 1*, translated by A. Armstrong. Loeb Classical Library. Cambridge, Mass.: Harvard University Press, 1969.

Preus, Anthony. "Plotinus and Biology." In *Neoplatonism and Nature: Studies in Plotinus' Enneads*, edited by Michael Wagner. Albany: SUNY Press, 2002.

Rousseau, Jean-Jacques. "Elementary Letters on Botany." In *Collected Writings of Rousseau*, vol. 8, edited by Christopher Kelly. Hanover: University Press of New England, 2000.

——. *Reveries of the Solitary Walker*. Translated by Russell Goulbourne. Oxford: Oxford University Press, 2011.

Russell, Bertrand. *History of Western Philosophy*. New York: Routledge, 2004.

Safranski, Rüdiger. *Martin Heidegger: Between Good and Evil*. Translated by Ewald Osers. Cambridge, Mass.: Harvard University Press, 1999.

Sayre, Kenneth M. *Plato's Literary Garden: How to Read a Platonic Dialogue*. Notre Dame, Ind.: University of Notre Dame Press, 1995.

Schlessman, Mark A. "Gender Diphasy ('Sex Choice')." In *Plant Reproductive Ecology: Patterns and Strategies*, edited by J. L. Doust and L. L. Doust. Oxford: Oxford University Press, 1988.

Silverman, Eric. "Anthropocentrism and the Medieval Problem of Religious Language." In *Anthropocentrism: Humans, Animals, Environment*, edited by Rob Boddice. Leiden: Brill, 2011.

Skeat, Walter, ed. *Concise Dictionary of English Etymology*. London: Wadsworth, 1998.

Sloterdijk, Peter. *Bubbles. Spheres*. Vol. 1, *Microspherology*. New York: Semiotext(e), 2011.

Spinoza, Baruch. *Ethics*. Translated by Edwin Curley. London: Penguin, 2005.

Swift, Jonathan. *The Works of Dr. Jonathan Swift, Dean of St. Patrick's, Dublin*. Vol. 7. London, 1765.

Von Uexküll, Jakob. *A Foray Into the Worlds of Animals and Humans*. Translated by Joseph D. O'Neill. Minneapolis: University of Minnesota Press, 2010.

Wade, Nicholas. "Lack of Sex Among Grapes Tangles a Family Vine." *New York Times*, January 24, 2011.

Ward, Julie K. *Aristotle on Homonymy: Dialectic and Science*. Cambridge: Cambridge University Press, 2007.

Wildon, D. C., et al. "Electrical Signaling and Systemic Proteinase-Inhibitor Induction in the Wounded Plant." *Nature* 360 (1992): 62–65.